THE SPIRITUAL BAPTIST FAITH

AFRICAN NEW WORLD RELIGIOUS IDENTITY, HISTORY & TESTIMONY

REV. PATRICIA STEPHENS

The Spiritual Baptist Faith
New World Religious History,
Identity & Testimony

Rev. Patricia Stephens

First published in Britain and the USA
by Karnak House 1999
300 Westbourne Park Road
London W11 1EH
England

Tel/Fax: 0171.243.3620

US Distributors:
Red Sea Press
11-D Princess Road
Lawrenceville, New Jersey 08648
USA

Tel: (609) 844.9583
Fax: (609) 844.0198

Typesetting produced by Ipet-Sut Imagesetters

Bibliographic information can be obtained from British Library Cataloguing in Publication Data and US Library of Congress

Cover Photo courtesy Deaconess Linda Thomas
CoverDesign Ipet-Sut
ISBN 1 872596 04 5

Dedication

To my mother, Edith Emelia Stephens and to the memory of my father, Jeremiah Ernest Stephens, to whom I shall be forever indebted; and to my son Nicholas Aramide.

ACKNOWLEDGEMENT

There are numerous persons to whom I wish to extend my heartfelt thanks for their unstinting support throughout this project. It is not possible to mention everyone, but I pray that all those who gave of their time and effort so generously and often at short notice will be blessed.

Thanks are due to my friend Senator Viola-Davis, the late Simeon Onyejiako, his daughter Joy, Glenroy Straughn and Marie Barratt for their support.

I remain eternally grateful to all those who co-operated in the study by giving interviews, making recommendations and contacts, and lending archival materials. In this regard, special thanks are due to Mr. John La Rose, Dr John Cowley, Dr. Fitz Baptiste and Mr. Reginald Clarke of the University of the West Indies at St. Augustine, Trinidad. Mr. Colin Rowe and Miss Elizabeth Williams at Partnership House Library in London, Ms. Abbott and Mrs. Lartey at Selly Oak Library, Birmingham, Rev. Hazel-Ann Gibbs de Peza and Curtis Jacobs were always eager to assist. I can only hope that all those colleagues did not find me too demanding.

Many generous souls within the Spiritual Baptist Faith were prepared to be interviewed, sometimes for many hours and to send material to aid the study. Special mention must be made of Archbishops Raymond Oba Douglas, Clarence Baisden,

Monica Randoo, Gertude Mundy, Senator Barbara Burke, John Noel and Phillip Lewis.

Archbishops Granville Williams in Barbados and Cosmore Pompey in St. Vincent were very generous with their time and hospitality. Bishop Rudolph Denzil of Guyana, who facilitated the efficient use of my time there. Bishop Magna Atherly in London not only gave generously of her time for interviews and discussions throughout the study, but also gave me invaluable physical assistance. Thanks also to Mrs. Cosmore Pompey in St. Vincent and Teacher Atherlene Reece in Barbados.

Mrs. Gladys Wells, Mrs. Kathleen Turner, Mrs. Elinor Stephens, Mrs. Adriana Gomez, Mrs Mavis Archer and Mrs. Joan Demas-Warner provided unfailing support and practical help during my research in Trinidad.

My brother and sister-in-law, Calver and Joy Stephens took a keen interest in the study and took great care of my needs so that I could be single-minded about it. I am greatly in their debt for their love and generosity.

My sincere thanks to Dr. Kimani Nehusi who introduced me to my publisher, Michael Francis and Nisma Bynoe who responded to my call for assistance with computing.

Finally, my supervisor Professor Werner Ustorf, gave me heaps of encouragement especially when I felt in danger of being overwhelmed. I must also thank Dr. Allan Anderson and Rev. Dr. R. Gerloff whose guidance contributed significantly to the final orientation of the study.

I must express my deepest gratitude to my friend and brother, Professor Reverend Gus John, who commented on various drafts of the manuscript and edited the final M.Phil. thesis. His critical analysis of the Spiritual Baptist Faith and its locus within Caribbean societies was as invaluable as the time he devoted to reading and commenting upon the manuscript.

I alone bear responsibility for whatever flaws remain in this book, which I trust has done justice to the contributions of all those mentioned and the many more who were not.

CONTENTS

PART ONE

IDENTITY & HISTORY

CHAPTER ONE

INTRODUCTION

SOCIO-BIOGRAPHY OF THE AUTHOR AS ADHERENT OF THE FAITH AND AS SOCIAL ANALYST

O n 21 January 1980, the editorial in *The Trinidad Guardian* read:

> Our university sociologists should undertake a serious in-depth study of those believers (The Shouters) who may well represent *our only indigenous group*. No such study exists and the lack of appreciation may well be solved by great understanding. We believe that the country as a whole should have an opportunity to know more about The Spiritual Baptists who are still largely a mystery to those who know little about their faith. What are their beliefs, their origins, their development? (emphasis added).[1]

I was visiting Trinidad at the time and making preparations for my first Mourning, a ritualistic tradition which is essential for one's spiritual development in the Spiritual Baptist Faith. The ritual is symbolic of death and resurrection, the Pilgrim goes through a period of sanctification for at least seven days, during which time s/he is instructed about the significance of Mourning and the laws of the iinner chamber, a small structure attached to the church that is set aside for this purpose. Some Spiritual Baptists describe Mourning as a period of "Godly sorrow," which

Figure 1
The author united in prayer with Teacher Jackie Robinson, London, 1994 (Photo courtesy Paul Miller).

can last from seven to twenty-one days. This has nothing to do with bereavement, and is based on the Old Testament, Daniel 10: 2–3, where Daniel mourned for three full weeks without bread, flesh, wine or anointing. The ritual begins during or after Sunday service with the washing of the pilgrims by the Mothers of the church. The Leader then sanctifies them by anointing the head, face, arms and feet with olive oil. These acts are of great significance and are justified by reference to Leviticus 8: 6 where the sons of Aaron were washed with water and in Leviticus 8:12, the pouring of anointing oil upon Aaron's head to sanctify him.

When this is over, the Pointer, who can be male or female, with the spiritual knowledge and understanding of Mourning rites takes charge of the pilgrims. The Pointer takes the bell, candles, chalk, cotton material of various colours to the inner chamber. The ritual of placing sealed bands on the eyes of the pilgrims and sinking them out of self into the spiritual realm takes place, then the pilgrim is placed on his/her back with a stone or Bible for a pillow, and lies with the head westward for three days and three nights. The pilgrim is now said to be in the grave.

After three days in isolation, prayer and fasting, the pilgrim *rises* and is taken out of the grave, changed around and placed eastward to continue his/her spiritual journey. The length of time spent in the inner chamber is determined by the Pointer under the guidance of the Holy Spirit. During the period of mourning, the pilgrim eats little or no food, drinks water by *measure*, exercises and is exhorted by the Word of God.

During mourning the pilgrims are expected to travel in the spiritual world, and at the end of their mourning a service is held at which they relate their experiences to the congregation, a process known as "giving tracks." Many mourners receive *gifts* in the Spirit, which dictate their office and the work they are called upon to do for the Lord. Some come out as Pastors, Mothers, Healers, Nurses, Shepherds and Shepherdesses, to name but a few. A person who is suspected of having made false claims of gifts on their spiritual travels is tested by a Prover, an elder with spiritual wisdom and with discerning eyes of faith. This situation seldom occurs, but most Spiritual Baptist churches have Provers in order to maintain the truthfulness of their work.

Among the many diverse gifts pilgrims may receive in the Spiritual world are the following:

PASTOR

This is a male office and the person who receives this gift in the Spirit inevitably takes on the leadership of the church. The Pastor is expected to interpret the Bible as revealed to him by God, counsel its members and support them in their spiritual development. Although most Pastors are not very literate, they are usually inspired by God with spiritual and metaphysical knowledge and understanding.

MOTHER

The work of the Mother is of paramount importance. A Spiritual Baptist Church traditionally must function with a Mother and a Father. The Father could be a Leader, Pastor or Shepherd. But most Spiritual Baptists will tell you there is an essence in the Mother that is not in the Father. In some churches a Mother could have more authority in the spiritual world than the Father, because God is not likened unto the flesh. Being a Mother doesn't imply that the woman is in a subservient role while the Father has the dominant role. A Mother must have depths of knowledge in the word of God in order "to give birth" to children in the spiritual world. She must be full of compassion and mercy, among other virtues. Since the Spiritual Baptist Church is likened to a family unit, the Mother and Father are the heads. However, it must be noted that there are Mothers of various ranks in the Spiritual Baptist Church.

SHEPHERD & SHEPHERDESS

A Shepherd is an advanced member of the Faith who usually assists the Leader or Pastor and deputises for him when necessary. A Shepherdess is a senior female officer, who like the Shepherd has the authority to conduct services, give advice, guide the faithful and assist the Mother of the church or the "Mother Superior" generally.

POINTER

A Pointer is the name given in the Spirit to an adherent of the Faith who has the full knowledge and understanding of the Ritual of Mourning. The Pointer is able to "point" souls to travel in the spiritual realm. The Pointer can be male or female and it is common to find a Mother/Pointer, Teacher/Pointer, Leader/Pointer or Evangelist/Pointer. Mother Virginia Sandy, a Mother/Pointer, who converted and mourned at Georgetown, St Vincent in 1945, describes one of her spiritual journeys in detail:

> I found myself in a very large house and there I met a gentleman. I stood in the middle of the floor and I saw him come in with a lovely foot machine. He placed the machine in front of me, he went back and brought me a chair, such that I had never seen in all my life. It was a chair the colour of mahogany, all made to curve at the back. He placed me there to sit in front of the machine. While sitting there he brought me twelve different coloured threads. He placed on the floor along side me a white basin of water, a plain glass of water and a white rose in it, a bell, a Bible, a strap and a bit of pencil. He said to me, I am going to make you an Evangelist/Pointer.[2]

After mourning, the Pointer is guided by a senior Mother/Pointer or Teacher/Pointer until s/he is able to take full responsibility in the Mourner's Room.

MATRON

The Matron is a very senior and a very respected person in the Faith. Quite often she is called out on duty in the Mourner's Room and is responsible for directing the Nurses and Midwives. In traditional churches, the Matron has the authority to overrule the Teacher's or Pointer's decision if a "pilgrim-traveller" or Mourner needs treatment.

BAPTISER

A Baptiser is one who is called and instructed by the Spirit of God on the mourning ground to baptise the converted. This is truly a specialist office. Leaders, Pastors and Shepherds are not necessarily Baptisers. A Baptiser is given the authority by God to sanctify and measure the water and conduct the ritual.

MOTHER DIVER

This office is very rare in Spiritual Baptist churches today, but traditionally a Mother Diver is a person who comes to the rescue in times of difficulties. She can dive in the spirit and save a drowning child. The Mother Diver's work is essentially in the Mourner's Room.

STAR GAZER

This office is not common today, but Star Gazers, like Divers, are spiritually skilled persons whose expertise is used in the Mourner's Room. Unlike most other officers who work in the hemispheric conditions, the Star Gazer looks up to the heavens and is able to see the Spirit of God coming down. He works by *revelation*.

WATCHMAN

There are few Watchmen in Spiritual Baptist churches today. However, according to tradition, each church must have a Watchman, whose duty is to protect the church from harm and danger. The Watchman sits or stands at the main entrance and keeps watch for spirits. He knows when danger is approaching and will advise or act accordingly on the spirit.

Messenger

A Messenger is a person who is used by the Holy Spirit to tell things past, present and future. Messengers usually go out and give warnings, which if not heeded can be catastrophic. A Messenger spiritually guides and directs the faithful.

MIDWIFE

This is another important office. When the Mother of the church gives birth to children in the Spirit, the Midwife is solely responsible for the safe delivery of the babies.

NURSE

The Nurse, unlike the Midwife, will be acquainted with the parts of the body. Spiritual Baptists insist that *as things are in the carnal world, so they are in the spiritual world*. A Nurse receives her training in the spirit, and is given a full nurse's uniform and is constantly on duty.

Being a social scientist and an adherent of the Faith, I decided to take up the challenge posed by *The Trinidad Guardian*. As though by design, I had a Cabinet appointment in 1984 as Adviser to the Minister of Community Development in the Trinidad and Tobago government, with direct responsibility for liaising with the Spiritual Baptist Community. This enabled me to do an informal assessment of the Faith. It then became apparent that although there is a fair body of published works on the history and development of African religion in the New World, there was still a need for socio-historical research on the Spiritual Baptist in particular.

G.E.Simpson (1980) states that:

> The origin and early history of the Spiritual Baptists have not been studied in detail, but apparently this syncretic religion with its reinterpreted Africanisms and Europeanisms developed in Trinidad during the nineteenth century without the aid of a strong revivalist movement.[3]

Having been brought up on Caratal Road in the village of Gasparillo, South Trinidad, a community that boasts a large population of people of Yoruba origin, the most widely dispersed group of Africans in Trinidad and Tobago (cf. Elder 1988), the Spiritual (Shouter) Baptist Faith has always been part of my experience. The Faith is essentially about righteous living, rootedness in African culture and the fear of God.

The following list gives an idea of the dispersion and concentration of people of African nations represented in Trinidad and Tobago. Variations on spellings are located in brackets:

NATION	LOCATION
1. YORUBA (Yaraba, Yuruba)	Bona Venture, Gasparillo, Mayo, Indian Trail, Patna Village, Cunupia, Moruga Road, Oropouche, St Francois Valley, Diego Martin, Morvant, Tunapuna, Point Fortin
2. HAUSA (Hausa Wele)	Mayo Town, Princess Town, Majuba Road, Manzanilla
3. CONGO including Kimbundu (Chimbundu)	Caratal, Belmont, Diego Martin, Tobago (Culloden Moor), Charlotteville, Pembroke Belle Garden
4. IGBO (Igbo Grenade, Scotch Igbo)	Bona Venture, Indian Trail, Company Village
5. RADA (Alada, Arada)	Belmont Valley Road
6. MANDINKA (Mandingo)	Mandinga Road (Naparimas), Lengua
7. TEMNE (Temene, Timene)	Migrant group from who Carriacou settled at New Village in Point Fortin (South Trinidad)
8. KOROMANTI (Koromantyn, Kromanti)	Small group of Asante (Ashanti) people asso ciated with the Nation Dance ancestor cult from Carriacou, Vance River, Point Fortin[4]

I am the third of nine children born to my parents, Jeremiah and Edith Stephens. My mother, a school teacher, is a devout Roman Catholic, and my father, a civil ser

Figure 2
The late Bishop George Noel of Mt. Zion Spiritual Baptist Church (left), accompanies blindfolded candidates to baptism (Photo by the Author).

vant, was an Anglican. My father's mother whom I remember well, Ma Lovette, was a Shouter Baptist and she had a church in Charles Street, Gasparillo.

My father's youngest brother, Pastor Theophilus Stephens, who at present lives and runs a Spiritual Baptist Church in Venezuela, had a church in Poonah. My great grandfather on my father's side, I was told, and this was confirmed in my research, was a direct descendant of African slaves and lived at the Kanga Woods Settlement. My grandfather lived at Mayo Village before he met my grandmother, who was a Kitson from Mt. St. George, Tobago. My father's first cousin, Joshua Salazaar, is a well known Shango-Baptist practitioner at Sum Sum Hill, Claxton Bay, and his niece, Katchura Manigro, is a Spiritual Baptist at Morne Diablo.

We lived in a very large extended-family home within yards of the Anglican church. My maternal grandmother was a practising Anglican, and we (my brothers and sisters) attended the Anglican church and were involved in its activities. As a child, I do recall the stigma that was attached to the Spiritual Baptist Faith, and my father guided us the orthodox way.

In spite of this, one could not escape the African religious and cultural traditions within our community. About four houses from where we lived, Ma Angee kept Nation Feasts annually. Her granddaughter, Thora Modeste, and I are contemporaries, we went to school together, and I still hold fond memories and vivid pictures of the happy crowds, the food and drink, music, singing and dancing at the Feasts.

Further up Caratal Road in Maryland, there were *Shango* (*Orisha*) feasts during the month of August, but we were not permitted to attend.

Nation Dance: Combinations Of African Elements

Nation Dance, sometimes called *Nation Feast* or *Bele Dance*, is another African retention, an attempt by the descendants of African ancestors to maintain their traditions, particularly those of music and dance, marrying these elements at the same time with their indigenous beliefs and practices in a simple ceremony.

Andrew Pearse (1958) describes it as a "cycle of dances" said to be of the following "nations" (as Africans call themselves in their own language): Koromanti, Igbo, "Scotch"-Igbo, Mandinka, Hausa, Congo, Chiamba, Temne, Bande, Moko-Bange and Moko yege-yege. "There is no possession, but an intensifying of the music marks the arrival of the spirits, invoked by the beating of a hoe. These are the "old people" or dead ancestors who intervene constantly in everyday affairs and communicate with the living through dreams. The dance placates them, and is performed at all critical junctures, along with the offering of food...(Parents' plate). Typical occasions are sickness, anniversary of a death, eve of a wedding, launching of a schooner, or a business transaction."[5]

Dancers from neighbouring villages are invited and the host would make elaborate preparations. A tent is erected, usually made from bamboo and carrat leaves, and bamboo seats are placed around the perimeter of the tent. Large quantities of food is prepared, e.g., *coo-coo* (a continuum from the West African *foo-foo*) made from grounded corn, callaloo, a mixture of ochroes and green edible leaves, cassava bread made from grated and dried cassava, black-eye peas and rice, and a pig was always reared especially for the feast. A portion of whatever was prepared for general use was cooked without salt especially for the ancestors and placed in a private room.

The women usually dressed in douilettes, long dresses made from coloured plaid material, with frilled petticoats and beautiful headties, while the men carried red handkerchiefs and towels around their necks. *Shak-shak*, small gourds filled with beads, and drums were the main musical instruments. In Gasparillo, the Temnes, a group of migrants from Carriacou (my maternal grandmother's parents migrated from that island), would sing the most rhythmic songs and were known for their suggestive dances.

J.D. Elder (1988) said that the Temnes who originated in Sierra Leone in West Africa, brought with them to the Caribbean "their culture, something spiritual and their oral traditions – their musical and choreographic arts... without them the ancestors would not enter the ritual dance."[6] It was this culture complex which formed a cluster in the daily activities of people in my village and members of my own family.

CHILDHOOD MEMORIES

In relation to my own experiences of the mysteries of spirituality, I remember my maternal grandmother's sister, Tantie Leatha, who was brought home very ill. She didn't speak, hardly ate and became more emaciated daily. I was about nine years old, when one day my uncle, Pastor Stephens, entered the house from the back round about the middle of the day and went to Tantie Leatha's room.

We heard him conversing aloud in a language we did not understand, at one point he appeared to be having a physical battle with someone, then moments after he began to sing and pray. Tantie got better, returned to her home at Santa Flora and lived to a ripe old age. We learnt later that the "magic" was exorcism and that Spiritual Baptists had the "gift."

Two days before my grandmother, Ma Lovette, died in 1957, she told me that her work was finished and that she was going "over yonder." On the day she died I was instructed to ride my bicycle to Poonah and convey the news to my uncle. I must have gone half the way, just after Bonne Adventure, when the bus approached. I got off my bike and moved on to the grass to avoid an accident with the bus. To my great surprise, my uncle, the Spiritual Baptist, called from the bus "me mother dead, ah get the message!" This was the sort of spirituality with which I was surrounded.

My father's ambition was that his children must be educated. My elder sister, Ionette, was a pupil teacher, my elder brother, Geoffrey, won a government scholarship to Queens Royal College (QRC), Port-of-Spain, and I won a place at St Joseph's Convent, San Fernando. QRC and St Joseph's were two of the most prestigious schools in the country. My father could not afford to pay secondary school fees and it was therefore fortuitous that five of his children won scholarships.

I was later converted to Roman Catholicism and at one time seriously contemplated entering a religious order. After graduating, I taught for a while at Delaford R.C. School in Tobago, Las Lomas R.C. and San Juan Girls R.C. before travelling to London in 1960. I attended the Roman Catholic Digby Stuart College in Roehampton and later lived and taught English at the Capitano Sisters Convent, Crespano Del Grappa, Italy.

I have always been rooted in and cannot be divorced from my peasant background and my African heritage. It was not surprising, therefore, that on my return to Trinidad in 1963, I had a most unusual vision. I was then employed as a Feature Writer at *The Trinidad Evening News*. I dreamt that I was walking up Providence Circular in Arima, about sun down. The road was gravelled, and as I turned the corner, there was a church on the left, perched on a hill. I entered the church, which appeared to be a Spiritual Baptist Church, with the women all wearing ìhead-ties and various uniforms. They were singing "What a friend we have in Jesus." I knew instantly that God was leading me.

The following day I took a taxi after work to Arima. It was Wednesday and I must have arrived in Arima just after 7 p.m.. Providence Circular was just as I saw it. The church was there, divine service was being conducted and when I entered they were singing the very hymn. I stood at the entrance in amazement and a woman shouted from the front, "a stranger has entered the camp!" The entire congregation turned around and I stood there for a while without being able to utter a word. The Leader, Elder Frank, came over and held me, gave me three sips of water from a calabash and a few sips of olive oil.

I introduced myself to the church and explained my vision of the preceding night in great detail. Elder Frank explained to me that many are called, but few are chosen, and that I was chosen by God to join the Spiritual Baptist Faith. I remember the church singing "Come to the Saviour, make no delay," as I knelt at the foot of the cross in full submission.

Arrangements were made for my Baptism and I returned the following Saturday with some white candles and five yards of white cotton material. After the service, I was placed on repentance ground for the night and was baptised around 6 a.m. in the Valencia River. This marked the beginning of a new life, I had become a member of the Order of Melchizedek (for further discussion of this order, see part two) and had made a covenant with God to serve Him to the end.

Important ceremonials on becoming a spiritual Baptist revolve around the Repentance Ground, Baptism and the Hands of Fellowship. The preceding two areas are developed at length in part two, but I shall state briefly the significance of the Hands of Fellowship. After baptism, the candidate is taken to the entrance of the church where the Ten Commandments are read. A Mother is assigned to the candidate and one is taught to bow at the entrance and touch the ground three times, recognising the Creator and simultaneously embracing the Father, Son and Holy Spirit. One is then taken to the Centre Pole (which represents Jesus Christ), in the middle of the church, to pray. The Mother then takes the candidate to the four corners of the church, a symbolic representation of the four cardinal points of the universe which are guarded by four archangels (see part two); then to the altar where the candidate kneels and prays. After this induction, the Leader introduces the candidate to one's spiritual family, then proceeds to the Hands of Fellowship.

This is executed by a firm and vigorous handshake, as a true and sincere greeting, uniting the officiants and candidate in one. The significance of this ritual is attested in biblical writing: "that which we have seen and heard declare we unto you, that ye also may have fellowship with us, and truly our fellowship is with the Father and with his son Jesus Christ." This is translated by a firm grip of both hands with index finger fixed to the under surface of each other's wrists, meaning, "I hold you from falling and you hold me." Three vigorous handshakes in quick succession mean, "we greet in the name of the Father, Son and Holy Spirit." The motion of both hands in firm grip with both thumbs clutched (cf. West African traditional handshakes and what, in modern times, has been characterised as the Black Power handshake), moving three times to each other's breast means:

Once	Your love for my love
Twice	My love for your love
Thrice	For the love of God

When both hands are raised upwards in a firm grip, means "we commend each other to the Almighty God." A warm embrace to each other's bosom three times means, "we meet in love and greet in the name of the Father, Son and Holy Spirit."

I travelled to Montreal, Canada, and spent the entire duration of Expo '67 reporting for *The Trinidad Guardian* and *Evening News*. Thereafter, I was employed as an Information Officer at the Nigerian Embassy in Washington D.C. I returned to London in 1970 and had repeated visions in which I was told to find a Spiritual Baptist Church. I was not aware of the existence of any Spiritual Baptist Churches in London and after much searching found the Mt Zion Spiritual Baptist Church, Boltwood Chapel, Kensal Green.

Bishop Noel had a very large congregation and branch churches in Kennington, Stoke Newington, Slough and Luton. We worshiped at the All Saints Church in Ladbroke Grove and I was appointed Chancellor.

I left Mt Zion in 1980 and began visiting other churches. There were quite a number of Spiritual Baptist Churches meeting in homes, in halls and very rarely in church buildings. I was concerned that there were so many autonomous groups of Spiritual Baptists operating in a vacuum. In 1983, under the auspices of the Greater London Council, I co-ordinated the first London Conference of Independent Black Churches, at All Saints Church. I thought at that time that it was possible for black churches to work together.

The conference itself was successful, but we did not achieve as much as we had hoped in our efforts to bring all Spiritual Baptist Churches together. However, in 1986 The United Council of Spiritual Baptist Churches was inaugurated with a membership of eleven churches. They were Mt Carmel S.B.C., Rt. Rev'd Magna Atherly, Mt Bethel S.B.C., Rt. Rev'd P. Sylvester, Mt. Paran S.B.C., Rt. Rev'd B. Simmons, Jerusalem S.B.C., Rt. Rev'd Arthur Welcome, Seventh Church of Melchisidec S.B., Rt. Rev'd P. Lewis, Emmanuel S.B.C., Matron F. Telesford, Mt. Salem S.B.C., Rev'd Mary Williams, Mt. Zion S.B.C., Rev'd P. Noel, Mt. Zion Halibethian S.B.C, Rt. Rev'd V. McGilvry, Germaine S.B.C and the Rt. Rev'd Ursula Lewis.

Our churches were encouraged to get out into the community, and as General Secretary of the Council I facilitated the formation of community groups attached to our unit churches.

On 12 February 1988, I was ordained into the Priesthood by The Most Reverend Elton Griffith in Port-of Spain, Trinidad. During the ordination ceremony I was prostrate on the ground when I heard the hymn "Forever with the Lord" being sung beautifully by the entire congregation. The late Rt. Rev'd Mother Superior Elaine

Griffith assured me that the hymn was never sung, and that what I heard was a hymn that was given to me in the spirit. I marvelled.

Against that background, I have had to satisfy myself that I could conduct this study of the Spiritual Baptist Faith with the detachment and dispassion appropriate to social analysis and social research.

When I began this project in 1994, I was convinced that I could conduct my interviews as an outsider and remain completely detached from the Faith. However, despite my efforts, this proved impossible. Once you are a member of the Spiritual Baptist Faith, you are discerned by others, particularly those with the gift of "The Eyes of Faith" who are able to see "the seal on my forehead." But there were advantages and disadvantages.

The methodology I chose was that of participant-observer and this enabled me to overcome the well-known pitfalls of being an insider. The researcher as insider, especially when engaged in qualitative research, is inevitably in a difficult position. For one thing, there is the risk of over-identification with the phenomena being studied, to the extent that critical questions could easily be side-stepped or avoided instinctively. Additionally, the research subject(s) may have expectations of the insider, which could fundamentally constrain his/her ability to adopt an impassioned approach to the issue under study.

In my case, as a practising Spiritual Baptist for some 38 years, I have a keen interest in the character and orientation of the Faith world-wide, but especially in Britain and the Caribbean. The question "where now for the Spiritual Baptist Faith?" is of direct relevance to me because of my concern as a member of the Faith, that the SBF and the church are failing to provide a continuity with the past and a direction for the future which could ensure the preservation of the Faith and its crucially important ministry to the young.

I characterise my method as "Participant-Observer" because I cannot establish a distinction between me as a Spiritual Baptist worshipper, Minister of the Word and follower of the Faith, on the one hand, and me the researcher, detached, dispassionate and clinical in my approach to the beliefs, rituals and everyday practices of the Spiritual Baptist Faith, on the other.

The method I employed enabled me to observe "the household of Faith," ask questions and draw conclusions based upon my knowledge of the Faith and the central figures upon whom the responsibility for shepherding the flock and propagating the Faith currently rests.

My ability to access information and interview the "High Command" of the Faith in Trinidad and the other nations has been due in no small measure to their knowledge and perception of me as a sympathetic but critical insider with the skills to represent the present condition of the Faith as sensitively and faithfully as possible.

In other words, unlike a totally detached researcher who might conduct such a study and move on, perhaps after having represented the Faith and the issues facing it in a not altogether sympathetic manner, the leaders of the Faith are aware that for me there is no hiding place. I have got to be seen to be accountable for what I write, the conclusions I draw, the questions I pose, and the way in which the Faith is perceived as a result of the ìtelescopeî I apply to it.

This is not to say that I am consequently constrained in terms of my findings and how I choose to communicate them. Rather, it is an acknowledgement of the fact that I have a special responsibility to bear witness and stand up for the truth, even though the message emerging may be a painful one for the Faith to engage with.

In 1989, when as part of the United Council of Spiritual Baptist Churches in Britain, we hosted a conference in London and had a number of guests from Trinidad, including amongst others, the then Archbishop Elton Griffith of the National Evangelical Spiritual Baptist Faith Archdiocese, it was evident that the Spiritual Baptist Faith was changing direction. I became aware that this was a crucial period in the life of the church and that the Spiritual Baptist Faith was transforming itself from within. I recalled *The Trinidad Guardian* editorial of 1980 and G E Simpsonís tentative statement which I read subsequently (Simpson 1980).

THE STUDY

This book, therefore, is a scholarly attempt to document the historical development of the Spiritual Baptist Faith. The aim of my research is to facilitate a self-understanding of the Faith and to give a general description and analysis of the Faith from a theological and sociological point of view.

The study began in July 1994 and was conducted in Trinidad, Barbados, St Vincent, Grenada and Guyana, where the rich oral tradition of the Caribbean peoples provides a helpful insight into the evolution of the Spiritual Baptist Movement. This religious group, or variations of it, can be found in all the islands, albeit they are called by different names. For example, in St Vincent they are called "Shakers" or "Converteds;" in Barbados "Tie Heads;" in Trinidad, Tobago and Grenada "Spiritual Baptists" or "Shouters;" in Guyana "Spiritualists," and in Jamaica "Pocomania." However, the Faith in all the islands with the exception of Guyana and Jamaica is thought to have a common identity. The "Spiritualists" and "Pocomaniasts" do not consider themselves Spiritual Baptists.

The religious practices and observances of the Spiritual Baptists were a source of ridicule in Caribbean society, and led to the social ostracism of the Faith's adherents. In Trinidad and St Vincent the Faith was outlawed by Prohibition Ordinances, and in Grenada its followers suffered the same hostility from the British colonial authorities and the established churches, especially the Roman Catholics, the Anglicans and Presbyterians. Where there were no definite laws prohibiting the practices of the Shouters, the Colonial establishment discriminated against those bodies. They were not given official status; their clergy did not receive legal recognition and this held true in the Caribbean as a whole.

This study to a great extent is ecclesiographical and historical. It relates and assesses the historical development of the Spiritual Baptists from a sociological perspective. It examines the development of the Spiritual Baptist Faith from its early beginnings as a loosely defined and interconnected movement of the oppressed to what is now an international religious body.

Qualitative methods and especially ethnographic models were used in order to look at various aspects of the Faith in different areas of the Caribbean and produce ethnographic accounts. Unstructured interviews were conducted with carefully selected informants who had specialised knowledge of the subject. In order to obtain information from as wide a cross section of the Faith's followers as possible, informal interviews were carried out also with ordinary members of the Faith. Socio-biographical statements and testimonies were collected. This study made full use of both primary and secondary sources. Services and rituals were audio-recorded and photographs were taken of special events.

The early 1950's saw immigration to Britain from most parts of the Caribbean. Amongst those who settled in London, Birmingham and Huddersfield were many hundred Spiritual Baptists. Followers of the Faith met in each other's homes to worship. What is commonly called "cottage meetings" were held in Shepherds Bush, Brixton, Hackney and other parts of London. One of the first Spiritual Baptist Churches, "The Household of Faith," was established at 47 Brackenbury Road, London W6, in 1964. Three of its foundation members, Archbishop Patrick Sylvester, Bishop Magna Atherly and Elder C. Flemming, were members of the United Council of Spiritual Baptist Churches (U.K) which was inaugurated in July 1986.

The first convention of the United Council of Spiritual Baptist Churches was held at the Aylesbury Community School, London NW6, on 25 October 1986. It was articulated then that the primary objective of the Faith in Britain was to establish a collective body that could represent Spiritual Baptist churches at various government departments and agencies. The Council sought to seek placements for senior ministers on statutory bodies such as prisons and chaplaincies, local health and education committees and any other bodies that make decisions which affect the lives of the African and Caribbean community. The Council also sought to provide training and other facilities to member churches in their community care projects and to develop itself as a community resource and information bureau with emphasis on the Spiritual Baptist Faith and African/Caribbean culture.

SOCIO-BIOGRAPHY OF THE SPIRITUAL BAPTIST FAITH

The Spiritual Baptist Faith is often thought to be just another "branch" of the Baptist Church, which originated in England and is regarded as one of the Protestant Churches. This is particularly true of the Faith and its adherents in Britain, especially among white English people the view is held that "a Baptist is a Baptist" and that black Baptists who call themselves "Spiritual" have simply developed foreign and exotic ways of professing the faith.

On the contrary, the Spiritual Baptist Faith is not just a church or a denomination. It is a "Faith," a "belief system" that is rooted within an African conceptualisation of religion and a deep spirituality which attests to the work of the Holy Spirit in shaping the Faith and governing the lives of the faithful.

After the British took the colony of Trinidad in 1797, slaves were brought in from other British-held territories and were distributed throughout the Caribbean nations. They brought with them their indigenous forms of worship and ritual and some doctrines of British churches. According to Edric Connor in his paper written in 1943:

> There were also slaves who used the English language which they applied to the practice of their African customs and disregarded the British churches and their rules. The "Shouters" we now know are descendants from the last mentioned group of outsiders who settled in Princes Town district, Moruga, Mayaro, Guapo, Tunapuna, Macqueripe, Morne Diablo and Santa Cruz. Their worship in many respects is similar to *Voodun*, and *Shango*. They concern the Order of Melchisidec, the outstanding difference is the fact that they use no drums. They use their voices to produce drum sounds which are in seven different forms and rhythms known as "Doption" from the English "adopt." I think these Shouters have furnished us with a large repertoire of good music. In my research I have found that the songs they used before 1890 are much better than those composed after that period.[7]

The adoption of guttural sounds is unique to Spiritual Baptists. Archbishop Randoo describes them as "the Song of God in man." She sees the Faith as emerging from the ravages of slavery to offer spiritual redemption, and believes that the cultural patterns surrounding the Faith were developed in order to enable its adherents to meet the challenges of oppression. It began as a movement of the lower class people in the middle 19th century. Those Africans who had their roots destroyed during slavery re-created an identity in an unequal social system.

As Warner-Lewis (1991) observed:

> Once legally free of direct involvement in this distorted social system, the slaves deserted the plantations..and set up villages. There, they reverted to patterns of life to which they were traditionally accustomed.[8]

Religion was one of their traditional patterns of life, as Mbiti (1975) explains:

> Religion dominates everything which adds up to the creation of the African personality... African religion gives its followers a sense of security in life; and through their religious way of life, they know who they are, how to act in different situations and how to solve their problems. The freed slaves used religion as a mechanism to adopt to their changed social environment.[9]

According to Brereton (1979), religious dances and the indigenous way of worship offered them:

> ...emotional release from economic hardships, political impotence and social humiliations.... religion provided a haven from rejection by the dominant classes and an index of status and authority within the black lower class.[10]

Slavery left a horrendous legacy amongst Africans in the colony. After full emancipation in 1838, freed slaves were poor, they were unable to purchase land, jobs were difficult to find or offered at starvation wages, and as a result they were forced to work at least part-time for their former slave masters. They squatted in their villages, often in tied cottages on the land of their former masters, they were insecure, but preserved a sense of themselves and positive self respect. It was this group of people that formed the nucleus of the Spiritual Baptist movement.

Pearse (1958) provides this brief overview of the Faith:

> The Shouters or Spiritual Baptists of Trinidad have modified the practices and beliefs of the Protestant sects, especially the Baptists, and added their rites from the African cults, their leaders often having served these cults. Though the music and words of the hymns come from the Protestant sects, they are thrown into intense and compelling movement by vocalised rhythmic breathing, (pumping) hand clapping and downward thrusting dance.
> In the older versions of the cult, the initiated dance around a central pole. In possession by the Holy Spirit their movements are similar to the manifestations of the African cults. The state of possession is accompanied by visions, the interpretation of which by the leaders, serves as their guide to action.[11]

The Spiritual Baptist Faith that emerged was a dynamic collision of African and Caribbean culture. One of the main characteristics of the movement is that it acted as an agent for mobilising the dispossessed into accepting the positive aspects of their African origin. They were a cohesive group because of their bondage in slavery. They were concerned with and worked to secure the welfare of their group.

In the early days, the theologies and rituals of the Spiritual Baptists were improvised. Over time, the practitioners adopted some of their masters' religious practices, thus creating a Creole religion. The Spiritual (Shouter) Baptists in the Caribbean then, not only struggled to carry out their religious rituals and traditional forms of worship without being discovered by their masters, but also had to come to terms with the intrusion of the master's religion into their belief system as an inevitable process.

Thus the gap between the African indigenous religions as practised in Africa and what the Spiritual Baptists constructed within the specific conditions in which they were placed is immense. It may be viewed as a broken continuum, one which relied on ancestral memory, something disjointed, ruptured and a gaping wound in terms of the original wholeness; a wound which could be healed by shaping the Faith around the struggle for dignity in the hostile environment of the slaves' new world.

The whole atmosphere of secrecy and illegality attached to the Spiritual Baptist movement, precluded the fact that it would become not only a form of protest, but that elements of its worship had to adjust and experiment with ways of expression which would utilise the body like a musical instrument, as opposed to the use of drums which were forbidden. One notes the guttural sounds which Archbishop Randoo describes as "the song of God in man."

The fact that the Spiritual Baptists were banned from practising their religion may be accounted for, in part, by the feelings of inadequacy and embarrassment which their former masters experienced in the knowledge that they never really controlled the heart and spirit of a people, and the fact that despite all their persecution and shameful brutality they could not kill the spirit of the people and their determination to practise their religion.

Should one deconstruct the Spiritual Baptist religious discourse, one would find that it privileges the African religious experience, placing Africa, its history and culture centre stage, while placing European religious orthodoxy on the margins of their existence.

Chapter Two

An Overview Of The History Of Trinidad
1783-1908

I t has been generally recognised that the modern history of Trinidad began in 1783, after the introduction of Cedula of Population. Williams, (1962) in his *A History of the People of Trinidad and Tobago* wrote:

> A On November 20th 1783, the Kings of Spain issued the famous Cedula of Population, opening Trinidad's doors under certain conditions to foreign immigrants.[1]

One of the conditions was that foreigners could settle and invest in the development of Trinidad. The conditions were that immigrants must be Roman Catholic and prepared to swear allegiance to the King of Spain. Land grants were given free of charge to immigrant families, the extent of each land grant was being determined by race, size of the family and the number of slaves each family bought. Immigrants were offered certain tax concessions and incentives..[2]

The importation of Africans and other peoples was part of the policy of the Spanish Government's attempts not only to establish, but to perpetuate the plantation system of agricultural production. After Trinidad was captured by Britain in

1797, the British continued the Spanish policy and larger shiploads of African slaves, of different tribes and from varying countries, arrived.

With people settling in significant numbers after 1783, the question of plantation supplies, including slaves, arose. The French, and to a lesser extent, the Spanish, had begun to supply slaves from their respective slave trading ports in Africa.

Slaves were also supplied from the same British slave trading ports that supplied Barbados and Grenada. Between 1783 and 1797 Barbados, unlike Trinidad, had become a long established plantation society, and according to Selwyn Carrington, "was saturated with slaves."[3] Trinidad, on the other hand, had an insatiable demand for slaves. During this period, Jamaica and Barbados became transshipment points for slaves bound for Spanish-owned Trinidad. By 1797, the origins of African slaves in Trinidad had become obscured.

The outbreak of the French Revolution in 1789 further resulted in revolts among the slave populations of Haiti, Martinique, Guadeloupe, Dominica, St Vincent and Grenada, and brought a fresh wave of immigrants seeking a safe haven in Trinidad. These refugees also brought their slaves with them, hence it became more difficult to ascertain the origins of the slaves in the colony.

The most critical implication of the British capture was that African slaves did not cease to be a valuable commodity. Slaves were in even greater demand and were now imported directly from British-held slave trading ports in Africa. They were also imported from other British-held colonies in the West Indies. Trinidad began to attract British settlers, not only from the British Isles, but also from the British and French West Indies.

1797–1870

A decade after the capture of Trinidad, the British Government decided to put an end to its own slave trade. Trinidad was still a relatively new colony, and the British had been actively pressing ways and means to make this a model colony. Trinidad received several companies of ex-slaves, former soldiers and free men, who had fought on the British side during the War of 1812 against the United States. These former soldiers reached Trinidad in 1815, and were settled in places, which eventually bore their name – the "Company" villages. This battalion, prior to their

departure from the United States, had been converted to the Baptist religion and
was noted by John Stewart (1976) when he wrote:

> ...the Baptist faith was in fact introduced [in Trinidad] ..Ö. by a number of black refugees
> who had themselves been members of the earliest Black Baptist congregation in the
> Southern United States of America. This early conflagration had developed along the
> Savannah River - which marks the state boundary between South Carolina and Georgia - prior
> to the American Revolutionary War, but was broken up and dispersed as a direct conse-
> quence of the war itself.[4]

Archbishop Raymond Oba Douglas makes the same point:

> The Baptist religion came to Trinidad by African ex-slaves in 1815 from America... The first
> boat load arrived in May 1815 by *HMS Levant* with 61 men, women and children, who settled
> in Naparima and the third, fourth and fifth company in Moruga.[5]

The story of the Anglicisation of Trinidad has been told in the *History of Modern
Trinidad 1783-1962* by Bridget Brereton. The implications of this Anglicisation policy followed by the British were significant for the colony's African population. The
first matter to be dealt with is the influx of Africans who were freed slaves into
Trinidad from Sierra Leone, West Africa. They were given indentureship contracts
and were to settle eventually as free men. Insufficient numbers of freed slaves from
Africa arrived and as a result they could not supply free labour to the planters from
that source as envisaged. Hence, an alternative labour force was brought in, mainly from India, and this resulted in the depressing of wages in the colony.

The second point is that the British Government encouraged migration into
Trinidad from other parts of the British West Indies. These new immigrants spoke
English, were Protestant in religion, and were accustomed to British rule. Anthony
De Verteuil noted, "...with the influx of immigrants from Barbados, St. Kitts and
Nevis, the population was becoming each day more Protestant and less Catholic."[6]

Brereton made a similar observation:

> The years after 1840, therefore, saw many different types of immigration into the island.
> Trinidad's black population was supplemented from two sources, there was A large, spon-
> taneous, and steady influx from the eastern Caribbean, nearly all of African descent, attract

ed by high wages, and the relative availability of land and jobs.

Another implication was the change of laws. The British government eliminated the social rights of black people which they previously enjoyed under Spanish law. Africans were no longer able to inherit property from their white masters and parents; they were not allowed to purchase land below a certain acreage, so effectively they were prohibited from land-ownership. The introduction of the Christians from England was a deliberate move to ensure that English-speaking immigrants from other parts of the West Indies were kept away from the charismatic Africanised religions.

In their desperate attempt to keep Trinidad British, the government allowed the entry of English and Irish Catholic clergy. This move was opposed by the Trinidad French Creoles and championed by Louis A. de Verteuil.[8]

After the Battle of Trafalgar in 1805, the British navy stood unchallenged on the seas. It would not fight a major naval battle until the first World War (1914–1918). In the mean time part of the British Navy was employed in the seizing of slave trading ships of other nations still engaged in the slave trade, particularly the French, Spanish, Portuguese and Americans. After these slave-laden ships were taken to Sierra Leone and St. Helena, the slaves were freed and given the option of either making their way back to their respective homelands or to go to work in the West Indies, particularly Trinidad.

Maureen Warner-Lewis informs us that a significant number of Africans who had briefly experienced the trauma of capture and slavery had been baptised as Christians at Freetown, capital of Sierra Leone, before leaving for the Caribbean, "Baptism was administered at Freetown in some cases..."[9]

Brereton confirms that not all of the Africans who came to Trinidad were Christian:

> Most of them had just been rescued from the slaveships, or had been liberated only a short time before they emigrated. They spoke no English; they were "Pagan retaining the full vigour of their tribal customs.... they were for the West Indies a throwback to those who had been transported to British islands before...1807.[10]

De Verteuil,. in his book, *Trinidad*, first published in 1858, also noted the trend, "About 4,000 Africans, liberated from captured slaves, have been added to that class since emancipation."[11]   According to De Verteuil, in the Trinidad Census of 1851, there was a total of 8,150 people born in Africa out of a population of 69,600:

Natives of Trinidad -	40,584
Natives of Africa -	8,150
Natives of Europe -	1,508
Natives of Asia -	4,200
Emigrants from other parts -	15,158
	69,600[12]

Indigenous Africans made up the third largest single group. Added to this group, there were Africans who included among them "natives of Trinidad", and "emigrants from other parts."

An education system in which the language of instruction was English was introduced around 1851, and this system was completely outside the control of the religious bodies. As a result, the dominant linguistic pattern changed gradually from French to English. The Christian missionaries also played a vital role by imposing Christianity from a British standpoint.

The British introduction of people from other parts of the world was not the only development in Trinidad which is of interest to us. Trinidad also received, with British support, a number of Christian missions, particularly those of the non-conformist branch of Christianity. This was an addition to the Church of England after the British capture. De Verteuil (1858) noted the presence of: "Roman Catholics; Episcopalians or Church of England; Wesleyan Methodist; Presbyterians; Baptist; and Independents and others."[13]

The introduction of these missions served at least two purposes; they catered for the spiritual needs of the faithful who had settled in Trinidad in significant numbers; and they saw in Trinidad an opportunity to gain new adherents for their respective faiths. For the British rulers, the entry of these non-conformists further diversified the linguistic and religious landscape in order to make Trinidad British.

In the particular context of the Baptist denomination, a British missionary, George Cowen began his ministry in Trinidad in the year 1843. This is reported by both Underhill (1862) and East (1892).

Figure 3

Mrs. Mabel Salazaar, age 95 of Marabella, Trinidad, whose mother Eliza Salazaar was born in 1871, was a direct descendent of indigenous African slaves (Photo by the Author).

The Baptist Mission in Trinidad was formed in the year 1843, when the Rev. George Cowen commenced preaching the gospel in Port of Spain.[14]

It was in 1843 that the attention of the Baptist Missionary Society was directed to it. This was by Mr George Cowen, a Baptist, who had long wished to be engaged in preaching the Gospel.[15]

What the story unfolding so far suggests, is that from 1783 to 1900 Trinidad became a melting pot of the world's races, religions, aesthetics, cultures, medicines, music, song and dance. Within this community a wide variety of ethnic groups emerged. According to Donald Wood (1986):

> The picture is somewhat clearer as far as the liberated slaves are concerned, although wide areas of uncertainty nonetheless exist. When they were being brought to Trinidad it was sometimes glibly stated that they were easily assimilated into the Creole population, but the process took longer and was more complex than the supporters of their immigration claimed.[16]
>
> Among the passengers in the Senator in 1844 were Atams, Ibos, and Kalabari from present day Nigeria, Popos from Dahomey, Kossos from Upper Volta, Shebros and Temne from Sierra Leone, Muslims and Wolofs from Senegal, Krus from Liberia and Contos.[17]

It was not expected that such diverse groups of people would integrate easily with one another nor with the "natives" of Trinidad or other immigrants.

Members of the same tribe tended to congregate once they had left the estates and, as they

Figure 4

Mrs. Mary Munroe, sister of Mabel Salazaar whose parents came to Trinidad directly from Africa. (Photo by the Author).

did in Sierra Leone, to form their own villages in which they could enjoy the security of common language and shared habits.[18]

J .J. Thomas stated in *Froudacity* that:

> The Congoes were the most numerous and important ethnic grouping, that practised their own religious cults very privately in an area known as Congo Wood in South Trinidad.[19]

It has been reported that a large number of this group were Yorubas and they settled in villages throughout the colony. Trotman (1976) notes that:

> The Yoruba immigrants to Trinidad came to a plantation society in its formative stage. By virtue of its recency and diversity of its population, the contours of the Creole culture were still being shaped. With large scale immigration and favourable economic and geographical conditions for group isolation, it was infinitely easier for the Yorubas to retain their group identity and practise their indigenous culture.[20]

By 1859, Trinidad was home to a growing population of *Orishas* and Spiritual Baptists. They comprised those who had nurtured the Faith and kept alive the various religious traditions within the harsh confines of the plantation, those who had been transferred from other islands, having been practising their faith irrespective of the structural constraints, and the now much smaller group that joined them directly from Africa.

The only thing all these groupings experienced in common was the unspeakable hostility towards their practice of indigenous religion and their cultural expression that reflected their defiance of the barbarism of slavery and their determination to affirm their African identity. The organised European churches kept alive among slave-owners past and present, and among African converts to Christianity, the notion that traditional African religious practices were hedonistic and that only conversion to Christianity would redeem those whose religious beliefs and practices were still rooted in Africa.

As a consequence, the established order placed the adherents of the African religious traditions on the margins of society and heaped hostility upon them.

In the pre-emancipation era, i.e., prior to 1838, the Spiritual Baptist Faith evolved within the strictures that were imposed upon the slaves. The established churches, Roman Catholic or Protestant, worked hand in hand with slave-owners in order to seek to impose christianity upon the Africans. Consequently, the Africans accommodated two traditions, namely, African religious customs and beliefs and the Christian tradition in the form of an amalgam of different rituals, practices and beliefs. But it should be noted that biblical christianity, both from the Old and New Testaments, provides the researcher with ample information in forging a comparison between African traditions of religion and what can be characterised as christian fundamentalism. The body of thought, philosophy, ceremonies, rituals and world-view developed by proponents of the Faith demonstrate (in part two) without a doubt that they inherited specific religious traditions which resonated easily with christian fundamentalist's practices.

Religious worship became a clandestine activity, conducted in different modes or "registers." Traditional rituals and ceremonies provided opportunities for full participation by the faithful. However, they also needed to practise the religious rituals the colonial church insisted upon under pain of flogging, enforced separation or worse.

Binding the head with a white cloth, ringing a bell at intervals during meetings, holding lighted candles in the hands, turbulent shaking of the body and limbs, shouting and the expression of guttural sounds, writing with chalk marks on the floor in addition to other practices were prohibited. Leader Archie, who had a church in Cocorite, St. James, often had two watchmen at the door to herald the arrival of police.   On seeing the police, the watchmen would shout loudly "Sampson, Sampson, the Philistines are upon you!" The entire gathering would then disperse with their paraphernalia, in order to avoid being arrested by the pursuing police. The interruption of such meetings meant that the faithful would switch registers to make it appear that they were adhering to the teachings and religious practices that were meant to displace their own.

Some respondents believe that the *Orisha* tradition no less than the non-*Orisha* Spiritual Baptist tradition is a rich synthesis of African traditional religion and of the practices of the established Christian Churches. In other words, over time, the two distinct registers merged giving rise to a distinctive and uniquely Caribbean Faith which is at one and the same time a cultural art form that gains expression through melodious singing and humming, drumming, pumping *doptions*, etc.

The Spiritual Baptist Faith, therefore, could be said to have evolved in a specific way because God's people kept alive a clandestine church, convinced of the guiding power of the Holy Spirit and of the Spirit of their ancestors. That the One, Supreme and Indivisible Spirit rewarded their faith and courage by manifesting itself during their religious ceremonies and giving guidance, teaching, healing and chiding.

CHAPTER THREE

BELIEFS & PRACTICES OF
THE SPIRITUAL BAPTIST FAITH

W hatever contestations there may be about the historical origins of the Spiritual Baptist Faith, it is more than likely that the Faith as practised in the Caribbean and by Caribbean settlers in North America and Europe is an accretion of beliefs and ritualistic practices that have evolved over three centuries.

The authority for the fundamental practices within the Faith, i.e., those which are "essential" in that they constitute the distinguishing features of the Faith, rests in "Holy Writ." The Faith sees its "mission" as being first and foremost to call sinners to repentance and to Baptism by the Holy Spirit in "living"/running water. In order for the reader to gain a thorough understanding of the beliefs and practices of the Spiritual Baptist Faith, however, a number of key terms require explanation, as follows:

Glossary of Symbols used in the Spiritual Baptist Church

Scale of Balance	Justice
The Balance Wheel	Righteous Living
The Cross	Deliverance, Victory over death
The Scale	Discernment in Personal Life
Eternal Light	God's presence
Cords	Strength
Seals	Closed mysteries
Incense	Prayer
Trees	Man
The Burning Bush	Holy Spirit
Goat's Hair	Atonement
The Star	Guide, Pointer

The following contain the primary symbols used in the Spiritual Baptist Faith and constitute only an introduction to their meaning.

BELL

The bell plays a significant role in Spiritual Baptist worship and has various uses:

Call to worship
Invocation of the Holy Spirit
Consecration
Benediction
Dispellation of evil
The toll of death
Silence
Amen

FLAG

A flag denotes the presence of a carnal sovereign or a spiritual deity. Spiritual Baptists use various flags in their churches, at baptism and in the Mourner's Room;

there are:

Nation Flags
Protection Flags
Messenger Flags
Conqueror Flags
Deliverance Flags
Defence Flags
Each flag has its individual colour and design.

CANDLES

Candles are used in all Spiritual Baptist rituals, and the colour of the candles also plays an important part in the rituals.

White	-	Purity, Truth and Righteousness
Red	-	Love, Fire and Blood
Blue	-	Healing, Happiness
Green	-	Prosperity, Peace
Pink	-	Success
Yellow	-	Spirituality
Brown	-	Positive, Definite
Purple	-	Victory, Royalty
Black	-	Strength, Remembrance
Mauve	-	Power

SWORD

Judgement
The Spirit that cuts all sins out of personal life
The Separator from evil

SHEPHERD'S ROD

The staff of God which is used for measuring the depths of water and to certify that the territorial boundary is safe to perform the ceremony of Baptism.

The paramount belief of a Spiritual Baptist, therefore, is a belief in the Holy Spirit and the power and presence of the Spirit in the life and the affairs of the faithful. The Holy Spirit "arrests" souls and elects them for baptism, sometimes when they least intend to pronounce the death sentence on their life in sin and embrace a new life with Christ in the Spirit. Conventionally, however, a pilgrim would be prepared for baptism during a period of repentance and instruction on "mercy seat."

That instruction would invariably focus on the Gospels of Matthew 3, Mark 1, Luke 3, John 1 and the Book of Acts. Instructions on the themes of repentance, justification and righteousness would be given, with numerous references to Romans 3, 4, 5, 6, 7, 8; John 14, 17; Psalms 1, 13, 14, 32, 131.

Other fundamental beliefs and requirements of the Faith are:

a)   A belief in the power of the revealed Word of God, and in the power of prayer. The need for ministers and adherents of the Faith alike to preach and interpret the Word. As an individual responsibility, the need to pray the Word, to study the Word, to meditate upon the Word.

The need to spread the Word and discharge one's responsibility to convert sinners to a life in Christ and away from sin.

b)   A belief in the cleansing power of Fasting and of Mourning, activities which assist the faithful in "taking self out of self" and in elevating the Spirit within so that s/he may more readily commune with God and experience a wholeness in the Spirit.

The authority for the above is also to be found in "Holy Writ" in diverse parts, including the four Gospels, the Letters of Paul, and Daniel 10: 20–21.

The liturgical practices of the Faith reflect these fundamental beliefs and responsibilities. The order of the divine service, the manner of singing hymns and of chanting, the Pointer's observation of pilgrims on Mercy Seat, Repentance Ground, in the Mourner's Room prior to Baptism, and during mourning, all play a major part in ensuring the integrity and continuity of the Faith.

BAPTISM

Great importance is attached to Baptism as entry to the Spiritual Baptist Faith. The early mission statement "repent and be Baptised, the Kingdom of Heaven is at hand," still holds true in most cases, because Spiritual Baptists believe that Baptism regenerates the soul. Archbishop John Noel of the Children of the Light Spiritual Baptist Shrine at La Sagesse, Grenada, affirmed:

> Some people get the notion that when they baptise, they have accomplished their goal. We are teaching them that when they baptise they *begin* the process of trying to accomplish their goal and not that they have accomplished anything. They are now born again and begin to grow in the spirit. So we have them *sanctify* themselves, that means they partake of nothing worldly for seven days prior to their Baptism and seven days after.

The late Bishop Clement Nain Griffith of the Spiritual Baptist Chapel of the Wildwood, L'Anse Mitan, Trinidad, explained in 1994 that Spiritual Baptists believe that "candidates are baptised backwards so that when they rise out of the water, they face eastwards where the sun and positive vibrations therefrom penetrate our planet."

MOURNING

Everyone who is baptised does not necessarily go to mourn. One must be called or have the desire to have a closer walk with God. Some Spiritual Baptists describe Mourning as a period of "Godly sorrow" and it is generally understood that mourning is necessary for spiritual development in the Faith.

It is symbolic of death and resurrection. In the inner chamber a candidate is placed westward for three days and three nights and it is said that the candidate is now in the grave. After three days, the candidate is changed around and placed eastward, but in doing so there is a ritual that is performed where you are risen from the grave, so that resurrection and death in the Mourning Room is symbolised.

Some candidates travel in the mystical plane, some travel to the continents of Africa and Asia and return to tell their experience. Bishop Magna Atherly, Leader of Mount Carmel Spiritual Baptist Church in London, gives an interesting account of her spiritual journeys (see Part Two).

A pilgrim is sanctified for seven days before Mourning and seven days after. The

Figure 5

Leader Leon Millette of the Tribe of Judah Spiritual Baptists during a baptismal ritual at Dhein's Bay, Carenage, Trinidad. The ceremony took place at sunrise (Photo courtesy *The Trinidad Guardian*).

period spent in the inner chamber or Mourner's Room can vary from 7 – 21 days. During the period of isolation and prayer, the candidate travels in the Spiritual realm.

BANDS AND SEALING

Bands and Seals are placed on candidates before they are baptised and before they mourn. The Bands are triangles or squares of cotton material that have been blessed, then writings are placed on them to cover the eyes so that the candidates are encouraged to look within themselves, in order to reflect on their relationship with God. The practice of placing Bands on candidates is taken from Ezekiel 4:8 "And behold, I will lay bands upon thee and thou shalt not turn thee from one side to another...." Most Mothers use blue and white bands for baptism and coloured bands for mourning. The white and blue bands used at baptism are for spiritual sight and for praying. The colour of the bands used in mourning would be determined by the spiritual standing of the pilgrim. Each colour has its virtues; red, the blood of Jesus Christ and victory; blue, truth and healing; yellow, spirituality and love; white, purity, etc. Symbols or signs are written on these bands with chalk or candle as guided by the Holy Spirit.

Specific reference is made to Revelation 7:3: "Saying, hurt not the earth, neither the sea, nor the trees, till we have sealed the servants of God on their foreheads." After placing the bands the Pointer whispers a password to the pilgrim, which is used to defend them against evil forces on their journey. The Password, Key or Sword is revealed to the Pointer by the Holy Spirit. Each pilgrim gets a different password, which could be a biblical quotation or a short phrase or sentence.

SINKING PILGRIMS

This ceremony is important, because it is said that unless the pilgrim is able to "come out of self and sink himself into the Spirit," he will not travel. Therefore, in order to assist him, the Mothers symbolically press various parts of his body down. A Bell, Bible, *Lotah* with water, flowers and a lighted candle are used to sink the pilgrim. Each part of the body that is pressed down in the ritual has great significance.

The head is the helmet of salvation; the shoulder is for bearing the cross; the back shields one from the blow of the enemy; the chest is the breastplate of righteousness; the abdomen is the bowels of mercy and compassion, and the rod and staff symbolise that Christ would comfort them throughout the journey. Each part of the body is pressed down with the Bible and *Lotah* whilst ringing the bell. When this is finished the pilgrim is spun around three times then placed to lie on the ground facing upward.

SURVEYING

Spiritual Baptists always survey their place of worship because it is not "an abiding place." They use the Bell, a *Lotah* or Calabash filled with water and a lighted candle to survey the four corners of the church, the entrance, exits, centre-pole and altars to invite the celestial order of Spirits to protect them and their work throughout the service.

The four Archangels are very significant in the Spiritual Baptist Faith; they have a great part to play in the worship and invocations that are made to them. Raphael rules the East, Gabriel the West, Auriel the North and Michael rules the South. They are the *Four Watchers of the Plane* and Spiritual Baptists accept that they are the keepers of the peace on earth and are actually holding the winds of strife.

The Surveyor also invites unseen guests by ringing the bell and sprinkling water, moving backwards as she does so. If and when it is necessary, evil entities are dispelled by surveying from the altar and the centre-pole outward to the main entrance.

The fundamentals described above constitute the distinguishing features of the Spiritual Baptist Faith. The rituals and liturgical practices within the faith have clearly undergone adaptation and change over some two hundred to three hundred years. As this research study has indicated, a critical concern among the elders of the Faith set the pace and direction of change.

The transcripts of interviews with elders and members of the ecclesiastical hierarchy provide vivid accounts of the role and importance of the various ritualistic and liturgical practices within the Faith. Those transcripts also provide evidence of the metaphysical character of the Faith in that its adherents are often able to influence events or phenomena in a manner that cannot be explained without an acknowledgement of the paranormal.

As the next chapter demonstrates, the Faith protected itself and survived during periods of persecution because of the seemingly inexplicable power Spiritual Baptists were thought to possess, as evidenced by what they caused to happen or by what was attributed to their involvement or direct intervention. Consequently, some of their practices were viewed with deep suspicion if not with fear.

What could not be explained was ridiculed and condemned. The African retentions in the Faith led sceptics, unbelievers and detractors to condemn the practices of its adherents no less than its forms of worship as "sinister," as inspired by "dark evil forces" and geared towards wielding undue influence over unsuspecting folk.

In this chapter, the reader engages with those charged to propagate the Faith, to lead, to teach and to inspire. Their accounts are central to an understanding of the Faith if only because it is not possible simply to present a description of the Spiritual Baptist Faith. The Faith is what its adherents practise. The custodians of the authenticity of its practices are its Elders. The teachings and preachings of Elders and of Mothers, Leaders, Shepherds and Ministers are often inspired by the Holy Spirit. As in oral traditions, seldom are there prepared texts, drafted, redrafted and finally honed (although ideas, subjects and procedures are relentlessly debated, scrutinised and measured).

The Faith has no accepted body of doctrines or dogmas. Consequently, in the transcripts, the Elders provide descriptive and explanatory accounts of the rituals, pastoral activities, spiritual gifts and metaphysical experiences of the adherents of the Faith. They explain the centrality to the Faith, of the Centre Pole, of the "Mercy

Figure 6

Mourners preparing to give "tracks" at St. Mary's Spiritual Baptist Church, Overland, St. Vincent (Photo by Author).

Seat," the use of the Bell, the use of chants, the number of hymns sung at the start of a service or a prayer meeting (for elaboration of these ideas, see part two).

Three crucial elements of the Faith are the *Centre Pole*, the *Mourner's Room* and *Mercy Seat*. They serve as central barometers of the Spiritual Baptist's faith and desire to progress spiritually within the framework of God, our Creator, and Christ

THE CENTRE POLE

All important ritual ceremonies revolve around the Centre Pole, which is the principal identifying feature of a Spiritual Baptist Church. The Centre Pole can be elaborate or simple, the top represents the centre of heaven and the foot represents the grave. The beams which secure the post to the roof form a star-shaped ceiling demonstrating the work of God in the heavens. Spiritual Baptists on entering the church, pray first at the Centre Pole – they believe that Jesus, the Christ, is always present there.

MOURNER'S ROOM

The Mourner's Room is the true temple of the Spiritual Baptist Faith. It is built on the design used by Moses to build the Ark of the Covenant, and the tabernacle described in the Book of Exodus 2:3: "And when she could no longer hide him she took for him an ark of the bulrushes and daubed it with slime and with pitch and put the child therein; and she laid it in the flags by the river's brink."

The traditional Mourner's Room is a small square building attached to the church. In the middle is a Centre Pole, which Spiritual Baptists say reminds them of Moses, who when he took up his priestly work, planted his staff in the midst of the temple. The floor of the room is never paved nor tiled, because Spiritual Baptists believe that when you mourn, the pilgrim must connect with Mother Earth.

Around the Centre Pole there is a raised pedestal on which lights, flowers, bells, flags, thunder stones and goblets of water are placed. There are benches around the side of the room and hanging from the roof is a wheel with lighted candles, the Balance Wheel.

MERCY SEAT

Most traditional churches have a bench set aside at the front of the church on which candidates for Baptism or for Mourning sit throughout the duration of their instructions. This bench is called *Mercy Seat* and the name is derived from the plea to God for mercy.

Crucial to the Faith and the nature of religious observance within it are the various injunctions which appear to be universally followed. These include strictures concerning the forms of dress women must adopt, e.g., having their heads tied when in church or worshipping in the open air, where they may sit, e.g., women may not sit at the altar with male leaders/ministers. Similarly, it is universally accepted that shoes are not to be worn by anyone in the Mourner's Room or around the altar. Indeed, some churches prohibit the wearing of shoes inside the church altogether.

There are other important events which characterise the adherent's indebtedness to God for answering his/her prayers. *Thanksgiving* is a fundamentalist Judeo-Christian activity as well as it has its more remote antecedents in Ancient Egyptian and traditional African offerings, either to the Sole Creator, a deity or ancestors.

Figure 7
The Mother rings the bell to invite the celestial order of spirits before the beginning of worship. The bell is used in conjunction with water and a lighted candle (Photo courtesy Andy Hypolite, *The Independent*).

THANKSGIVING

Most Spiritual Baptists believed that *Thanksgiving* originated when the children of Israel came out of Egypt. Moses laid a table and gave thanks to God, and this tradition is carried on by Spiritual Baptists today. When something significant occurs in the life of a Spiritual Baptist, s/he is encouraged to lay a table and give thanks as a recognition of the blessings received.

Bishop Ruby Hunt of St. Peters Spiritual Baptist Cathedral, Gonzales, Trinidad, explained that there are different types of Thanksgiving.

> We have Thanksgiving of Lights, where the individual may be spirituality directed to have plain white lights or coloured lights on the table and again prayers are being offered giving God thanks for the Christ Light in their lives. Then we have Thanksgiving of Sweets, which is a sweet table where everything that is offered is sweet. This signifies that the Word of God is sweet and by offering this table is a form of the Word made flesh and dwelling amongst us in the form of radiating light. This table is giving God thanks for spiritual elevation and transformation of life.
>
> We have *Food Thanksgiving*. The Spiritual Baptist Faith is built on inspiration so at times an individual may be asked to give a table of food, with meat or without meat.
>
> Prayers are being offered and the food is blessed, consecrated and shared. The sharing of the food is a form of the Word of God, when they eat the food, they are both being physically and spiritually filled.
>
> We have *Nation Feast Thanksgiving*, which consist of food, a combination of all the sacrifices together which are Prayers, Lights, the Sweet Table, the Food Table and food of different nations like Africa, India, China, all being cooked, blessed and served to the poor and

Figure 8
Thanksgiving table given by the Author. See previous pages
for explanation.

all those who are needy.

All these are central to the practice of the Faith, the insights to be gained from
the accounts of Elders who have been practising the Faith for many years will provide the reader with an essential backdrop to the story of the prohibition of the
Faith and its struggle for survival during a lengthy period of proscription.

This story is told in the next chapter.

CHAPTER FOUR

PERIOD OF PROSCRIPTION
TRINIDAD 1917 - 1951

On 28 November 1917, the Government of Trinidad passed the Shouters Prohibition Ordinance, with a view to suppress the Shouter Baptist Movement in the colony. The Ordinance failed in its objective and on 26 April 1951, the Legislative Council of Trinidad voted to restore the Spiritual (Shouter) Baptist's rights to worship. The fact that this religious group was able to survive the period of proscription which was meant to legislate them out of existence shows their adherents' determination to hold on to their Faith in face of the legalised persecution at the hands of the state. In Trinidad, the research conducted by M.J. Herskovits for his books, *The Myth of the Negro Past*[1] and *Trinidad Village*[2] suggests that the Spiritual Baptists had begun to increase in numbers in spite of the Ordinance. In 1949, a colony-wide petition circulated by the West Indian Evangelical Spiritual Baptist Faith placed their membership at 30,000.[3]

At the time of the passage of the Ordinances, Crown Colony Government was the order of the day for most of the British West Indies. All executive power was vested in the office of Governor who administered the colony with the assistance of colonial officials, for example, the Attorney-General, the Comptroller of Customs and Inspector General of the Constabulary. Completing the Legislative Council were the unofficial members, all of whom were nominated by the Governor.

Bridget Brereton gives an explanation of the reasons why the British Government decided to introduce Crown Colony Government in Trinidad at the start of the nineteenth century, and a wholly nominated Legislative Council by 1831:

> By the middle of the 19th century, Crown Colony Government had come to be viewed as the only form of government suited to Trinidad. The men in the colonial office were convinced that the illiteracy of the mass of the population made any public opinion impossible, and representative government therefore unworkable. The mixture of races and nationalities, the doubts about the 'loyalty' of the French and Spanish Creole, the influx of Indian immigrants, all reinforced the idea that Trinidad could never be trusted with representative institutions. Indeed, the Colonial Office felt that Crown Colony Government had worked well in Trinidad, and that the Governor and officials had protected the ignorant and the weak against the planters. For this was the official justification for the Crown Colony Government: the Crown was the best guardian of the propertied few.[4]

There was a difference, Brereton pointed out, between theory and reality:

> It was a great myth of Crown Colony Government that governors and officials were impartial administrators, and at the same time, the special protectors of the poor. But the written constitution was one thing, reality another. It was too much to expect that British officials would have operated as impartial arbiters between the social groups. The poor had no access to the policy makers, while the propertied interests could lobby effectively. The practice of appointing Unofficials to represent the large property interests of the community made it inevitable that they would influence the decisions of the local government. Through the unofficial members of the council, this group was able to influence and even make government policies, especially on domestic issues like taxation, finances, immigration and economic policy in general.[5]

The process by which the Shouters Prohibition Ordinance was passed reflected Bridget Brereton's observations. The procedure did not take into account the interests of the Shouters, who were regarded as dispossessed without access to those who exercised power in the colonial society. For example, in Trinidad and Tobago, on the eve of the passage of the Shouters Prohibition Ordinance in 1917, a group of eight Shouter Baptist Leaders sent a petition to the Governor of the colony, Sir

John Chancellor, requesting that the Ordinance be not passed.[6] Their petition was ignored and ironically two of the leaders, Moses Jones and Joseph Bailey, were among the first Spiritual Baptists to be charged for violating the Ordinance.[7]

The Attorney General, in leading off the debate on the passage of the Shouters Prohibition Ordinance, said that the specific intention of the Bill was to deny the Shouters their rights to worship. It is interesting to note that members of the Legislative Council were mainly Roman Catholics and Anglicans of the planter-merchant ruling class:

> The next bill for the consideration of the House is one of exceptional character. As perhaps the House will realise, it is very far indeed from the desire of the Government to do anything which interferes with the liberty of the subject and the right of the individual to choose the way in which he should worship. But, unfortunately, a condition of affairs has arisen in the colony by reason of the practice of a set or body calling itself the Shouters which so far as the Government sees, made it necessary to come to this House and submit proposals for interference of the practices of that body.[8]

This opening statement by the Attorney-General clearly refers to the Spiritual Baptists as a religiously distinctive body.[9] An examination of the *Hansard* record of the Legislative Council Debates reveals other references to the Baptists as a religious body. For example, the Inspector General of the Constabulary's contribution ran in part:

> There is a building in connection with this ceremony which is called 'Mourner's House'. In this those being initiated are placed and not allowed to come out for a considerable period of time...There is a tremendous crowd there, and they shout and holler while they are getting 'possessed by the Spirit' as they call it. There has been writing in Scriptures in support of their practices..

The Ordinance itself did not specifically state that the Spiritual Baptists were a religious body. There were, however, references to some of the rituals and practices of the group:

(1)   A "Shouters" meeting means a meeting of two or more persons, whether indoors or out, at which the customs and practices of the body known as Shouters

(hereafter in this Ordinance referred to as 'the Shouters') are indulged in. The decision of any Magistrate in any case brought under this Ordinance, as to whether the customs and practices are those of the Shouters shall be final, whether the persons indulging in such customs or practices call themselves Shouters or by any other name.

(2)   A "Shouters" House' means any house or building or room in any house or building which is used for the purpose of holding Shouters' meetings, or any house or building which is used for the purpose of initiating any person into the ceremonies of the Shouters. The decision of any Magistrate in any case brought under this Ordinance as to whether any house or building or room in any house or building is a Shouters' house shall be final.[10]

The two sections quoted above are the two most direct reference to the Shouters as a religious group in the entire Ordinance. In 1931, Albert Gomes had put forward the view that the Ordinance had made the Spiritual Baptists into "criminals":

> It could not be in an endeavour to restrict mere noise that there is in our statute books an Ordinance whose purpose is expressed to 'render illegal indulgence in the practices of the body known as Shouters'. Were such the reason we would be the first to commend it. But the Shouters are regarded as a social evil; and the spirit that has sought to suppress gambling, brothels and the like moved here.[11]

Why did the law make them "criminals" and avoid calling the Spiritual Baptists a religious group? It is likely that those whose interests the passage of the Ordinance represented wished to suppress the formation of what appeared to them to constitute a people's movement, and in order to evade disallowance under the 1865 Colonial Laws Validity Act, they tried to present it not as a religious movement, but as one *endangering* public order. This act, passed by the British Parliament, established supremacy of that Parliament over its colonial legislative. Under the 1831 constitution of Trinidad, its Legislative Council was authorised to pass Ordinances which were subject to assessment by the Governor and the British Parliament.

This Act, when applied, disallowed the passage of any law by a Colonial Legislature that was found to be repugnant to the British Constitution. It is more likely that an Ordinance suppressing the freedom of adherents of any faith to worship and proclaim their faith would have contravened the Act.

Albert Gomes in his 1931 editorial in *The Beacon* journal stated:

> Why may we not be allowed to shout in peace? There are no longer persecutions of anyone professing to even the remotest forms of Christianity; 'Infidels' go unguarded; Mormons daily infest Hyde Park; the Salvation Army strikes up at every corner.[12]

The Beacon editorial argued that, in the heart of the British Empire – London, there was a certain level of religious tolerance; the Attorney-General in spearheading the 1917 debate, implied that freedom of worship was a freedom guaranteed by the British Constitution. The reasons why the colonial government was willing to pass this Ordinance in the face of these legal realities must have been pressing indeed.

What is also significant about the debate on the passage of the Ordinance is the part played by the head of the Police Force. Apart from the fact that it was the Inspector-General of the Constabulary himself who seconded the Attorney-General's motion to pass the Bill, the debate also showed that he had done the research work which had gone into the drafting of the Bill. This is clear from the *Hansard* records of 16 November 1917:

The Hon. Dr. E. Prada: Is there any book which describes the customs and practices of the body known as Shouters?

The Attorney-General, The Hon. H. Cowper-Gallan: Perhaps the Inspector-General of the Constabulary will be able to inform you.

Inspector-General of the Constabulary, the Hon. G.H.May: Not that I am aware of, but there is a report which I put in describing the whole procedure.[13]

The Ordinance known as the Shouters Prohibition Ordinance which became law on 28 November 1917, was understood by the Spiritual Baptists to be a declaration of was against them. They therefore prepared themselves for the challenge.

The Spiritual Baptists placed their fundamental spirituality to the forefront; they seem to have heeded the epistle of Paul to the *Ephesians*, Chapter 6, Verse 12: "For we wrestle not against flesh and blood, but against principalities, against powers, against the rulers of darkness of this world, against spiritual wickedness in high places."[14]

This emphatic statement of Paul may have given the Spiritual Baptists an understanding of the forces against them. In my perspective, the Spiritual Baptists applied to themselves this quotation from Paul. The Spiritual Baptists then, and the Spiritual Baptists now, believed that *Ephesians* 6, Verses 13 – 17, showed them how to lead their lives as people true to the Faith in order to be able to withstand the persecution they were to endure.

13.   Wherefore, take unto you the whole armour of God, that ye may be able to withstand in the evil day, and having done all, to stand.

14.   Stand therefore, having your loins girt about with truth and having on the breastplate of righteousness;

15.   And your feet shod with the preparation of the gospel of peace.

16.   Above all, taking the shield of faith, where with ye shall be able to quench all the fiery darts of the wicked.

17.   And take on the helmet of salvation, which is the word of God.[15]

Spiritual Baptists reflecting upon the prohibition years often claim that those admonitions of Paul prepared them to deal with police raids on their services and other rituals such as baptism , the smashing of their makeshift churches, the beatings of their members, the fines and imprisonment imposed by the law, and the harassment, contempt and ridicule they received from the public. As far as the Spiritual Baptists were concerned, they were prepared to disregard the Ordinance which made the practice of their faith a crime punishable by fines and imprisonment.

The colonial authorities' attempts to suppress their practices have been told in newspaper reports, the lyrics of calypsoes and by historians. Eudora Thomas writes:

Government's efforts to suppress and discourage the spread of the faith led to defiance among the faithful. A few cases are as follows: Teacher Patrick of Picton Road, Sangre Grande, was arrested along with some members of her church while performing a baptism in a river. At the court hearing, the members were released, but the leader was imprisoned for three months.

Leader Roach, alias 'Braveboy', and his wife, Teacher Violet Roach, lived and maintained a

Shouter Baptist Church on Belle Eau Road, Belmont. They were often pelted with rotten eggs and fruit peelings while preaching on street corners. The violence did not deter the leader from bravely continuing his mission. His faith and belief indicated the appropriateness of his alias name.

Leader Harold Lackeye (Lacaille) was raided by Police while preaching in a church. He was arrested, brought to trial, and sentenced to pay a fine or be imprisoned for six months. He elected to go to prison because he had no money to pay the fine. His wife thereupon explained to the magistrate that her husband had recently been discharged from the hospital and said that she was willing to serve his prison term. The magistrate acted with sympathy and placed the leader on a six month bond instead.[16]

The calypsoes of the period also reflected the attitude of the establishment towards the Spiritual Baptists. Gordon Rohlehr's book, *Calypso and Society in Pre-Independence Trinidad*, deals with this phenomenon. He reproduces the words of a calypso recorded by the Growling Tiger, one of the best exponents of the art. The calypso is "Is This a Religion?/What is a Shouter?":

We have the Roman Catholic, Anglican and Salvation
But what is a Shouter Band?
I am tired with this nonsense: give me an ease
The unknown twang on River Jordan that is the thing I can't understand
The Catholic make their ceremony
Which is known universally
Very charitable is the Salvation
The Anglican I could understand
But the Shouters want to see Zion when they die
And bawling car-im-boother cico ih
With candle and a cross and a cycle bell
Invoking Lucifer in Hell..
I read at Mt. Hope the other day
They had chased some Shouter away
With their head tie in white, with some long night gown
While the Police had them surround
In the height of the feast they began to moan
Five miles apart you could hear them groan
A fellow said he come from Kiracoo (Carriacou)
They burst his head with the police butoo.[17]

❦

In the preceding calypso, the ceremonies and rituals of the Spiritual Baptists are caricatured, and one sees the petty nationalism of the calypsonian who ridicules the association of Grenada ("Kiracoo") and the so-called perceived backwardness represented by the Spiritual Baptists. The point can also be made of the distinctiveness of the worship of devotees which is characterised by the calypsonian as associated with devil worship. Whether this is expressive of the popular imagination is doubtful, but it certainly represents a view which supports colonial prejudices. In another calypso, Radio is levelling another accusation at the Shouter Baptist leader; sexual promiscuity. This is not the only lyrical attack which is launched at the Spiritual Baptists. Another type of attack is also found in Rohlehr's work:

> All the members sang that night
> And the spirit held me tight[18]

The 'spirit' turns out to be a pint of rum with which the preacher is baptising the neophytes. The experience is described as a 'spree' and the hymn is called a 'letgo' (that is a leggo, a Carnival road March chorus). Again, the distinctiveness of the African tradition of worship which recognises ancestral veneration and saintly powers through the offering of drink, is here reduced to blatant ridicule.

The idea of the Shouter Baptist ceremonies as being indistinguishable from fetes, festivals and sprees had become deeply rooted by 1937.

> Oh the rum was passing free
> Vermouth and Whisky
> Johnny Tay-Tay drank so much gin
> And ran out of wind
> Teacher Sookhan shouting 'give me more'
> And hit Papa Tookhan with the flambeau
> Oh yes, every teacher had a pal.
> That was festival[19]

The Spiritual Baptists were determined to practise their faith in spite of the persecution they suffered at the hands of the state and the contempt poured upon them by that important medium of popular culture, the calypsonian. It is ironic that calypsonians who like the Spiritual Baptists were "the underdog," appropriated the judgmental and condemnatory language of the colonial establishment in order to confirm the Spiritual Baptists as social pariahs.

The American anthropologist Melville Herskovits made similar observations of the Spiritual Baptists of Trinidad:

> They strikingly resemble the early Christians in their communal co-operatives, in the measures they take to exact discipline and morality within their own groups, and in the gentle non-resistance with which they persist in carrying on despite the edicts against them and what they regard as constant persecution resulting from enforcement of the law which makes them subject to frequent raids and fines and jail sentences..[20]

Herskovits made a similar observation in *Trinidad Village*

> ....it is clear that the interdictions under which they carry on their activities give them, as a group, an inner cohesion, and as individuals a depth of conviction that strengthens them in putting their weakness in numbers and resources against the legal sanctions of the state. Sharing what little they own, meeting for crucial rites of initiation and worship in secret, refusing to pay fines levied against them, choosing instead to 'go to jail for Jesus', their convictions make a deeper impression on their co-villagers.[21]

In spite of this constant harassment by the authorities, the Spiritual Baptists were busily engaged in organising themselves as a group to have the Ordinance repealed. Rhoda Reddock in her study *Elma Francois*, shows that the Negro Welfare Social and Cultural Association (NWCSA), an organisation of which Francois was one of the leaders in the 1930's and 1940's in Trinidad, had some contact with the Spiritual Baptists. Reddock reveals this in her description of the NWCSA's efforts to mobilise support for a particular cause, "They also held discussions with organisations such as the Clarks Union, the Amalgamated Building and Woodworkers' Union, representatives of the persecuted Spiritual Baptists and other labour movement activists."[22]

From the evidence it appears that the organisation of the "persecuted Shouter Baptists" at the time of Elma Francois was both of a religious and secular nature. One of its objectives was the repeal of the 1917 Shouters Prohibition Ordinance. Cuthbert Joseph, the parliamentary representative for Port of Spain East, delivering a feature address at the laying of the foundation stone at St Peter's Spiritual Baptist Cathedral in Gonzales, a district of Port of Spain, on 29 September 1974, made reference to that petition.

> As we close, let us throw back our minds to those before us who laboured that this day could be fulfilled. Let us recall the petition to the Governor made fifty-seven years ago by the defenders of the Faith. On the eve of the passage of the Shouters Prohibition Ordinance in 1917, they pleaded that "they should not be deprived of their spiritual privileges in serving their Creator... according to God's own plan of Salvation.

> The prayers of these eight humble petitioners can still be heard:

Rev. A.A. Dalzell	-Tunapuna Tabernacle
Pastors William Patterson and Phillip Maxwell	- Caroni
Pastors James Huggins and Moses Jones	- Chaguanas
Pastor George Yearwood	- Curepe
Teacher Amos Frederick	- St Joseph
Teacher Joseph Bailey	-Cunupia

> Let us on this Day of Fulfilment raise our voices with theirs and repeat the prayer they wrote in their 1917 petition: Ezekiel 36, Verses 26–28:

> 26   A new heart will I give you,
> And a new spirit will I put within
> You and I will take away the
> Stony heart out of your flesh, and
> I will give you an heart of flesh

> 27   And I will put my spirit within you,
> And will cause you to walk in my stattutes,
> And ye shall keep my judgements,
> And do them.

> 28   And ye shall dwell in the land
> That I gave to your fathers;
> And ye shall be my people,
> And I will be your God.[23]

From a careful study of Cuthbert Joseph's account of 1917 and Rhoda Reddock's account of the 1930s, it can be concluded that the Spiritual Baptists kept alive for 25 years their campaign for freedom to worship alive for almost twenty-five years their campaign for freedom of worship.

This meant that Deacon Elton Griffith's fight to repeal the Ordinance was not conceived by him, but constituted a concerted line of continuity, with mass support from adherents of the Faith, with the earlier efforts of Spiritual Baptists to wage an unwavering campaign for over a quarter century to reverse the heinous ordinance imposed on them.

In the midst of the colonial authorities' attempts to suppress the Shouter Baptist Faith, and ridicule by journalists and calypsonians, the Spiritual Baptists had their sympathisers amongst the colonial intelligentsia who were associated with *The Beacon* magazine between 1929 and 1931. They were C.L.R. James, Alfred Mendes and Albert Gomes.

The Beacon was published for two years before it went out of existence. However, its editor, Albert Gomes, devoted the editorial column of the August 1931 edition, "Legalised persecution of the Shouters of Trinidad and Tobago," to a defence of adherents of the Faith.

It is evident that Albert Gomes was one of the early members of the colonial (albeit vociferously anti) establishment to publicly support the Spiritual Baptists. In his autobiography published more than forty years after the editorial in *The Beacon*, Gomes gave the reason for his interest in the Spiritual Baptists.

> Of all the crusades of a rather maverick political life, I like to remember most the one that had to do with the cult of the Shouters. Perhaps the reason is my fondness for the bizarre. Also, being able to cock a snook at smug convention always had a special fascination. Indeed, I think it is more than just a spontaneous urge and that I deliberately cultivate dissent because I know that it renews vision and purpose. Conformity, on the other hand, implies the ageing process. There is a little death in all acceptance, all life being a protest of some kind. It is the Don Quixote who preserve their usefulness, not the heroes of success stories who come to rest at a point of self-fulfilment and first stagnate there. In this sense, the fight to free the Shouters met all the requirements... That the Shouters could in turn produce a tailor-made burlesque of such basically travestied Christianity provided a vicarious retribution for one like myself who, fettered by the inhibitions of active political life was more often under the constraint to swallow one's protest and instead mouth some deferential platitude.

It was in this way that many aspects of the way of life of the ordinary folk of Trinidad became a way of life for me also, more meaningful even than the one which my position constrained It was indeed not only politics that drove me to the calypso tent, to the defence of the steel-band boys, to the Shango ritual, to moral outrage at unjust ban against the Shouters. In many ways, *I was defending my own way of life, the things in which I deeply believed, the things which I had assimilated and made a part of my own integrity and self respect*. I crave them not only because to do so provided the ideal political image, but because indeed they had become the *essential image, the only one that I had found myself prepared to accept*[24] (emphasis added).

By the end of the 1930s, we find the Shouter Prohibition Ordinance still very much on the law books of the colony and being rigidly enforced by the colonial authorities. The newspapers and the calypsonians were still busily heaping scorn and contempt upon Spiritual Baptists as a group.

The Spiritual Baptists' determination not to forsake their faith in the face of the enforcement of the Shouter Prohibition Ordinance was beginning to gain the sympathy of their persecutors, particularly the police. Earl Lovelace takes note of this change of attitude in his novel, *The Wine of Astonishment*:

All of them had their duty to do, but they know we is not the criminals and they use a little reason; they leave us alone once we don't broadcast that we have a Baptist church going on in the village. True, we used to send them, now and then, a bunch of plantains or some pigeon peas, and Corporal Busby used to get his regular chicken because he used to tip us off about the days they was going to raid the church. They was police, but they was human too.[25]

This suggests much more than Christian forgiveness on the part of Spiritual Baptists. Like the calypsonians, the police were predominantly working class and it would be surprising if many of their own relatives were not Spiritual Baptists. Indeed, stories are told by Spiritual Baptists who lived through the prohibition period of police men having to turn in their own parents or siblings for fear of being proceeded against by their superiors. "All of them had their duty to do..." implies an acceptance on the part of the Spiritual Baptists that the police were enforcing the law irrespective of their roots within those same communities. There seems to be little question that the police took courage from the determination and unassailable force of the movement of persecuted Spiritual Baptists themselves.

Herskovits also noticed this trend when he did his field work in Trinidad in 1939:

> This power is made most manifest in the way police raiders are believed to be turned away by the strength of the Shouters' words: "Mother Margaret was a little ol' woman. You never think she have power like that. But when she live at San Fernando an' the police came, she just told them of her power in Jesus an' the Corporal say, 'I believe you,' and get in his car an' go right back to the station.[26]

In addition to these, there were people among the colonial establishment who saw that the passage and enforcement of the Shouters Prohibition Ordinance was unjust, and who were already predisposed to defend publicly their cause when the time came.

One of the most crucial events in the history of the restoration of the Shouter Baptists' rights to worship in Trinidad and Tobago was the arrival of Elton Griffith at Port-of-Spain from Grenada on June 21, 1941. Archbishop Clarence Baisden, head of the National Evangelical Spiritual Baptists Archdiocese in Trinidad and Tobago, describes the Griffith story as "unique."[27] He continued:

> In 1941 while a member of the Glad Tidings Pentecostal church in Morne Jaloux, Grenada, he had a vision and call from God to go to Syria and deliver the church. The nearest Syrian Community was in Trinidad, so he came to Trinidad as a missionary." Arriving in Trinidad he became interested in the Spiritual Baptist Movement, which he felt resembled the liturgy and work of the early apostles. In a personal communication to me, Griffith said that he was appalled by the harsh persecutions and wicked sanctions directed against this innocent minority group whose only fault was that they were indigenous to the West Indies and that in his opinion came from direct contact with the early apostles of John, Jesus and our slave ancestors.

Griffith was determined to concentrate his efforts on obtaining freedom for the Spiritual Baptists. He spent some time assessing the situation and befriending the leaders. What is of great significance is that Griffith noted that Henry Gollan (an Englishman who was Attorney General of Trinidad at the time of the enactment of the law) stated that he refused to have anything to do with it, as it was entirely a religious matter and that he could not dictate to His/Her Majesty's subjects how to worship God.

Figure 9

The late Archbishop Elton George Griffith (centre) addressing the gathering at the Spiritual Baptist Liberation Day celebration, Jean Pierre Complex, Port of Spain, before his death in April 1992 (Photo courtesy *The Trinidad Express*).

Griffith made a tactical move and applied to the Governor of the day, Backward Wright, for permission to begin his own mission and to visit institutions where his converts were being treated. Strict warning was given to him not to do anything close to Spiritual Baptist worship.

> He was even summoned to the police headquarters, severely warned and instructed in how the law expected him to worship his God. Acting within the framework of his instructions, he continued his mission. In 1943 Griffith applied for and obtained permission from the Colonial Secretary to use the La Horquette River for baptism. He invited the registrar general Mr Deeble, Hon. Albert Gomes and other dignitaries to his first baptism of converts. The Holy Spirit blessed the service and a woman in the crowd was seized with the Spirit and cried "baptise me now or never." She was baptised and the officials were impressed. Later it was discovered that the woman was the wife of a police official living in Carenage.[28]

Some evidence of the ministry of Elton Griffith in Port-of-Spain during the 1940s is recorded in Thomas (1987):

> ...George Elton Griffith, who was then a deacon and started his spiritual ministry in an open yard using a carpenter's bench as an altar. He held nightly meetings in his chapel in Port-of-Spain around 1942. His ministry of converting souls, preaching, and healing of sick bodies was so successful that he had to accommodate the crowds that flocked to his temple.[29]

Sometime in the middle 1940's, Elton Griffith began to mobilise the Spiritual Baptists and forged links with businessmen and politicians according to Bishop Nain Griffith. Some of Griffith's contacts formed during this period, who were helpful in the advancement of this cause are listed below.

URIAS PHILIP GRANGER, Grenada-born member of the Trinidad and Tobago contingent which served in the British West India Regiment in World War I. He was also a staunch supporter of Marcus Garvey both in Trinidad and the United States, where he had lived and worked for a time after the war. In Trinidad he had been involved in previous attempts to have the 1917 Ordinance repealed before he became one of Griffith's mentors and supporters after 1941. As a barber and hairdresser, his shop on Park Street and later Charlotte Street, Port-of Spain, was one of the major meeting places for Shouter Baptists in Port-of Spain during this period.

MOTHER CLARISSA ADAMS : She is believed to have been born in St. Lucia. One of the most famous of the Spiritual Baptists who rose to prominence during the period after 1951. She was one of Griffith's earliest and strongest supporters.

ALBERT GOMES was one of the earliest supporters from the Portuguese community who publicly defended the Spiritual Baptist cause. As editor of *The Beacon* he often argued the case against the Prohibition Ordinance and was the highest placed politician to join the campaign to repeal the Shouters Prohibition Ordinance.

ASHFORD AND MITRA SINANAN, two brothers themselves the descendants of Indian indentured labourers, attorneys by profession, who were in a position to offer legal advice to Griffith during the public campaign to repeal the 1917 Ordinance. As members of the Legislative Council of Trinidad and Tobago in 1951, they were able to give support to the motion to repeal the Ordinance on March 30.

C.B. MATHURA was another of the East Indian politicians who had been active in Trinidad and in local politics in the Port-of-Spain area during the 1940's and 1950's. His support of the Spiritual Baptist cause was such that he was one of the first signatories of the petition of the West Indian Evangelical Spiritual Baptist Faith in

September–October 1949.

ANDREW J. BALFOUR was one of the spiritual sons of Urias Philip Granger whom Griffith was able to enlist in the drive to repeal the Shouters Prohibition Ordinance. He served as Deputy President of the West Indian Evangelical Spiritual Baptist Faith during the early years of the organisation.[30]

TUBAL URIAH BUTLER born in Grenada from where he emigrated to work in the oil-fields of south Trinidad, became the leader of the British Empire Workers and Home Rule Party. A Spiritual Baptist himself, he championed the anti-Ordinance cause and commanded massive support in South Trinidad.

The formation on 26 March 1945 of the West Indian Evangelical Spiritual Baptist Faith launched Elton Griffith's campaign to repeal the 1917 Ordinance.

Certain developments took place in the British West Indies during 1945-1951, which had important implications for the campaign to repeal the Shouters Prohibition Ordinance: In 1949, Albert Gomes was the first politician to make over-tures to the Spiritual Baptists. He promised public support in return for their votes and an alliance was formed. Gomes' alliance with the Spiritual Baptists lasted until 1956.

In 1947 to the advantage of the Spiritual Baptists, the book *Trinidad Village*, researched by an American anthropologist and his wife Frances Herskovits, appeared in Trinidad. This book dealt extensively with the Spiritual Baptists and portrayed the religious group in a most favourable light. They wrote:

> The shouters must be given a place of prominence in any consideration of the religious life of Trinidad. This is true even though their places of worship are humble in character. For it is from beliefs and practices such as are found among the Shouters, and in acceptance of div-ination and magic as techniques for controlling the immediate problems of living, that the Tocoan attains a sense of being part of the Universe that can provide a place of dignity and security in this world as well as the next.[31]

From 1945 Elton George Griffith and the West Indian Evangelical Spiritual Baptist Faith had been quietly going about the business of organising themselves. In

September of 1949 they circulated a petition, calling on the government to repeal the Shouters Prohibition Ordinance of 1917.[32] Albert Gomes tabled the petition at the meeting of the Legislative Council of 28th October 1949, and moved a motion that a Select Committee of the Legislative Council be appointed to enquire into the petition. The motion was carried and a Select Committee was appointed. Its members were L.C. Hannays, K.C. (Chairman), Albert Gomes, Victor Bryan and Georgina Beckles. The petition read:

> We, the officers of the Spiritual Baptist Faith, commonly known as the Shouters, humbly beg that this Ordinance, the Shouters Prohibition Ordinance, Chapter 4, No. 19 has become an annoyance to us, and has outlived its twenty five (25) years duration.
>
> We, as African descendants crave indulgence of the Honourable Speaker of the House and the Honourable Legislative Councillors to use their good office by assisting us to modify or repeal the "Shouters Ordinance".
>
> We consider that this form of religion or sect is our ancestral heritage. Owing to this Prohibition Act of Shouters, Chapter 4, No. 19 has affected thirty thousand (30,000) members of the faith.[33]

The select Committee submitted a report on August 28th 1950, and recommended repeal of the 1917 Shouters Prohibition Ordinance.[34]

The Trinidad Guardian newspaper on 30 March 1951 gave front page coverage to the Spiritual Baptists' campaign to have the Ordinance repealed. Thirty four years earlier it had given front page coverage to the Ordinance in its edition of 17 November 1917 under the headline "Shouters' Meetings Prohibited." Its 30 March 1951 edition carried a lengthy and persuasive editorial which argued in favour of freedom of religious expression and warned that to continue to proscribe the Spiritual Baptists would engender in them a deep sense of injustice and encourage them to make common cause with those who harboured other grievances against the establishment.

> It is a far cry from the "body known as Shouters," as the Ordinance describes them in 1917, to the present-day sect of Evangelical Spiritual Baptists as the Shouters now call themselves. The Ordinance for some reason avoided calling them a religious group, but included references to the initiation ceremonies and other things. We are not specially concerned today with questions of ritual or ceremony, though the group seems to have grown in wisdom and stature, and is apparently in less disfavour than at the time when the 1917 law was passed.

We do wish, however, to ask the government this question;... Will it continue the ban on a religious organisation, whose practices (whatever anyone may think of them) are entitled to the protection commonly accorded religious bodies and all citizens so long as they do not offend public order or decency?

The Bill seeking to lift the ban comes before the legislature today after investigation by a committee appointed to consider a petition sent in more than a year ago by the Spiritual Baptists. The committee will probably not wish to be associated with a ban that cuts across those religious liberties whose maintenance is a cardinal tenet of democratic faith, and we presume it has thoroughly satisfied itself on points in doubt.

Besides, as a member of the committee has well said, the maintenance of the ban tends to create a needless tension in society and to drive adherents of the sect underground. It practically invites an anti-social complex by making these persons a hunted and outlawed group smarting under a sense of injustice, and therefore the more ready to join forces with other men with a grievance – men who may not have as valid a claim on our tolerance. We hope that the tyrannical and proscriptive law now enforced will be changed.

The members of the Legislative Council who assembled on the morning of Friday, 30 March 1951, seemed to agree with the views expressed in the editorial column of *The Trinidad Guardian*. At least one member of the Council, the Hon. Roy Joseph, expressed the view, as he piloted the Bill, that the Repeal Ordinance would not be a controversial one. In addition, Mr. Joseph was aware of the wider, international significance of the Bill to restore the Spiritual Baptists' legal rights to worship:

> The present Bill is not, I am sure, going to be a controversial Bill, but I think it is only right to say that since the Colony has accepted the Charter of Human Rights in which is enshrined the principle of freedom of worship, it is very appropriate to remove from the Statute Books any law which forbids the individual from practising the religion of his choice.[35]

Mr Joseph was correct. The Bill itself was not controversial. The entire Legislative Council seemed to be of one mind on the question of passing the Shouters Prohibition (repeal) Ordinance of 1951. *Hansard* did not record a single dissenting vote when the question was put before the Council. A controversy erupted over the role played by Members of the Legislative Council in championing the cause of the Shouters. Finally, the Legislative Council voted to restore the Shouter Baptists' rights to worship by its repeal of the 1917 Shouters Prohibition Ordinance on 30 March 1951.

Archbishop Granville Williams, now based in Barbados, previously worked with Archbishop Elton Griffith and others for Repealing the Prohibition Ordinance in 1951. With this heightened sense of achievement, Pastor Williams left Trinidad and returned to his native land where he founded the Sons of God Apostolic Spiritual Baptist Church, Ealing Grove, Christ Church.

During the last forty-two years, his ministry developed and the Zion Apostolic Spiritual Baptist Temple was established at the Richmond Gap, St Michael's. Archbishop Williams' knowledge of the Faith and his African-centred views gained him the respect of those in authority. Both churches have exceptionally large congregations, their members are well informed not only of the Bible, but also of their social responsibility and their African ancestral links.

The Archbishop and his community are unrepentant in their philosophical position regarding Africa and have learnt to accept the positive aspects of their African origin. Almost half of the memberships are young persons and there is a large percentage of male adherents.

It is interesting to compare the proscribed history of the legal situation which obtained in Trinidad & Tobago with that of St Vincent in its dealings with adherents of the Spiritual Baptist Faith. This I set out to do below albeit briefly.

St Vincent 1912–1965

The history of the Ordinance to render illegal the practices of "Shakerism" in the colony of St. Vincent enacted in October 1912, is similar to that of Trinidad's. The Shakers of St Vincent were as determined to preserve their Faith despite being subjected to beatings, arrests and imprisonmentís as a consequence of the Prohibition Ordinance, as the Shouter Baptists in Trinidad were to become following their proscription five years later.

The Shakers of St Vincent have a great affinity with the Spiritual Baptist community of Trinidad. As early as 1881, Spiritual Baptist leaders emigrated to Trinidad from St Vincent. Archbishop Baisden stated that Teacher Clearer from Calliaque emigrated to Trinidad and had a church at Carapichima, in Central Trinidad. She mourned Archbishop Kenneth Ash, current Head of the Mount Hope Spiritual Baptist Archdiocese at Fort George, St James.

Figure 10
Archbishop Granville Williams, Primate of the Spiritual Baptist Apostolic Spiritual Baptist Cathedral and Zion Apostolic Spiritual Baptist Temple, Barbados (Photo courtesy Teacher Atherlene Reece).

Teacher Bonnie Andrews who died in 1964, aged 100 years, was a *Converted* from Riley, near Evesham in St Vincent, who emigrated to Trinidad with her son Enoch Andrews and they had a "Praise House" which is a church, in Trinidad. Pointer Olivierre of Mesopotamia also emigrated to Trinidad and was well known.

In those days the *Converts* or *Penitents* as they were called in St Vincent, wore white dresses and aprons, and blue headties. They were devoted practitioners of mental prayer and relied much on dreams, visions and revelations. Many of them were clairvoyant and had gifts of healing. At the hours of prayer they were often seized with "The Whipping Spirit" and when they were not in a state of Spirit possession, they entered into prayer and intercession. Sometimes they prophesied.

Although an affinity exists, some of the practices of the Spiritual Baptists in St Vincent differed from those of their counterparts in Trinidad. The phrase "Spiritual Shouter Baptist" was taboo in St Vincent. The Faith was first known as Shouters, Penitent, Converted and in 1951, Christian Pilgrim, thus being identified with John Bunyan's *Pilgrim's Progress*.

Archbishop Cosmore Pompey of the St Vincent and the Grenadines Spiritual Baptist Archdiocese asserts: "We as servants of God, we acknowledge that whether we change to Spiritual Baptist, we are still Christian Pilgrims; not many Spiritual Baptists know this." If one reads *Pilgrim's Progress*, there is definitely an identity with the Christian Pilgrim and the Spiritual Baptist convert.

In St Vincent, Archbishop Pompey explained:

> When they started the Spiritual Baptist work here it was mourning alone until the Elders started going through the bible and they saw where Baptism is essential, so they started to baptise. But the original way was just to mourn people, but then as they said, to the "low ground of sorrows"... So Mourning or Fasting, whatever you want to call it, in the earlier days the least the people used to take was twenty-one days [see part two for further elaboration].

In Trinidad it is different. One has to be baptised before one mourns, and Baptism is the most important requirement for entry into the Faith. Many rituals and practices vary. But what is most significant is the fact that although the Faith was proscribed in St Vincent in 1912, their community was not ridiculed and ostracised as their compatriots were in Trinidad. The Ordinance remained on the statue books until 1965, but the Shakers enjoyed a much more tolerant attitude from the authorities.

Jeanette Henney (1973) in her work, *The Shakers of St. Vincent, a stable religion*, observes that:

> In their sermons, Shakers stress that the sufferings of Jesus and other biblical characters far exceeded the tribulations of the Shakers, being favoured by God even as the biblical examples should expect – even welcome – suffering since it brings them into closer affiliation with that heavenly group.[36]

In spite of being ridiculed and persecuted, the Shakers, who were mainly Africanand of the lower class, remained passive. But there was persistent lobbying in the Legislative Council by George Augustus McIntosh, a Vincentian politician, from 1939 as recorded in the Legislative Council debates of 13 April of that year.

> McIntosh was intensely aware of the oppressive conditions under which the majority of the black population lived. According to (Jim) Banette, however, McIntosh was seen in the society as "good but godless." He challenged the Scriptures and the power of the established church. In particular, he is remembered for his defence of the Spiritual Baptist religion.[37]

The son of a Scottish father and an African mother, McIntosh had an understanding of the way of life of the poor, powerless and dispossessed in colonial society. In 1919, McIntosh helped to form the St. Vincent Representative Government Association, in order to secure the introduction of elected members in the St. Vincent Legislative Council.[38]

In the course of the debate of 13 April 1939, all the elected members present supported Macintosh's motion, along with one of the nominated members. Holding the position of the colonial authorities were the Attorney-General, Colonial Treasurer and the other two nominated members.

Macintosh's motion calling on the Government to either amend or repeal the 1912 Shakerism Prohibition Ordinance was put to the vote:

> That government be requested to introduce a Bill to amend the Shakers Ordinance to define what is Shakerism; secondly, to give the right of appeal and in every other way to give freedom of the worship of God as is intended by the principles of right and justice under the British Constitution..

The Legislative Council voted in favour of the motion, but the Government failed to act upon it. McIntosh therefore continued his campaign for at least another eleven years. He moved another motion on 5 October 1950.

Eudora Thomas writes that during the debate, McIntosh made it clear to the Council that he had no personal interest in Shakerism, but 'merely wanted the government to take a sober view of the matter.' He thought it unfair that "any vagrant or criminal from abroad can come here and set up a religious body and is given recognition by Government but when the people of St. Vincent say we have a right as others to form a religion of our own, they are denied that right.' "[39]

George McIntosh again failed in his attempt to induce the colonial authorities to amend or repeal the 1912 Shakerism Prohibition Ordinance. However, he was a member of the upper class and able to wield a certain amount of power as a politician. He was thus able to challenge the control that organised religion and the established churches had in the colony.

McIntosh argued:

> That although he was not a member of the Shaker community and had no personal interest in their religious activities, the continued retention of the 1912 Ordinance on the law books was a disgrace to the colonial administration:

The Honourable Member for Kingstown (George A McIntosh) then said that in moving this motion he considered that this Ordinance created a blot on the Statute Books of the colony. On looking through this Ordinance he had not seen a clause which did not amount to placing a hardship on a certain set of people because they were poor. Under the British Constitution people had the right to serve God in whatever manner they pleased...[40]

According to Jeanette Henney, the Shakers were subjected to beatings, arrests and imprisonment as a result of the 1912 Ordinance. However, from the early 1930's a more lenient policy was adopted toward the community:

A more tolerant attitude toward the Shakers began to prevail in the thirties, and they were permitted to hold their meetings without further interference. Their status was still questionable, however, until the Ordinance was repealed in 1965...[41]

During her research, an informant had told Henney that the last case against the Shakers was brought before the St. Vincent courts around 1932. The practice of the faith, however, remained illegal until 1965 when the Shakerism Prohibition Ordinance was repealed by the Legislative Council of St. Vincent. This was not the case in Trinidad. The campaign for the repeal of the Shouters Prohibition Ordinance only picked up momentum with the advent of Elton Griffith.

It is difficult to ascertain exactly what took place in St Vincent in the period between Macintosh's second motion in 1950 and the repeal of the Ordinance in 1965 since no oral or written evidence appears to be available.

The passage of the Shakerism Prohibition (Repeal) Ordinance in 1965 implies the existence of a political and social process which adopted a more tolerant attitude towards the Shaker community during the period after 1945. This occurred at around the same period that Britain was preparing to divest itself of its colonial possessions. As a direct result of the decision to grant independence to its colonies, the British Colonial Office began to grant increasing measures of self-government to the colonial Legislature.

Henney describes the process:

St. Vincent has been undergoing significant economic and political changes. Universal adult suffrage was not established until 1951 when a new constitution went into effect providing for the election of the majority of the members in the Legislative Council. Election to public office has been one avenue to power and prestige for Vincentians, and the interest in political affairs has been intense.[42]

The granting of self-government was accompanied by the expectation that there would be responsible government. The expansion of the number of areas over which the Legislative Council had total autonomy was underpinned by the granting of Universal Adult Suffrage. The conditions were right, therefore, for the Shakers to become a political constituency, a special interest group, with the political resources and numerical strength to make their presence felt in the society.

The passage of the 1965 Shakerism Prohibition (Repeal) Ordinance coincides with the coming to power of Ebenezer Joshua, who had earlier migrated to Trinidad from St. Vincent. While in Trinidad he had become one of the leading members of the political organisation of Tubal Uriah Butler. The evidence suggests that Joshua became a Spiritual Baptist minister in Trinidad.

Upon his return to St. Vincent from Trinidad he helped to form a political party which continued Macintosh's struggle to repeal the 1912 Ordinance from the Laws of St. Vincent. It was not surprising, therefore, that the Shaker community of St. Vincent formed the nucleus of Joshua's political power in the colony, and his government's sponsoring of the Repeal Ordinance shows a commonality of interest between the Chief Minister – Joshua himself, and the Spiritual Baptist community of St. Vincent. Henney summarised the reaction in St. Vincent after the passage of the 1965 Shakers Prohibition (Repeal) Ordinance:

> Some of the clergy of the organised denominational churches in St. Vincent expressed resentment over the governmental action legalising Shakerism. They interpreted the move as a political gesture to win Shaker votes, which they felt was unnecessary because the Shakers were essentially being given the religious freedom before the Ordinance was repealed.[43]

Henney's account suggests that the churches were convinced that the Shakers had enjoyed a more tolerant attitude from the authorities since the 1930's, and had in fact been granted religious freedom. This may have been so, but the 1912 Ordinance had nevertheless remained on the statute books, and its continued existence therefore gave the authorities the legal right to enforce it. The repeal of the

Ordinance in 1965, then, may be seen as bringing the law into line with the practice.

At least one member of the Council, the Hon. Roy Joseph, expressed the view, as he piloted the Bill, that the Repeal Ordinance would not be a controversial one. In addition, Mr Joseph was aware of the wider, international significance of the Bill to restore the Shouter Baptists' legal rights to worship:

> The present Bill is not, I am sure, going to be a controversial Bill, but I think it is only right to say that since the Colony has accepted the Charter of Human Rights in which is enshrined the principle of freedom of worship, it is very appropriate to remove from the Statute Books any law which forbids the individual from practising the religion of his choice.

LIBERATION AND TRANSFORMATION

T he Shouter Baptists in Trinidad were liberated in 1951. The Faith in Trinidad had spent thirty-four years in the "wilderness" and the leaders were determined to organise all Shouters into one body. They had already given full authority to the Rt. Rev. Elton George Griffith, whose efforts to liberate their flock had been so richly rewarded.

The Shakers, (Spiritual Baptists) in St Vincent, however, were to endure prohibition for a further fourteen years before, in 1965, their Ordinance was finally repealed. The Most Rev. Clarence Baisden, head of the National Evangelical Spiritual (Shouter) Baptist (NESB) Archdiocese recalled that in 1949

> One hundred Shouter leaders and heads including Richard Bobb of Arima, Brown from Goofor, Serge from Enterprise, Harvey from Carapichima, Jade from Sobo La Brea, Laker from Laventille, Jake Williams from Morvant, Marga from Jumbie Bridge, Barataria, Albany, Leaders Palargree and Jarvis, Leader and Mother Le Caille, Pastor Smith of Tobago and others met upstairs of Coelho's building under the chairmanship of Pastor Henry Granger, father of Makandal Daaga.

They elected Griffith as the Bishop of the Shouters and gave him a mandate to represent all Shouters in the territory. Griffith was hailed as the anointed one from God and his job was to shepherd the flock. The Spiritual Baptists celebrated, throughout the Eastern Caribbean territories, their freedom to worship God without restraint, their freedom to build temples and their freedom to preserve the Faith passed on to them through Jesus Christ.

Their mission then was to call sinners to repentance:

> Repent and be baptised. The Kingdom of Heaven is at hand. Heal the sick, cleanse the leper, raise the dead, cast out devils, freely you give, freely you receive.

This became their rallying cry. Spiritual Baptists believed that they were an invading force with orders to invade Satan's Kingdom in the name of Jesus and occupy it till Jesus comes. During the 1950s, Spiritual Baptists' churches or "Prayer Houses" were made of tapia and mud. They had rafters made of bamboo or wooden poles and arranged in the form of an umbrella, a star or a wheel, a central pole supporting the roof, and bamboo altars and seats.

PRAYER HOUSES

Prayer Houses were made of ordinary timber sawn by human hand, the roof covered with thatched leaves (consisting of the palm fronds from coconut trees) and other leaves , or sometimes with galvanised iron sheets. In some places they would take the trees and make posts and rafters. Then they would mix dirt with water and in some places would add white lime to cover the sides of the building. The floor was never paved, it was dirt. The Prayer Houses were beautiful little buildings to serve God.

The Prayer House is where the faithful assembled to pray. In the early days, an advanced member of the Faith could build a Prayer House out of wood, the leaves of trees and earth, and bring the local adherents together. Because Spiritual Baptists were disenfranchised, they worshipped God in the simplest way. However, the centre of worship today is the Church, a more modern structure, usually made of bricks and concrete. The roof is designed to represent the heavenly canopy. The Centre Pole is the sole support holding the leaves and earth apart. The Centre Pole

Pole not only represents the earth's imaginary axis, it is also the Ladder of Jacob, the Sacred Staff of Moses, the Rod of Aaron and the Wood of Lebanon, of which the temple was built thousands of years before Christ came.

The Faith was hinged on the operation of the Holy Spirit. Their worship had a rich syncretic character that was controlled only by the guidance and direction of the Holy Spirit.

The Most Reverend Raymond Oba Douglas, of the Mt Pisgah Archdiocese, explains that in the 1950s leaders of the Faith were for the most part inspired, emotional, virile and charismatic, but not necessarily literate. Its priests and priestesses were Pastors, Leaders, Shepherds, Mothers, Matrons and Nurses, according to their work.

> The Mourner's room is the true temple of the Shouter Faith and the church structure an outhouse for congregational worship. It closely resembles the design used by Moses to build the Ark of the Covenant and the Tabernacle described in the Book of Exodus. It consists of a large covered area, in the middle of which is a centre pole.
>
> Around the centre pole in the ancient mourner's rooms, there were raised circles of earth on pedestals upon which were placed lights and flowers, bells, flags, thunderstones and goblets of water. There was a hollow in which a candle burned constantly, this was called Zion Fireside and has considerable ritual significance.
>
> All important ritual ceremonies revolve around the centre pole, the top of which represents the centre of heaven and the foot of which is the grave. Radiating from the top of the pole and forming vertical lines, squares, intersecting lines, equilateral triangles, and other designs are the beams which secure the post to the roof, forming a star-shaped ceiling demonstrating the work of God in the heavens, and perhaps saying in silent language, 'God the great architect of the universe geometrizes.'

When you enter a Spiritual Baptist church you bow at the front door and touch the ground with your hand three times and leave your shoes there. Then you go and kneel at the centre pole to pray, after which you greet your elders and the entire congregation, then take your seat and pray or "hum" until the service starts.

The Most Rev. Monica Randoo explains:

> The earth is the Lord's and the fullness thereof. You are paying recognition to God as you come into His Holy Temple. So you can embrace the Father, Son and Holy Spirit. Then you go to the centre pole that represents Jesus Christ and so you pray there.

Changes had already begun to take place within the movement. "Pastor Boatswain of Tunapuna headed a movement of change after a vision in which he reported that a woman appeared to him and gave him a rosary instructing him to keep nine days of prayer."

Baisden recalls that there were many Catholics converted to the Spiritual Baptist Faith and the leaders needed no excuse after that to include Roman Catholic rites in the the worship. In the middle to late 1950s the churches in central Trinidad around Chaguanas and Enterprise, where there was a large East Indian community, experienced marked changes.

The leaders began to replace some of their indigenous vessels with the *Lotah* and *Tarya* and the church fireplace, all of which are vessels and implements commonly used in Hindu religious observance. The Indian *Kurta* and *Dhoti* began to appear as acceptable dress and prayers to Baba and Mahadeo were said.

The Indians (commonly known as East Indians in the Caribbean) were introduced to Trinidad as indentured labourers during the immediate post-emancipation period. Emancipated slaves were not willing to continue working with their former slave-masters on the plantations in sufficient numbers to guarantee the viability of the plantation economy. The Indians were brought in and paid lower wages and given fewer rights than the freed slaves were demanding. But in the same way as Africans, even in bondage, had found the means whereby they could ensure some continuity with the past, Indians gave expression to their religious beliefs and to the culture that had shaped their identity to date.

Indians similarly were affirming their right to freedom of religious expression and introducing into Trinidad and Tobago the beliefs and religious practices of Hinduism and of Islam. They fasted before major feasts, venerated the saints and planted flags in honour of the saints. Like their African counterparts, religion played a critical role in their social and economic existence as well as in their spiritual lives.

Over the years, Hindus have been keen supporters of the Spiritual Baptist Faith not so much because of a commonality of class and of status within the society, but because the Hindus believed that Spiritual Baptists worshipped the same One and Indivisible Spirit.

Spirit possession in the Spiritual Baptist Faith is not confined to Africans. Indian spirits manifest themselves as do Chinese and the spirits of other nationalities. It is not unusual to find Spiritual Baptists with pictures of Indian Saints and Bhagavans (Bhagwans), or to hear chants (especially *Orisha* chants) to Ramari, or Ram Sitaram. Indeed, many Spiritual Baptists are governed by Indian spirits and the "sit down Puja" (Indian) prayers form part of their worship.

In the early 1960s, the social and cultural character of the Faith was very explicit. Spiritual Baptists were exclusively lower class and black and they sought to broaden their understanding of the culture and religion of the other major ethnic grouping that shared an identical class position, if not identical social and political status in the society, the Indians.

The Spiritual Baptists played a vital role in the lives of poor people; they provided them with status. Their long hours of undisturbed faithful prayer relieved adherents of stress and infused them with a new spirit of determination. The church began to grow in numbers and in vigour.

By this time, i.e., the late 1950's and early 1960's, the Spiritual Baptists were a political force in the country. This was not surprising, however, since throughout their struggles in the period of proscription, they aligned themselves with working class political movements. Three important figures, C. L. R. James, George Padmore and Henry Sylvester Williams, who were associated with the liberation of Africa from colonial rule and had been involved in Pan-African conferences (Williams as leader in London, 1900, Padmore and James in Manchester 1948) were sympathetic supporters of the Spiritual Baptists.

Eric Williams (1944) had lived in Britain as an Oxford scholar in the middle to late 1930's and produced the seminal work *Capitalism and Slavery*.[2] While in Britain he had been partially involved and was partly influenced by major figures in the anti-colonialist movement, and provided useful information to the struggle in Trinidad itself.

He returned to Trinidad in 1954 and formed the People's National Movement, becoming Premier in 1956, Prime Minister in 1962, the year of independence. The Most Reverend Monica Randoo recalls that the Spiritual Baptists stood solidly behind the P.N.M., "for 38 years, we were with them from its embryonic stage."

Having studied the transcripts of some fifty major interviews with adherents of the Spiritual Baptist Faith, including Archbishops and others in the hierarchy of the Church, it is clear that the evolution of the Spiritual Baptist Faith in the Caribbean parallels the emergence of a number of other cultural forms, many of which were forms of cultural resistance to the oppression of organised labour, inhuman working conditions, and the suppression of religious and cultural practices originating in Africa and other countries.

Among these other cultural forms, the development of which paralleled the evolution of the Spiritual Baptist Faith, are: Canboulay; Stick-fighting; Tamboo-bamboo; the Kaiso (Calypso) as a medium both of social protest and social commentary; Steelband playing; Carnival; Nation Dance; *Saraka* and *Orisha* feasts. The debate about the possible genesis of the Spiritual Baptist Faith within the practices and belief systems of the Early Christian Church on the one hand and within African Traditional Religion on the other is an important one which the research so far has not fully illuminated.

The ongoing discussion within the Faith about its history is informed by a range of positions, each based upon a set of assumptions. It is difficult to establish a set of historical facts within that debate. What follows therefore, is a presentation of positions adopted by certain Elders within the Faith as part of the discussion of its origins and historical roots rather than an exposition of historical facts as such.

Two distinct strands have emerged which are elucidated below.

THE ORIENTATION OF THE SPIRITUAL BAPTIST FAITH

The Spiritual Baptists in Trinidad and Tobago have developed in different directions. How do Spiritual Baptists see themselves? This question was asked throughout my fieldwork and the responses made me conclude that the Faith is struggling with the question of identity, even after forty-six years of liberation.

Father Clyde M Harvey, an African/Caribbean Roman Catholic priest, in an article written in Trinidad's *Catholic News* pointed out that there are three distinct strands in the development of independent African-centred Churches.

The first strand, properly called Spiritual Baptist, claims unequivocally to be Christians for whom the Apostles' Creed is the norm of Faith.

The second strand, called Shouter Baptists, *Shango* Baptists or African Baptists, seek to combine Christian faith with Egyptian, Cabalistic, Traditional African and even Hindu thought and practice.

The third strand, is the strong emergence of the *Orisha* movement. People in the first strand are very clear that they are not *Orisha*, some even condemn it. The *Orisha* movement seeks to give African traditional religion pride and place in Trinidad and Tobago as part of a restoration of black pride and dignity.

Reverend Hazel Gibbs de Peza stated categorically at the National Congress of Independent Spiritual Baptists of Trinidad & Tobago Conference in Port-of-Spain, 23 March 1996, that "the Spiritual Baptists belong to the world-wide fraternity of the British. They are paralleled by the Baptists of Jamaica, more recently called the Revival, the Shakers of St Vincent and the Black Baptist Church of Sierra Leone. The Spiritual Baptists are of Trinidad and Tobago."

There is therefore no doubt that a crisis of identity exists amongst Spiritual Baptists. My research revealed that, as Father Harvey argued, there is a group of Spiritual Baptists who wish to purge themselves of African traditions and are committed to Orthodox Christianity. This group I refer to as the Non-*Orisha* orientation of Spiritual Baptists.

The Spiritual Baptists with the *Orisha* orientation are the Shouters, principally those who publicly declared that they would maintain their African religious traditions and fought for the repeal of the Ordinance in 1951.

a. The non-*Orisha* orientation of the Spiritual Baptist Faith would tend to suggest that certain fundamental practices, for example, Fasting, Mourning, Baptism in freely running waters, have their origins in the practices of the Early Church.

b. The Spiritual Baptists with *Orisha* orientation locate the development of the Faith, its practices and rituals much more directly within African religious beliefs and practices. They would argue that the specifically Caribbean tradition of *Orisha* in the Spiritual Baptist Faith has to do with the manner in which colonists introduced Christianity and insisted upon adherence to it at the expense of the indigenous practices and religious lore of the slaves themselves. Venerating of Saints, for example, is seen as having origins in the need to demonstrate to slave-owners and indeed to the civic authorities in the post-emancipation era, that they were actually indulging in legitimate forms of worship.

In other words, the clandestine and the "legitimate" merged over time to produce the specifically Caribbean version of *Orisha*, which in some islands, Grenada and Trinidad in particular, represents the dominant tradition in Spiritual Baptistry.

In the course of this study, a number of respondents gave graphic accounts of the syncretic nature of the Spiritual Baptist Faith and particularly about the *Orisha* orientation within the Faith.

Ninety-five year old Mabel Salazaar for example, tells of her mother, a Spiritual Baptist who died in 1981 at the age of 110. People such as her mother would have been critical of the development of the Faith and would have been concerned with the preservation of African retentions both within it and more generally in the cultural traditions of the society. The responses of Mabel Salazaar and Mary Munroe (see Part Two) therefore, are most illuminating and aid our understanding of the relationship between Spiritual Baptists and *Orisha*.

Salazaar and Munroe describe how their mother and they themselves would begin a feast by having Spiritual Baptist prayers and then in a ceremony with separate rituals, chants and songs, engage in traditional African religious practices.

Q. The Spiritual Baptist Church in those days, did you hold feasts in them?
A. Yes. They used to keep the prayers first. We used to keep the prayers first and after the prayers, the whole night, you see like Monday night, Tuesday night, prayers, and after the prayers we start on Wednesday morning. Wednesday, Thursday and Friday is the African Feast.

Ella Andall argues that while the *Orisha* movement in Trinidad and Tobago exists in its own right and is not confined to the Spiritual Baptist Faith, the tradition was kept alive by Spiritual Baptists.

Q. Explain to me Ella, are you both Spiritual Baptist and *Orisha*?
A. Well, you know I have to be all of it, because all is one of it.
Q. What exactly do you mean by all is one of it?
A. If you deal with the history of the *Orisha* religion as far as I know, for

it to be kept alive, it was kept by the Baptists. What I know is that we have to thank the Spiritual Baptists for keeping this culture alive for us.

Andall goes on to argue that the *Orisha* religion is not a Christian religion as it existed long before Christ came.

Q. If you are having the Spiritual Baptists' prayers before the feast and that is Christian, can it be correct to say that the Orisha is non-Christian, when you have combined both?

A. But the *Orisha* is non-Christian. If you go into the trueness and purity of the religion, when you go to Nigeria you are not going to hear the   Christian prayers. So we are talking in the diaspora now.

Archbishop Clarence Baisden argues, on the other hand, that the distinction between Spiritual Baptists and *Orisha* as suggested by Andall, Salazaar and others may be too rigid. He suggests that the origins of the Spiritual Baptist Faith could be in the practices associated with "The Early Church" and its evolution within African societies with a rich blend of mystical traditions and spiritual customs. As he puts it:

> Many Shouters today believe the Shouter Faith came from Africa as an off shoot of African religion and much reference is made to the similarity of dress and liturgy in the work of *Orisha* worshippers. The Shouter has always worshipped Jehovah God in the name of His Son Jesus Christ. We have always tarried, fasted and prayed for the baptism and anointing of the Holy Ghost with the evidence of speaking in tongues. Older Shouters refer to the Spiritual Baptist Faith as the Converted Way, The Penitents, John's Work, the Baptists' Faith, which again refers to the faith or expectation of John the Baptist as a forerunner of the Messiah. They firmly believed that we are an invading force with orders to invade Satan's Kingdom in the name of Jesus and to occupy it till He comes. The battle cry was always repent and be baptised in the name of Jesus. They healed the sick, cleansed the leper, raised the dead, cast out devils and unlike the modernised church they did it for free in Jesus' name.

Archbishop Monica Randoo locates the development of the Spiritual Baptists Faith, its practices and rituals within the context of African beliefs and practices.

Those who say that the Spiritual Baptist Faith evolved in the Caribbean share the same view, not surprisingly, with those who say that the Faith evolved as a protest movement and has a cultural link with carnival, calypso and canboulay. This perspective is appealing in that the Faith did not evolve separately from the people. The people of the Caribbean evolved and developed a Caribbean identity. They were principally working class people, their expression of the Faith, their living and practising of the Faith were part and parcel of living as workers and labourers.

In the same way that other cultural traditions like stick-fighting and tamboo-bamboo emerged, these cultural traditions were part of the evolution of social cultural forms within the society, which had a lot to do with how working people on the plantation system organised their leisure. So the relationship between culture and leisure, work and leisure, leisure as cultural resistance and protest about work, was critical to the life and soul of the people. Their faith was clearly a central strand in their economic, cultural, social and political life, in that it governed and informed their daily living. It made their living with oppression more bearable.

Those influences, those cultural forms that emerged side by side with the Spiritual Baptist Faith, influenced the development and form of the Faith. Therefore, the Spiritual Baptist Faith cannot be separated from the other conditions of their existence, and they themselves made no such distinction.

There are those who see the Faith as having a link with all the cultural precursors of tamboo-bamboo, stick fighting and calypso, which are cultural forms deeply rooted in Africa. Therefore, the Afrocentric forms of culture that evolved within the diasporic crucible of the Caribbean amongst African/Caribbean people were an adaptation of the cultural forms and practices that had shaped them in Africa or had been revealed to them by the Spirits of their ancestors within the diaspora itself.

This underscores the point that culture is dynamic and gains expression through the animated externalisation of people's creativity, their spirituality and their capacity to interpret their social world through whatever medium. Visual art, verse, prose, percussion, chants, geometric shapes, the crafting of tools and other implements for day to day living, cuisine, traditional medicine, rituals and beliefs, all form part of the rich tapestry of *culture* that people in every age and in all societies have woven in the long march of human evolution.

Fundamental to the origins of the Faith among the people of the African diaspo-

ra in the Caribbean was their pattern of social organisation in a situation of enslave-
ment and of cultural bondage. How their labour was organised, how their social
units were organised, how they effected systems of mutual support and solidarity to
counterbalance the effects of the barbaric rule of their slave-masters, helped to
define them as a group and gave them an identity that was *other* than that of chat-
tel or bonded man or woman.

The material conditions of their existence determined what forms of culture they
generated and created, in the same way as they determined how they worshipped
and to a large extent the theology that informed their worship, religious and ritualistic practices. This came out very richly in much of the data and some people were
more eloquent about it than others.

Issues about the historical origins of the Spiritual Baptist Faith are also reflected
in the belief systems of adherents of the Faith. For example, all Spiritual Baptists
affirm the centrality of the Holy Spirit to the Faith and see the Bible in its most lit-
eral form as the revealed word of God. Intercession to Jesus through His mother
Mary or through His Saints, however, is not something all Spiritual Baptists counte-
nance.

Spiritual Baptists, with *Orisha* orientation especially, also believe in the revealed
word of God. But central to their Faith is the belief that the Holy Spirit manifests
itself through the Saints and that the Saints are extensions of the Holy Spirit,
"labourers in God's vineyard deployed to work with God's faithful" and guide souls
to a closer walk with God. Saints are therefore to be venerated as people through
whom one rightfully and righteously makes intercession to God.

An important point to be borne in mind is that the Spiritual Baptist Faith,
Orisha or non-*Orisha* orientation, is a phenomenon of the African diaspora, irrespective of whether or not it is thought to have originated on the African continent
itself.

A key question arising from the data, but one to which few coherent answers have
emerged is: How self-confident is the Spiritual Baptist Faith as we approach the 21st
century, and what degree of social acceptability does it see itself as enjoying?

All respondents made vivid reference to the period in which the Spiritual Baptist
Faith was proscribed, and the degree of persecution the Faith endured. What is
clear is that even after the repeal of the laws proscribing the Faith, the Shouter

Figure 11

Archbishop Raymond Oba Douglas of Mt. Pisgah Spiritual Baptist Archdiocese, former president of the National Congress of Incorporated Baptist Organisation of Trinidad and Tobago (right) with Archbishop Vernon Vaughan at Liberation Day Celebrations 1981. The current president is Archbishop Amilius Marrin (Photo by the Author).

Baptists in the popular consciousness continued to have associations with dark and clandestine practices, and a Faith shrouded in as much mystery as Masonic orders.

In the last twenty years there has been a burgeoning of leaders holding high office within the Spiritual Baptist Faith, with the ordination of priests and the consecration of Bishops and Archbishops. Civil law now accepts the priestly functions of the Church, such as conducting infant baptisms or more
accurately, the dedication of infants, marriages and conducting funerals.

There remains a body of adherents to the Spiritual Baptist Faith who feel passionately that the pendulum has swung too far in the direction of ecclesiastical orthodoxy, with all its structural trappings and that the *essence* of the Faith is in danger of being diluted as a result. Insofar as this matter goes to the heart of the question: where now for the Spiritual Baptist Faith?

It is clear that contrary to what many Spiritual Baptists themselves remember of the Faith, and contrary to abiding popular belief, the Spiritual Baptist Faith in all the islands researched has been attracting large numbers of young people. On 1 January 1997, at the St John Spiritual Baptist Church, Point Pleasant Park, Laventille, Trinidad, for example, its leader, Shepherd Baker, baptised twenty-one candidates, all of them below the age of 23 years.

Archbishop Granville Williams said in 1996 that almost half of the membership of his churches in Barbados are young persons. "Young people form a significant part

Figure 12

Former Prime Minister Mr. Patrick Manning is greeted by Senator Archbishop Barbara Burke at Liberation Day Celebrations, 1996. (Photo courtesy *Newsday*)

of the Spiritual Baptist membership and constitute an integral part of the churches activities. They are highly regarded as the future of the church and it is imperative that greater responsibility be entrusted upon them so that they can fully participate in the daily spiritual and secular affairs."

The question this raises is why? What accounts for their attraction to the Spiritual Baptist Faith? One cannot answer this question simply by looking at the Faith itself. The question needs to be posed in the context of the religious revivalism that is now a feature of Caribbean societies.

The "electronic Bible" being peddled by massive superstructures within the United States of America, the emergence in Caribbean societies of Faith ministries, Pentecostals, Open Bible churches and other forms of Fundamentalism, and the growth of the Charismatic Movement within the more established churches (principally Roman Catholic and Church of England), have all been responsible for much higher levels of youth participation in the active life of churches in recent years, than up to even a decade ago.

Finally, the question of where the Spiritual Baptist Faith sees itself going towards the millennium. This question could be further subdivided as follows:

The future of the Spiritual Baptist Faith in relation to its mission and witness to the world. Winning souls for Christ ("repent and be baptised") has traditionally been its core business. More and more, however, believers as well as non-believers take their burdens to the Spiritual Baptist Church. That includes people seeking healing, seeking prayers for the relief of stress, relief of debt, resolution of domes

Figure 13

The Prime Minister of Trinidad and Tobago, Mr. Basdeo Panday greets Bishop Deloris Severight of the NESBF Canada Archdiocese at Liberation Day Celebrations, 1996. (Photo courtesy *Newsday*)

tic conflicts, disputes in the work place, some come wanting magic or hoping for miracles. Irrespective of motives and expectations, however, what is clear is that the church is concerning itself more and more with the oppression of poverty, of economics and of class, of gender subordination and of the control apparatuses of the state no less than it is with the oppression of sin and of the individual's fall from grace. Does the Spiritual Baptist Faith therefore see it as its business to pronounce or take action as an organised collective body on the major social issues of the day?

Does it see "standing up for Jesus" as necessitating "standing up for Justice"? (John: 1996).[3] The future of the Spiritual Baptist Faith in respect of its structures and organisational forms: Can it avoid the march towards modernity and relativism? What with churches springing up in the Caribbean, in North America and in Europe at a startling rate, how will the Spiritual Baptist Faith ensure (indeed can it ensure?) that there are key distinguishing features which identify a church in London or in Brooklyn as a Spiritual Baptist Church?

If more and more Spiritual Baptist ministers are being ordained, who sets standards for the clergy, who defines "codes of practice" and to whom do the faithful or other ministers complain about the unacceptable conduct of the clergy?

These are all crucial questions for a church/faith which was made to operate outside the mainstream and is now projecting itself centre stage. Issues of credibility, accountability and public standards are already emerging as being paramount in the concerns of some of the Elders who took great personal risks for the preservation and the propagation of the Faith during the period of proscription, and since.

Conclusion

"To Serve This Present Age
My Calling to fulfil
And may it all my powers engage
To do my Master's Will"

This study has attempted to chart the growth of the Spiritual Baptist Faith and the evolution of its historical identity. The method used in this study to a large extent has been oral historiography. Questionnaires were sent to a selected group of Spiritual Baptists, Socio-Biographical statements and testimonies were collected. My research made full use of both primary and secondary source materials. Services and rituals were recorded and photographs taken of special events.

Although I conducted interviews in Trinidad, Grenada, St Vincent, Guyana and Barbados, I determined that it was impossible to give an account of the Faith's development and history, because of the diverse ways in which the Faith evolved in the Eastern Caribbean, and the wide range of positions held by individual groups of Believers within the Faith and the Elders within those groups as to the origins and historical identity of the Faith.

The Study has endeavoured to represent faithfully the various accounts of the history and essence of the Faith as given by its adherents and especially by its Elders and Leaders, the majority of whom were from Trinidad or had associations with Archdioceses in Trinidad.

It is noteworthy that although the Faith could be seen to have been given expression in Caribbean society at least as early as the beginning of the 19th century, remarkably little has been written about it, even by its own adherents.

The Spiritual Baptist Faith emerged in the 18th and 19th century as essentially a "religion" of God's people in bondage, the dual bondage of slavery and of sin. Sin, or the condition of coming short of the grace of God, created the agenda for Spiritual Baptists charged to fulfil their calling, i.e., to bring sinners to repentance and baptism and to a fuller life in and through the Spirit of God.

But there was also the sin of Empire, the "sin of the nation," that was visited upon them by the system of slavery and by their systematic exploitation within the plantation economy and for the advancement of mercantile capitalism. The Faith survived and advanced, taking on new identities here and there as the faithful insisted on serving their God at all times and in their own unique way, irrespective of the obstacles erected to control, suppress and frustrate them in that task.

What the study reveals, crucially, is that the Spiritual Baptist Faith pre-dates Euro-Western missionary institutions and their activities in the Black African diaspora, albeit the Faith has borrowed extensively in ritual, in hymns and anthems, and more recently in the structure of its organisation, from Wesleyanism, Catholicism and to a much lesser extent, Anglicanism.

The one conclusion on which the majority of Spiritual Baptists agree is that the Spiritual Baptist Faith is essentially a Caribbean phenomenon, the existence and evolution of which cannot be divorced from the colonial, economic and social history of the region and its place in the triangular trade (Africa, the Caribbean, Britain) in the heyday of the growth of western mercantile capitalism.

The Study has succeeded in illuminating the links between cultural forms of resistance among essentially the working class and peasantry in Caribbean societies and the growth of the Spiritual Baptist Faith as a protest movement and a religion of the masses within those very societies.

While there is a strong and ever growing *Orisha* movement in Trinidadian society at the present time, a movement which has an identity separate from that of the Spiritual Baptist Faith as such, the study reveals that there has always been a strong *Orisha* orientation within Spiritual Baptistry. The latter could properly be described as a "settlement" between orthodox Christianity (especially Roman Catholicism) and African Traditional Religion, a settlement forged within the economic, social, labour and religious activities and circumstances of the poor and disenfranchised in Caribbean societies.

Respondents such as Ella Andall goes as far as suggesting that the Spiritual Baptist Faith acted as a "Culture Carrier" for the *Orisha* tradition for almost two centuries, thus enabling *Orisha* to win space in the society for self-expression and to project Caribbean people as essentially linked to Africa and its traditions in an organic way.

Whether or not Spiritual Baptists of a non-*Orisha* orientation believe that the Faith's origins lie in the Caribbeanisation of the African diaspora, what is clear is that no other religion in the region, however long established, has so much of an essential "folk" element as does the Spiritual Baptist Faith.

Inevitably, therefore, adherents of the Faith adopted given traditions and practices and adopted new ones during the long march of the Faith from those early beginnings to the elements that characterise the Faith in "this present age."

The Faith has never published nor has it insisted that its adherents subscribe to a *dogma* that it considers to be the *sine qua non* of Spiritual Baptistry. It does not have a catechism nor does it have a book of *canon law*. Neophytes are instructed to see their calling, no less than the authority of the Faith or of the Shepherd/Leader/Mother, as deriving from no other source than the revealed word of God Himself.

Adherents to the Faith receive their calling from, or have their special individual gifts identified for them by, the Spirit of the Most High God. They learn the rituals of the Faith by doing, and in the course of any prayer meeting or divine service, once the conditions have been created in which the presence of the Holy Spirit could be encouraged, the Spirit guides the faithful in terms of how they might create the most positive vibrations, e.g. by raising a particular hymn or by ringing the bell.

It is for all the above reasons that many people refer to the Spiritual Baptist Faith as a "folk" religion, with its beliefs, forms of worship, styles of liturgy, etc, being handed down from one generation to the next.

Knowledge of its traditions are thought to be handed down from one generation to the next with variations and adaptations being introduced along the way, usually as a direct consequence of the physical constraints placed upon the practice of the Faith, as in Britain and the United States, or as a consequence of the specific guidance a Leader or Mother. It is perhaps not so surprising, therefore, that Spiritual Baptists appear to be straining to secure a consensus about the *true* history and origins of the Faith, its genesis, growth, persecution, liberation and transformation. In one important respect, this preoccupation is healthy. In an inquiring and increasingly sceptical age when just about everything is thought to be capable of rational if not scientific explanation, a religion or Faith such as the Spiritual Baptists' cannot hope to attract the children of "the present age" unless it is able to state not just that its authority rests on Jesus Christ and on the revealed Word of God, but where it has come from as a *religion* indigenous to black people, what it has come through, what it stands for now, and where it is going.

What this study reveals is that there is some confusion about those very issues even among older adherents of the Faith themselves. It is important that the Faith addresses itself to those questions, however, if only because, as the preceding chapter has outlined, the increasing tendency to erect an ever expanding ecclesiastical superstructure around the Faith, i.e. Archbishoprics, archdiocese, and the rest, and to organise the ministry and mission of the Faith around such structures could result in a glittering top-heavy steeple sitting atop tottering foundations.

Not only is this the stuff of which schisms are made, the danger is that so much effort and spiritual energy could be expended in establishing these structures and becoming like unto the "established church" that the true mission of the Spiritual Baptists as defined and revealed by God would be compromised.

Far from seeing this challenge facing the Faith as a crisis, terminal or otherwise, I feel it should be regarded, rather, as an opportunity for the Faith to reflect, regroup, re-launch, and re-dedicate itself to the service of Christ in "this present age," adopting only those structures that are considered essential in enabling it to do so, given the nature and challenges of present conditions.

The research study has highlighted the tension within the Faith both in the

Caribbean and in Europe, a "tension" between the so-called traditionalists and those who would break with and be purged of tradition, and move ahead.

Lanternari (1963)[1] comments upon points of crisis in popular movements such as the Spiritual Baptist Faith which is considered in the same way by some of its adherents:

> ... movements of the people within the religious dynamics of their society, they highlight the critical moment at which tensions and differences have reached a climax – the moment between traditional forms too static to move ahead and the new challenge to religious life.

Breaking with tradition is not a new phenomenon amongst the Spiritual Baptist community. In 1949, a group of Spiritual Baptists broke with tradition and denounced the practising of certain rites. That group received their own Bill under another name and the Spiritual (Shouter) Baptists remained outlawed and ostracised.

If this study succeeds in enabling the Faith to reflect upon its present condition as articulated by a cross-section of its members, and to see this period as signalling the potential for clarification, consolidation and growth, then I would feel I have made a modest contribution towards the process of bringing the Faith away from the margins and into the mainstream of social and theological debate about faith, ministry and mission of the "Church of the Oppressed."

PART TWO

TESTIMONIES

Figures 14 & 15

These represent the younger generation of SBF adherents who take pride in participating in the Faith's activities. Young people are steadily joining the Faith.

CHAPTER ONE

SOCIO-BIOGRAPHY OF AN ADHERENT
LLOYD CHARLES, TRINIDAD

My name is Lloyd Charles. I presently reside at 74 De Nobriga Street, Morvant. Phone No: 627-7695. I was born on 11.11. 1952 at 16 Cassia Street, Morvant. I was christened at the Cathedral of the Immaculate Conception on Sunday 1 January, 1953. I grew up in a Roman Catholic tradition. I made my first communion and confirmation. I also attended a Roman Catholic School and was married in a Roman Catholic Church. I was not at that time considered to be a regular church going member. I went whenever I felt like it. My social and economic standing is considered to be of the middle income bracket, or middle class.

I was called to the Spiritual Baptist Faith by my Lord and Saviour. I was later told that my calling was to free me from my friend and my wife who had me in trouble. Certain things were happening to me at times, so I knew that it was a fact.

There are several ways by which I can identify myself as a Spiritual Baptist. These are as follow:

▲ I was shown who was to baptise me. I was also given two seven day periods in two different months beginning and ending on the same days. Before baptism,

I was given my word which was the same that was given to me by my Spiritual Leader after baptism.

▲ *On the day of baptism just as I was about to be taken into the water a rainbow appeared over the water. When I was banded and dipped the third time the light was blood red and the sea roared like thunder. As the bands were removed the light became normal, the sea was calm, the sound stopped, the rainbow remained.*

▲ I was also told before hand what day I was to be dismissed from the mourning ground.

▲ I was shown the light and was told I am not to venture from the light.

▲ My hands were anointed and I was told to use these hands to do no evil. I was also given a prayer to say when I had to use it. I did it on someone who also was shown to me and it came to pass.

▲ I was shown the cow and told not to eat of it. I was told that I must not partake of the meat of horned animals which is the goat. My experience with that one is lasting.

I cooked rice, which I still have; it turned to blood. I was told a few days later when I asked for an explanation that it is the sweet savour of the blood of Christ. I was also visited by St Francis. One evening he appeared to me dressed in a brown suit with yellow bands around the waist and cuffs, there was no head but a yellow cloth in the place of a head which looked like the head of a turtle. He said nothing to me.

I was made a king, and I was given a name, crown, sceptre and a robe. I was also covered by a sheet, which I was told happens when you make the covenant with God. I was told I am a Citizen of God's Spiritual Kingdom.

It is now one year and six months since I became a Spiritual Baptist. I can go on and on about my identity as a Spiritual Baptist. I am presently documenting my spiritual travels which is almost every night. My life is changed. I am somewhat more quiet, all my troublesome friends have been moved away from me, so that there is no distraction. I am shown what I have to eat. I have no regrets, it is an experience. I am happy to talk about it with anyone who wishes to become a member of the Faith or who is willing to do research in order to teach or educate others.

I do not know what my true role and function is as a Spiritual Baptist as I am still in the learning or preparation stages. I am constantly by myself, something that I could not do before and I never feel lonely. I am always at peace with myself and for some reason everyone around me is always quiet; no rowdiness or violence. *I have since found myself giving people prayers to say whenever they have problems, something that just comes naturally.*

There are so many things that I can bring to mind, one of which is St John Chapter 14-17: "Even the spirit of truth; whom the world cannot receive, because it seeth him not, neither knoweth him; but ye know him for he dwelleth with you, and shall be in you. " That's how I feel; it is a unique experience.

CHAPTER TWO

ARCHBISHOP MONICA RANDOO
TRINIDAD

W hat did the repeal of the Prohibition Act in 1951 mean to you? Was it equality with other religious bodies? Did it bring dignity, liberation and freedom?

MR.   What the repeal of the Prohibition Act in 1951 meant to me: it was that triumphant moment when our people and myself as a whole could worship God in the way that they knew without having to hide, or to be harassed or to be jailed for the act of worshipping God as we the Spiritual Baptist Shouters did. The repeal of the Act was something that brought great joy. Also, our ceremonial articles, the bells, or *taryas*, our *lotahs*, the external things that were displayed in our worship in a sense of belonging without anyone having to take them away from you. Again, also the manner in which we worship by using our flowers, our different lotions, our shouting, our mourning, our preaching by the wayside, this brought about a release by which we were able to do without looking over our shoulders.   God really through his *power* had brought his Faith into the very open.

Did it bring us equality with other religions? As for me, if we had sought to have equality with other religions, this would not have been the path that we had cho

Figure 16
Archbishop Monica Randoo giving thanks to God in Woodford Square (photo courtesy *The Trinidad Express*).

sen. We wanted equality with other religions in this sense: that we would be able to practice our religion and in doing so be able to marry our people and do whatsoever we had to do for the nation of Trinidad and Tobago and all people as a whole without having to have other religious persuasions dictate to us, or the government, through the various powers restrict our movements.

You asked about dignity? When I received Christ into my life, when I was born of my mother and father, when I grew as a child and was taught by them, I had acquired from my childhood days the sense of dignity in worshipping God and also that particular training that I had. I would say that I did not acquire dignity with the freedom of the Act. I feel that way. Dignity was always a part of me. Being a Shouter Spiritual Baptist, even though our people were restricted by laws my dignity could not have been taken away from me.

[I can speak of] liberation only in the sense as to where a restriction applied. I was always liberated. From my childhood days [I was] one who knew about liberty, even though at times the restraints were there, my spirit was always free and I could not walk with God feeling that I was not liberated. My spirit was always liberated. I only felt the change that was put there by others and that could not stop me, because I was always a free person. So freedom brought me a type that you can extol to others without having to look over my shoulders. I was free to actually dance the dance of God, shout the shout of God, speak in his name using the symbols of the Faith without any sense of fear because of the way I worshipped God. In a sense, in the actual thing I was always free. So I hope that answers you questions.

Q.   Did the breaking of the laws take away the above?

MR.   The breaking of the laws did not take away my dignity. What it did, it caused me to see man in the different labels of worship, how they attempt to snuff out those whose worship is not like theirs before they try to find out what you are doing.

Q.   What was your interpretation of the repealing of the law?

MR.   The law [which] was repealed was placed into action by a colonial government at the time. My interpretation of the repealing of the law was that our people who were misunderstood, a people whom the *intelligentsia* of the community were afraid of. We exuded *power*, unknown *power* that they could not understand. We acquired knowledge that although they were schooled, educated, in the [highest] echelons of society, they could not understand. *Fear* was in their minds. Those who understood us in the Conformist Church, those who knew that we were the authentic thing, they also had *fear*. They knew that we would grow, they knew that we would release the captives, they also knew that we were going to expand in such a way that it was going to trouble their numbers. Because you see, we were a people that were working in the actual paths of Christ. We were searching the ghettoes, going among sinners. They didn't want that role, but we were *masters* at that. We were trained by the Spirit of God for the role of loosing and binding and setting free. The same road as Jesus Christ [had taken] and they recognised it in us. So I would say that the repealing of the law in that sense went into that particular area, where we walked into hallowed gates and manifested the natural order of life. We were advancing into every nook and cranny.

Q.   You spoke to me about mourning but you did not mention death and resurrection. Can you explain this with regards to mourning?

MR.   Mourning experience is symbolic of *death and resurrection*. In the inner chamber a candidate is placed westward for three days and three nights and it is said that the candidate is now in the grave. After those three days, the candidate is changed around and placed eastward. But in doing so there is a spiritual ceremony that is performed where you are risen from the grave, so the resurrection and death in the mourning room is symbolical.

Q.   Could you please describe the importance of baptism as a ritual?

MR.   Baptism as a ritual, is a must for every person in the Christian faith. High or low, every person must go there to experience that inward grace and the outward manifestation of it. Baptism is very important. Now, as a ritual in the Spiritual Baptist Faith, we have a bench that is called *repentance bench*, where you sit, think back, and try to assess the things one has done through prayer, to ask God's forgiveness. So you are actually sitting on *Repentance Bench*. You sit for a period of time there. Three weeks, three months, or it could be even longer until the date for your baptism is set and during that time you are taught the scriptures, you are given advice into holy living, you are counselled and strengthened through prayer. The night of your baptism, letters are written on bands, or strips of cloth, that's the ritual part. You are proved by the word of God, which is the bible. You are banned with these bands which signify that you are going to die, and you are given your *word* and it is constant praying and singing until you are immersed in water. Then the bands are loosed and you are a *new person* symbolically, and rise up and come out of that watery tomb. Then you are given prayer bands that would assist you in prayer.

Now I'm moving onto something else. My father was an African and my mother was an African mixed with Scottish blood. My father was from Tobago and my mother was from Barbados. My father was a very proud man, the one who taught me about black people long before I heard it in the streets. I knew it as a child. He was Anglican, but he was also one that visited the Hindus and the Orishas, so my mother was Anglican and when she was much older in life she became a Pentecost.

You asked about my attraction to the Spiritual Baptist Faith. I was invited by a man called Wilson who is deceased now, to go up to Star of Bethlehem Spiritual Baptist Shouter Church; it was not called a church at that time, it was called a camp and they were taking off mourners. I went up there and I saw this lady, she is still alive, Rita, and she was giving out what you called tracks. I did not know that at the time. She had on this colourful dress and she was speaking this African language and that was my connecting link. Instantly, I wanted to know much more about what this lady was talking about. How this lady could say that she went to Africa? She was in the camp here and speaking this African language. I made up my mind that I too must go to Africa just as she did. I told Wilson about it and he laughed and started to tell me about the Spiritual Baptist world. The information that he gave me only strengthened my determination to find our much more.

I decided that I would become a candidate for baptism in the Spiritual Baptist Shouter Church. I was taken by Wilson to Mother Weekes and she introduced me to Leader Weeks, his name is Theophilus Weeks and they were both from Barbados. Now when I told them that I wanted to get baptised they told me the things that I had to do. I had to come to church, be placed on the bench and take the instructions that they would give me and that others would give me. So I said OK and we began to walk that path, and during that time I became involved in a prayer circle with the very said Wilson and the membership of the Star of Bethlehem Church was engaged in that activity and it is in that prayer circle that I started to speak with brethren on the bible world and they started to speak to me about the world of spirit. I was able to understand them clearly, because as a child, hero and heroines of the bible were very real to me.

I remember well, some Canadian people used to keep Wednesday evening bible class under a tree and my mother would send me. When they narrated the story of Sampson and Daniel and all of them, I was actually in the den with Daniel. I used to traverse the shores of Galilee. I could see John, I used to hear his voice. All these things used to happen, my mind used to go on, so I could have understood the brethren when they talked to me about the world of travel with the Spiritual Baptist Church. So it was easy, I felt that I belong[ed] with them. That's how I came about to choose my Spiritual Mother, Mother Weekes, a brilliant woman, one who couldn't preach but one who could convert the vilest of sinner through her prayer. When she knelt to pray; you shake from head to foot. She and her husband were fondly called Ma and Pa; he was the preacher. And as I told you, it was a camp, it was an earth church made out of clay dirt and we had bamboo and wooden benches. The setting is still the same as in all Spiritual Baptist churches. You will always find it, the *four corners* [i.e., the four cardinal points of the universe] *has the lights*, the door, the entrance, the centre pole, the altar. You will not find that in no other church, the Anglicans, the Catholic, you will not find that sort of arrangement where there is light to the entrance of the door and that is why when you are in the Spiritual Baptist church, *you have come into an order*. You look at the four corners, you look at the centre pole, you look at the altar, the place where the leader and the mother sit and the different grades of members, the *Mother Warrior*, the *Prover* and all of these things. In those days the constitution of the church wasn't [based] on conferences, the liturgy of the church was quite different in this sense. The church commemorated Christ's death, burial and resurrection through the Lord's supper. The church at that time was made up of baptised believers. The church hadn't any roll call as such. It had a treasurer and you had a choir. Practically the whole church was the choir.

The church was very strong in the baptismal work, because John, whom they emulate, he was the Baptist. Now if one study the church that Jesus Christ assembled you will find that the disciples of John were Baptist and were in that assembly to make the body of the first church. You will find that the head of the Church of Christ was Jesus himself who was baptised by John. So the gospels declare that in the beginning Jesus Christ came to John and that he was baptised by John. Now the flag that floats over the Spiritual Baptist church is that of Jesus. The principles that govern and that have given the authority to the Baptist is that of Jesus. Although John's disciples were there with him and they assembled themselves with Jesus, they had something to receive from him and that was the *gift of the Holy Spirit*. You see, John never talked about that gift, it was Jesus Christ. So the liturgy of the Spiritual Baptist church in the sense of singing, clapping hands, rejoicing, bell ringing, trumpeting, is not as it was before. Our people are becoming very, very socialistic. The way we used to sing, they cannot do it now. Imagine you can take a hymn from the Anglican church and when they hear that hymn, they wonder and stand in their shoes with awe. So, you look at this hymn, "Thee we adore eternal name" in the prayer chant and in the song chant, you find that [with] the younger people the liturgy is changing, it's modernised. The basics are there, like *surveying*, the bell ringing, but certain aspects of the faith are gradually moving away and this is what we have to be careful about. Because now that we are seeing that it is being taken up by the Roman Catholic churches and the other churches, so that in the beginning when you were practising your religious persuasion in a very *authentic African* melodius way, you were criticised for that. *But they are taking that now* and using it because it has life, in an African way.

Each race of people has their solemnisation of their songs and so on and you find that the Shouter Baptist had that sweet melody of the African people. The hummings, the intonations, they were so pronounced in our Faith, but we are moving away. And as I told you, we hadn't these Synods and conferences and all these sorts of things. So the liturgy as it stands today, the bosses are there but we do not need to add too much to it, or else we will find ourselves with a problem. Hope I didn't go off there.

Now, I have returned to the old liturgy, but one must be very wise because you are in the age of change and as we move on and as we progress, knowledge is increasing, so you find that a word that was not used in our time when I was baptised, like shouting *Alleluia*! and shouting with your hands in the air *was not* in the Spiritual Baptist assembly. With radio and television and the different Evangelists that you have, people are looking and changing. But we have the basics and we have got to work on it.

You asked whether I had any problems in my job as a civil servant, being a Spiritual Baptist. I had no problem. As I have said, I always maintained the dignity of the Faith, I always walked with the beautiful manifestations of the word of God exhibited inwardly and outwardly. I want to say that I wore the appellations of equality, dignity and all the other things, about it, liberation, freedom, I wore them inside and they manifested strongly outside. As a civil servant I was able to move among persons of different races, I was able to move among the *intelligentsia* in the civil service, I was given opportunities to speak, I counselled some. For me, mine was a journey of pure joy. I loved it because God gave me a basket filled with gems and I was able to take them out and apply them to people and help them along. I always kept the Faith, everybody know that I am a Spiritual Baptist Shouter.

Wherever I go they knew me, from the time they see me coming they know that the ancient of days was there. I always had the will always to do that, God being my helper.

From the time I was baptised, they tied my head when I came out of the water and I wore that as a *crown*. I understood that this was no *ordinary* piece of cloth, I looked at it as my *spiritual crown* and my earthly crown. I looked at it as my father is a king and I am a princess, I want to be a queen someday, but I am a princess right now. When my head was wrapped I knew that I had reached the stage of His command and every time that I tie my head and I wrap it I feel as a child. When I was banned on one of my thrones, in the inner chamber, I was given swathing bands. It reminds me all about Jesus and the signs they found him by. My headtie is mine to reach out to the world through it. To tell the world that I belong to an ancient order from time immemorial. Therefore I wear it as a symbol or a sign that I belong to the living God.

You have asked about if it affects my work. Not at all. I have had no problems with my headtie. I work at the general hospital and the nurse told me that I must wear a nurse's cap. I studied it out and at the time I didn't have the knowledge then, so I wore the cap. But when I went to St. Ann's hospital I was more mature spir'tually, so I went there with my headtie and when I arrived I came in and the supervisor [who] was a Spiritual Baptist told me you look so lovely in your headtie. It was white and she said if all the Spiritual Baptists would use their white headties in the institution there would be a balance with the nurse's cap. So my headtie is no problem and has given me none at no time.

Chapter Three

Archbishop Clarence Baisden
Trinidad

Could you give me your personal interpretation of what it means to be a Spiritual Baptist?

CB.   A Spiritual Baptist is a person who has received a call in their soul, mainly the area of the mind so deep and insistent that it overrules all other religious intents and causes that person to seek entrance to and fellowship in the Faith which further develops the Christian personality in the areas of devotion to God and acknowledgement of and communion with the Holy Spirit mainly as teacher, comforter and guide and may lead to attainment of special gifts in the areas of preaching, healing and spiritual deliverance and insights.

Q.   Do you see the Spiritual Baptist Faith as having a direct connection to Black Africa?

CB.   It is undeniable that the early Spiritual Baptists (Shouter) practised traditional healing rites and herbal treatments and lustrations and used languages of Africa, mainly Ethiopian and Yoruba. The Mourning rites in many ways resemble the traditional rites of the Bokono Sages' initiations. This together with the method of their arrival and tradition, mainly oral, would naturally lead to the belief in a direct connection with Africa.

One cannot discount the presence of Christianity in Africa by contact with Apostles Mathew in Ethiopia, Thomas among the tribesmen of North and West Africa and the resemblance to Jewish synagogue religious practice in almost all Shouter praise houses even today.

Q.   In what ways does the Spiritual Baptist Faith help people to resolve their identity?

CB.   I am unsure as to which identity you refer. There are people adopting a pattern about blackness and African identity which is certainly not he mindset of a true Spiritual Baptist who lives looking for a city whose builder and maker is God.

The disciplines of the Faith require constant meditation on the sacrifice of Christ and preparation for evangelising and spiritual cleansing. The Rites show us types of death, burial and resurrection, practice of the Holy Presence as a means of attaining spiritual revelation and interaction with the Trinity if this is what one seeks, as one should. There is one identity, that of the Redeemed of the Lord.

Q.   In your view, what is the Order of Melchizedek?

CB.   My personal view is that it is not as some believe, a lodge or priesthood but rather a type of personality, a shadow of Christ without being like Jesus who had the beginning of human existence by birth and suspension of human life by a reason of death. Rather, the Christ which resurrected all of us in Him when He was raised up, has thereby made us a generation of Priest Kings. As Melchizedek was referred to in the Bible, I have not placed a lot of importance to this order, or even the shadowy figure of Melchizedek.

Q.   What is the role of the Spiritual Baptist Church towards economic and social progress in your country: for example, cultural and community groups, self-help projects, soup kitchens, etc.

CB.   Many Spiritual Baptists are involved in social welfare, craft teaching, community cultural groups and feeding the poor. Not as a church group but as part of our natural charitable works to the extent of our own economic ability. The church though is moving towards this pattern of community behaviour in many villages.

Q.   What were the important factors which had led to the survival of the Spiritual Baptist Faith?

CB.   Faith in God and the confident trust and reliance that He who called us would be faithful for the strength of Israel is not man that should lie. He who calls us will confirm his word with signs following. Even in the time of the oppression and persecution He was always strongly evident undertaking us. To quote an ancient key, "O Lord I am oppressed!, undertake for me."

CHAPTER FOUR

ARCHBISHOP GERTRUDE MUNDY
TRINIDAD

Could you give me your personal interpretation of what it means to be a Spiritual Baptist?

GM. A Spiritual Baptist is a person called by God into the Faith by dreams and visions;* having accepted Jesus Christ as the Way and as Saviour and Lord and receiving Baptism according to the rites of Faith. After the Mourning rites the confirming signs [are] Mark 16 Vs. 15-18 and 20 and the gifts of the Holy Spirit.

Q. Do you see the Spiritual Baptist Faith as having a direct connection to Black Africa?

* Acts 10 Vs. 30-48. Acts 9 Vs. 5-19. Acts 8 Vs 26-29.

GM.   There is a body of evidence that by 300 A.D. even "primitive" tribes in Africa had been evangelised by the apostles and disciples and Sephardic Jews of African descent.   It is unusual for a Faith whose leaders were mainly unlettered to have a church service resembling the Jewish Synagogue worship in the early church and traditional African practices of Healing by herbs, fastings and aromatic baths, etc., without African links.

On the basis of theses and the close resemblance of dress to the Black Sephardic Jews and the African, I would have such a perception. Also, all of the early leaders in each West Indian colony claimed African slave ancestry.

What I would like to explain here and what you have to know [is] that Moses and Aaron in the Old Testament gave different offerings to the Lord. The Orisha people deal with the Old Testament. The Spiritual Baptists who are called Shouters deal with the New Testament. According to our belief, Jesus Christ shed his blood once and that's finished and we must sacrifice our lives now, not the goat anymore. You will find Orishas who are Spiritual Baptist and wonder how they become that.

Q.   In what ways does the Spiritual Baptist Faith help people to resolve their identity?

GM.   It is my perception the Spiritual Baptist Faith does not seek to aid in resolving any identity other than that which identifies us as sons and daughters of God after the Way of Jesus Christ. Any other search must be a personal goal.

Q.   In your view, what is the Order of Melchizedek?

GM.   Melchizedek was a type of priest-king in ancient times. The Christian is described as a generation of priests and kings: see Hebrews 5 Vs. 1-6.

Q.   What is the role of the Spiritual Baptist Church towards economic and social progress in your country, for example, cultural and community groups, self-help projects, soup kitchens, etc.

GM.   From the inception of the Faith, Spiritual Baptists have been involved in almsgiving and helping to train seamstresses, handicrafts and trades persons.   Bearing in mind our own economic status, we have done these within the limits of our ability and the full extent of our capability.   I personally have two homes for the needy and give out food packages, hampers etc., with food and clothing.

Q.   What were the important factors which had led to the survival of the Spiritual Baptist Faith?

GM.   Unshakeable faith that God hath called us to the Faith and He would deliver and keep.

Q.   What is your organisation called?

GM.   Ezekiel Spiritual Baptist Gospel Assembly Ltd.

Q.   You were consecrated a bishop in the Spiritual Baptist Faith?

GM.   Yes.

Q.   Then you were elevated?

GM.   No, it's the same operation but my title is *Arkhiereus*.   I didn't like the word *Archbishop*.   I found it too Roman.   I didn't want to be the head of an organisation. The time came when the Lord said that I had to go on my own.   When it came to a title I said I didn't want that title of Archbishop.   I said to Bishop Baisden, I have to consecrate soon and I don't have a title.   I don't want Archbishop, could you find me a title?   He looked for a title for me and he told me what it means.   I have a niece in America.   She came in March, she asked me what title I was taking.   When I told her, she said "Oh, High Priest in Greek?"
    Let me add to what we have been discussing: for the past twenty-five years, I have been all about Trinidad, St. Vincent, giving out clothes etc.   Since I doing it I have encouraged people who have more money than me to give me money to build homes.

Q.   How involved is the Spiritual Baptist Faith in Trinidad and Tobago in social activities?

GM.   We are involved 100 per cent. We made the greatest mistake of our lives. I was reading this book. In the book the woman was giving out one box. I does go a lot of places and give out thousands of dollars in goods. I call it missionary work. The people of the Spiritual Baptist faith have been doing these things for many years. Our mistake is we never tell you come with a camera and take photos in a little book and sell it.

Q.   So the Spiritual Baptist have been doing this all these years and it hasn't been recognised?

GM.   That's right. I don't think there is anybody that does social work like us. Every Spiritual Baptist Church in Trinidad and Tobago does social work, when the month, week or day comes. Our problem is we don't record what we do, neither take pictures so the public can see. We don't make a little pamphlet and give it out to say the covenant did this for the month. This is what we have to do now. I am on that project to take pictures of anything we do to make a little pamphlet.

Q.   You think there is need for structure?

GM.   Yes, in that capacity. To show the government and people of the country the things we do.

Q.   I have been told that the faith is not growing in Trinidad and Tobago, That it is developing rapidly outside the country. For instance, it is growing in the USA and Canada. Is this true?

GM.   When you say not growing, what do you mean?

Q.   The membership.

GM.   What! That's a complete lie because for Mother Jean alone she has so much baptism every week or every night she has 17.   If you say growth for Baptism sake, it growing.

Q.   Why are they saying the faith is not growing?

GM.   Who is saying this?   I haven't seen this.   The problem is the politics in the faith.   What is failing the Baptist today is , I've been looking at it in recent months, ten Archbishops sit down at a table and come to an agreement and that must stand. That change my mind.

The Baptist is a force to reckon with.   If the Baptist come together,watch out government, watch out everybody.   If we form a party, we bound to win.

I have taken my time and looked at the constituencies.   You have 36 constituencies in our country.   And if you check how many members we have in each constituency, if the Spiritual Baptist form a political party, we must win.

ARCHBISHOP COSMORE POMPEY,
ST. VINCENT

Archbishop, the Spiritual Baptist Faith in St. Vincent, was it always known by this name?

CP.   No, it was called Shakers, Penitent, Converted. I understand the name was converted because of the scripture reading, "Except ye be converted and become as little children then you cannot enter into the kingdom of heaven." The word Shaker signifies what we call today, shout and rejoice. It was also called Shouters. There are so many names. Afterwards, the name was changed because the Government had wanted a substantial name. Therefore Bishop Leon Samuel who, before he departed this life, gave it the name Christian Pilgrim which was somewhere around 1951. That name went on until 1983, then it was renamed as the Spiritual Baptist and on our side is Spiritual Baptist Archdiocese.

Q   So where did the name Christian Pilgrim come from?

CP.   Well, when the Government wanted a name, they didn't want Spiritual

Figure 17

Archbishop Cosmore Pompey (holding staff) escorted by members of the clergy after ordination service in St. Vincent, 1994 (Photo courtesy *Spiritual Baptist News*).

Baptist because they believed that when you say Spiritual Baptist you still shake. They wanted another name so they chose Christian Pilgrim, which comes from the Pilgrim's Progress, John Bunyan. He was the first pilgrim who went on and was pointed as we are today by a man called Evangelis who pointed him beyond the wicked, so he can behold the shining light. From thence Christian was going on; his name was Christian also. His name was graceless before and after he turned to Christ his name was called Christian. This is where we got the name Christian Pilgrim. We as servants of God acknowledge that even if we change to Spiritual Baptist, we are still Christian Pilgrims because one of our old chorus says "Christian Pilgrims we're bound for Jerusalem." And when we sing those choruses we have the big shaking and rejoicing.

Q.   So your faith identifies with the story Pilgrim's Progress?

CP.   Sure.

Q.   In what particular way are they similar? Can you elaborate?

CP.   I believe the statement from John Bunyan is actually true. Not many Spiritual

Baptists know this but today in the Faith, I am definitely one who believes in it. At one time a man by the name of Holy Wiseman took Christians out of the way. God then sent Evangelis in his own time to point him [man] back into the right direction. At times when our pilgrims are on their journey, they are turned round by the evil ones.

Q.   Are you referring to the ritual of mourning in the Spiritual Baptist Faith?

CP.   Yes.

Q.   So you say mourning can identify the pointing of the way to Jesus Christ?

CP.   Sure.

Q.   How long have you been in this faith?

CP.   I joined this faith on the 16th of June 1955. Therefore I am at least 41 years.

Q.   What religion were you before ?

CP.   I was confirmed with the Anglican church at age 10 and about four years later I joined the Methodist Church as a junior member and Sunday School Teacher. I did enjoy my years in the Methodist Church and that was in 1946–1948. In 1954, I got the call to become a Spiritual Baptist.

Q.   How did you get this call?

CP.   Well, there was something strange happening to me whenever I attended a Spiritual Baptist service. I always felt a difference in my body. I felt as if I was cold, and I would put myself in all kinds of fashionable clothing so that no one would really perceive it. Later, when I read the Pilgrim's Progress I realised what was happening to me. Christian had this same problem and he was afraid to say it to his wife and children because they wouldn't listen. One day he was able to speak his mind to them. I remember one evening I spoke to my mother about what was happening and I asked her how she had felt when it had happened to her.

Q.   Was your mother a Spiritual Baptist?

CP.   No, she wasn't at that time but she used to have the same operation as a Spiritual Baptist. One Wednesday night in September 1954, some Shouters came to Overland on an open-air mission. While I was there I started having a different feeling. I had two friends and one told the other that I was going to go off so he came over. He asked me a question, then I just raised my hand, and I was off the seat. That was it. I never knew anything was happening until after everything was over. From that time I just turned my whole life over to God and decided to be a Spiritual Baptist when the time is right. I prayed and asked him to call me as the other Spiritual Baptists prayed, but I didn t hear the call. Then I turned to another faith. I asked the Lord to send me where He will send me. "Only thou hast guided my way. May your grace through life attend me. May thee only shall I obey." This is where I got the answer. He did send me and where did he send me? To a man I never knew. To a village I never knew and I obeyed his call because I always liked to be obedient to the will of God. So I went down on the North Leeward side to a man they call Denzil Prince. He was young and he told me how young he started the pointing. He says that when he became a pastor he had to go in long pants so that people could see he looking like a man. He was one of the blessed servants of God. I remember in the room when he came in, he would say "My son, remember two men went up to the temple to pray. The Pharisee and the Publican." And he was always saying to me what the Publican boy was saying, "I smite upon my troubled breast with deep and conscious guilt of Jesus Christ on his cross my only plea, Oh God be merciful to me." These are words that strengthened me and gave me courage to endure. At that first throne of grace I took seventeen days mourning and when I came out, I came out a Shepherd.

Q.   Were you already baptised?

CP.   No, I was not.

Q.   Do you usually mourn before you baptise?

CP.   Yes, I understand when they start the Spiritual Baptist work here. It was mourning alone until the Elders start going through the bible and they see where Baptism is essential so they start doing Baptism. But the original was just to mourn people, but then, as they say, to the low ground of sorrows. So mourning or fasting, whatever you want to call it, but in the earlier part the least the people used to take was 21 days.

Q.   So this was the initiation to the Faith?

CP.   Yes, and this comes through the book of Daniel, Chapter 10 where Daniel was mourning for three full weeks. There is no change of garment until you finish mourn. Today it is different with some Pointers but not with all. I still hold the old standard and the old teaching.

Q.   So you mourned for how many days?

CP.   I mourned seventeen days the first time and from the time I left home to the time I return it was 22 days.

Q.   And you were not baptised?

CP.   No.

Q .   And what was the experience then?

CP.   When I went back the second time which was three months later, I went back for Baptism. The Baptism was postponed and I had to take another mourning before Baptism. Then I was baptised a Thursday morning at a beach. One of the things I experienced at my baptism [was] I was standing on the bank of the River Jordan; I saw a great light and a gentleman came on a horse to the water. My baptism was a pleasure for me. I feel when I receive my water baptism I was really a new man inspite [of the fact] that I mourned before. I got my call very early because I was just entering my 20's. All in all I love Christ, I love the Faith. There is absolutely nothing that can remove me from being a Spiritual Baptist.

Q .   So when you mourned the first and second times what did you gain?

CP.   I have a lot of experience from my mourning. Things that I never knew, I knew then. Things I had seen, as you can say, in the outer world. Mourning is something you must be wise to ask questions. Sometimes you have a track and you think that you've reached to Kingstown and it's not except you ask. Where I am? What is the name of this place? According to Evangelis' direction to Christian, you must ask question and somebody is always there to give the answer. Mourning takes a lot of prayer and in fact in everything is prayer. You stand up is prayer; you sit down is prayer, you lie down is prayer, you kneel down is prayer. I personally will eat and still pray, I go to the wash room I am still praying, I never cease from praying, I pray all the time.

Q.   I gather mourning is advancement in the faith. What was your office after mourning ?

CP.   After my first throne of grace, I came out a Shepherd. The second time I came out to be a full Leader. I was crowned as a Leader so that I can lead the flock, lead anyone. When I went back to the third and fourth throne of grace I became a full Teacher/Pointer Evangelist whatever you want to call it. The real name I had at that time was Teacher.

Q.   That was one of the highest posts in those days?

CP.   Yes.

Q.   Pointer Teacher?

CP.   Yes.

Q.   I realised you donít say leader but Pointer Teacher. Tell me more about the mourning experience, you said you were crowned, but before that, can you describe the preparations for mourning?

CP.   Of course, we must get bands and the candles. There are some people who eat while mourning and some who do not. Like Daniel did, he ate no pleasant thing until three full weeks was completed. For mourning you have to lay aside those things stained with sin. Going to mourn you must prepare your body because some people go to mourn and they are corrupt. Of course we are sinners and no saints go to mourn.

It must be sinners, but when you go to that journey your heart must be set only on the things you are looking to achieve, which is something in Christ. Mourning has the holy cities like Jerusalem, Zion. We go to the river and when we ask the question, they say this is the river Jordan. I remember one time in my mourning but before taking the journey I told the Pointer I want no noise around this place because I am going on a journey. That Journey I was praying and asking the God of heaven to give me a golden sinker and the diving belt. While I was there I received them. A very broad belt around my waist and the golden sinker were two things on my hands that is going to sink me down.

I was lying on my back and when I go off in the spirit and take the first plunge to go down to the sea, I came back. When I took the second, I came back. When I took the third I was down in place. I found myself with a fish in my hand and an anchor. When I float, I was told this place is in Ninevah. So with mourning comes a wide world experience. There is something very thrilling, touching, but sad to say some people do not keep it. Those of us who love the Lord have to keep mourning. I do not see anything in this world to change my mind from the Spiritual Baptist Faith. Anytime the spirit call me to mourn, I am going.

Q.   So how many times do you have to mourn?

CP.   There is no limit.

Q.   Why do you keep going back?

CP.   Some people go by choice, others make plans to go every year. I donít believe in this especially if you are not living the right life. I believe when the spirit calls you, it calls you. You should always prepare and be obedient to the call because *sometimes the Father wants to reveal something to us, but the conversations in the home prevent this.* But when He calls us out on this journey, we are separate from the rest of the world. We are going to a new city, a new place and He will reveal His secrets unto us. Even when I became a Bishop it was on the mourning ground and for me I always get something new when I go on the mourning ground. The coloured bands we get them there and so on. Lots of things we get there, so I just believe in mourning.

Q.   You said the third or the fourth time you were crowned?

CP.   Yes, robed and crowned.

Q.   Can you describe this robing and crowning? How you got the garments? How did you know the garments were real?

CP.   The garment that was given to me on the journey. At one time I was given one and was told this is the old Pointer Bloucher's robe and the work that he started was not finish. When the lady handed it to me, she said "Take this, press it out, it's yours." It was the old Pointer Bloucher's own.

Q.   The old Pointer Bloucher's own?

CP.   Yes, that's the one who died in Trinidad.

Q.   What was this robe like?

CP.   It was a black robe. She said the work he started here he didn't finish and you will have to finish it. That was even before I started Pointing, that was at least 36 years ago. I just set myself in order. When I became a Pointer I travelled to a place where I saw a house. When I reached the house, it was closed, so I came back to myself, as you say, the spirit came and I was out again. I went back to the said place and I met the house open. Within the house was very, very clean. Wattles and daub and trash house. I saw two long benches, one table, one chair, a pile of enamel plates and cups. When I came back to myself I received the other things to be a Pointer.

Q.   What are the things you receive to be a Pointer?

CP.   Basin, towel, the leather strap, scissors, tape, tape line and the robe. It was really a black robe. When my spiritual mother crowned me that night and they delivered these things to me, I almost fainted because I wondered how a young person like me could take up this great responsibility.

Q.   So when you say your spiritual mother crowned you, did she put a crown on your head?

CP.   She placed the *sago* and tied flowers.

Q.   You mean the palm?

CP.   Yes, the *sago* palm made a crown. Then they gave me a plate with lighted candles and they gathered all the members around me and with the bible resting on my head, the plate on the bible and somebody had the bell. They began to sing "Jesus loves to hear little children sing," so we will crown him with roses to wear. And one of the main hymns they were singing was, "All hail the powers of Jesus." That night again it was a world wide experience.

Q.   So that is the crowning ceremony. You use the *sago* palm and make a crown with candles on a plate and you ring the bell and sing?

CP.   Yes.

Q.   What is the significance of ringing the bell?

CP.   You chime the bell to the sound of the hymn or the chorus.

Q.   So you were launched out then to do your work?

CP.   Yes.

Q.   You got a church?

CP.   Yes, when I was crowned there I had a church. On the first, second and third throne of grace I hadn't a church. I shouted at Orange Hill, that was the place I used to worship, but at this particular time in 1959 I had a church.

Q.   Where was your church ?

CP.   In Overland here just to the back of the house. The church was very small, it was the same wattle and daub, it was twelve by sixteen. After the spiritual family began to increase, I rebuilt in 1961. At that time it was part wall and part wood with some trash on it. After that I started moving out and using concrete blocks and gal-vanise. I rebuilt again and extended the church, the more children, the bigger the house.

Q.   You are referring to the spiritual family and the church?

CP.   Yes.

Q.   So as your size developed you built a bigger church and now you have a Cathedral?

CP.   Yes

Q   How many ministers you had? Who were responsible for the running of the church?

CP.   In 1961 it wasn't really under any Diocese.

Q.   I know that, I mean was there a mother running the Church?

CP.   In 1961, I was the only pastor in the church. When I point our spiritual children, some turned out to be Leaders. I had four leaders. Leader Caesar, Leader Williams, Leader Griffith, Leader Edwards. Some became Pointers. Leaders Caesar and Williams became Pointers. Then my wife mourned with me and she became a Pointing Mother, which she is now. There are other people from different places, these are only people who belong to the village, but there are people from other villages who came, some turned out to be Leaders, Pointers, crowned and robed. When somebody mourn and they came out a Pointer for the first time, I will always question the person. Then I would say to them, I am putting you out as an assistant teacher. Do not tell the world you are a full Pointer, you are only an assistant teacher. Well, they came back to renew and to elevate further on.

Q.   So in the 60's it wasn't organised?

CP.   In the sixties it didn't belong to any Diocese.

Q.   What I meant is that you didn't have a hierarchy? Just a simple church?

CP.   Yes

Q.   A simple, unstructured church?

CP.   Yes.

Q.   Was it happy in those days?

CP.   Sure.

Q.   Flourishing in those days?

CP.   People from all about would come to visit me, one of the things that was really true, the said Pointer, Pointer Bloucher, who had died, I was able to mourn many of his children. Pointer Baptiste at Sandy Bay, who was a Pointer before me, took two thrones of grace. Another Pastor from him by the name of Mother Mo, took two thrones of grace from me. Lots of people were coming to me. I remember one day I had a baptism of 25 candidates.

Q.   It lasted all day?

CP.   No, because I always worked fast no matter what the task. The pointing of them that night went on until almost early morning, because I point my candidates Thursday night. I raise them on Saturday morning and in the evening we have a whole night of prayers with them. I had very big [people], physically I mean, to mourn and God gave me the strength and the courage to cope with them. I remember Pastor Caesar telling me, "Daddy, you will have to get Bishop Samuel to help you with the pilgrims," but I knew I was not going to do it myself and that I would do it with the help and the authority of God. It was really amazing that day, when I tell you about twenty-four candidates I had to Point. I had people from Fair Hall, Belmont, Orange Hill and Overland. We had lots of people come to the Baptism. Before I had the commission to baptise, Pastor Olivier used to baptise for me.

Q.   Do you work with the operation of the Holy Spirit?

CP.   Sure.

Q.   Is this the way the Spiritual Baptist Faith operates?

CP.   Yes, if we mean to be guided by the spirit, this is the way we operate because as I was telling you of the house I saw in my sleep. One night before I built the house, I had the church but this house was the mourning room. I dreamt I was going up the street to the church and I met a gentleman sitting at the gate. He said to me, "You will have to build a house." I said to him me? I don't want no house,

I got a house already. He said, "You will have to build a house, the house you saw is yours." I am to build it and furnish the same as I saw it. Then I get some men to get stick and we build the room and prepare one table, the benches and the chair and I use enamel plate. After awhile I followed those who were using the calabash. I cut from the *boli*, but when I think it over I forgot about it and just use what the spirit show me.

Q.   What did the spirit show you?

CP.   Enamel plates to use for my pilgrims. I donít use calabash except somebody came to mourn and they requested that. In my room I use enamel plate, I use two basins, one for the feet and one for the hands. I use two towels, one for the feet and one for the hands. The hands and feet because the pilgrim must be washed to go down on the ground. The more I grow in the spirit, there are other things added time and time again.

Q.   So there is absolutely nothing you do unless instructed by the Holy Spirit?

CP.   Sure.

Q.   You were telling me in the late 50's, early 60's the church was [a] loosely organised, unstructured body. In those days you just had a leader and a mother and you carried on. There is no sort of hierarchy in the church. Now, after 30 years, have things changed?

CP.   Things have changed. We have deaconess now.

Q.   You are saying to me you only do things when instructed by the spirit. As Archbishop of the Spiritual Baptist Archdiocese in St. Vincent do you have Spiritual Baptist manuals for the ministers to follow?

CP.   No.

Q.   You haven't had any done here in St. Vincent?

CP.   What we had were some small ones from the Christian Pilgrims. It was only few people in the Christian Pilgrim at that time and it wasn't properly done. We are still in process of doing that to get our own manuals.

Q.   Therefore the instructions in the manual are from man. How do you relate that? If you are operating by the spirit and you begin to use manuals by members of your faith, how do you relate the use of manuals with your spiritual operations?

CP.   We use the manuals for Sunday morning worship, funerals and weddings.

Q.   So you have no objections to the Spiritual Baptist making their own manual?

CP.   No.

Q.   But do you think it is necessary – this transformation?

CP.   As time goes by, we should have everything as Spiritual Baptist. Of course there are some Spiritual Baptists that use the Methodist hymn books and it sound so strange on the radio when they say hymn No.1 from the Methodist hymn book.

Q.   So is high time you have your hymn books for yourself?

CP.   Yes. We do ordination now like women to be deaconess, men deacons, priests and so on, but the spirit itself making you to be what he wants, like a Leader, Shepherd, Mother, Diver, Warrior, Captain, Surveyor. All these things are spiritual and somebody could mourn and get the gift of a prayer and still receive a crown. Somebody could get the gift of a Mother or a Nurse and receive a crown because she is a Mother Nurse. The first two female I mourned were two sisters, one came out a Mother Warrior and the other a Mother Nurse. The first time they mourned they both receive colours because the Mother Nurse came out in [a] brown dress and a pinafore. The Mother Warrior came out in a mauve dress and an apron. They are still in the church.

Q.   How many years ago

CP.   I think that was in 1964.

Q.   You said they came out with colours. Were colours always used amongst Spiritual Baptist here in St. Vincent? When I say colours I mean you were not a church of only white. I mean bands and uniforms, you use colours?

CP.   Yes, my bands increasing more and more in different colours. If you notice the Pilgrims last night you will see they have plaid and some of the colours they have I never carry them as yet which is the plaid until I had to take another throne of grace. I received this cloth when I have pilgrims. I remember one time I had a man who came to me on his journey; he was going on but when I saw these two colours, different plaid and I cut them for him, he went on like when somebody flying. When he came out he was great, I believe some of these colours have some kind of upliftment.

Q.   What do the colours mean when you are going to mourn or baptise?

CP.   When I started baptism, I started two colours and that was from my pointing. The same Mother Sandy, she was one of the first set of candidates, she told me is white and blue she used. So I brought white and blue and since then I use that. That went on for some years, not until I went to Mother Daniel in 1982 I started to use white above and this was a dream I got on my pilgrim Journey. I met some fellows, Overland young men. It is true that the group I met there I never associated with them. When I came back to myself, I said to myself this is not good enough for me as a Pastor, to go to this river, meet these people and not say anything to them. I took a journey and I went back; when I went back, I met just one gentleman. When I look at him he was in the water and he had three pieces of white, one after the other. He didn't say anything to me. I didn't ask him anything. When my spiritual mother come into the room, I asked her what colour she does baptise with. She says white only, then I give her the vision. She said to me that the spirit showing you is white above you should use. So from then, I use white above.

Q.   But for mourning?

CP.   Yes, there is one thing that I don't know if this mightn't be good to talk. I heard some Pastors saying I do not band. I doubt the fact that this is true. As I was saying they trying to fool the public.

Q.   So each Pastor writes differently in the band? What do you write on the band? You write in English, in Greek or what?

CP.   This is the *secret* and this is what I am saying. Every Pointer carry a different seal. I get something different to put on a band. For example, suppose the spirit tell you to write "must Jesus bear the cross alone" and he tell me to write "How sweet the name of Jesus," you think you could read my band or I could read yours? When yours carry a different word. But if I could read is different words, you can't read them.

Q.   So the secret of mourning is in the writing and these writings are given to you in the spirit?

CP.   And the words to give the Pilgrim.

Q.   Which is called a sword?

CP.   Yes.

Q.   So you give that person a sword, which is a word?

CP.   When Evangelis point Christian, he gave him a particular roll and Christian shove it in his bosom. I believe the words that we give, some people when I was young and I hear them talk, they say "password" but I don't believe in the "password." It's your *secret*, your *key*, your parchment roll and you must go with it.

Q.   So each candidate is given a separate word?

CP.   Well, I have that for Baptism and for mourning.

Q.   So each person gets a different word?

CP.   They get the same word.

Q.   And for mourning they get the same word?

CP.   Different colours.

Q.   What's the meaning?

CP.   When a person go to mourn the first time, they don't get all the colours. Every time somebody come, their colours add unto them. I remember at one time I receive some colours for a pilgrim but more and more other colours come in, different colours in plaid and so on.

Q.   What does the plaid mean? Is there a specific meaning for the plaid material?

CP.   I think so, as I told you. I think there is some real spiritual strength in the plaid. I do not give every pilgrim that, there are certain pilgrims,   [it's] according to your qualification or if the spirit reveal it to me to give you it while you on the ground.

Q.   What is the meaning of the colours ? Let's say red, for example.

CP.   Red, is a colour I never really like whether bands or cloths but the Red signify the blood of Christ. I was told one night in a dream: I saw a shirt hanging up and the shirt had so many different colours and I was told I must choose my colours from this. I pick out the colours that I want, I do not like to wear a mix colour shirt, it must be one colour like blue, yellow or green. I mourn a pilgrim after and he had a choice similar to that with a set of bands. Well I believe we cannot be on one colour all the time.

Q.   You said you don't like red. What is the meaning of blue, for example, in mourning?

CP.   Blue signifies real victory. As my spiritual Mother told me once when I went to her, she said my blue should be deep instead of light blue. They told me the deeper the blue is the higher you mourn.

Q.   What about yellow?

CP.   Everybody describe the meaning of them different.

Q.   So all Pastors will put different meanings for the colours they use?

CP.   Yes, candidates get a different one from mourning but what I was saying [is that] the secret of this whole thing is in the seal. So what you write on the band will decide where the pilgrim goes to.

Q.   What country he travels to?

CP.   That will carry them right through to any city. But one of the things pilgrims need to do is to ask questions while they mourning. If they don't, they won't be wise. If you listen to one of the pilgrims last night, he said "Somebody light is pointing further." That is what I told them in the room. I said they must not answer punctual as it could be somebody else. You must not say too punctual you reach Trinidad, it could be Africa. If I answer punctual if I reach England, it could be America. Except you ask the question and that was what was given to you. Too many people come out of the room without knowing the right thing. There's another thing that people do when they go to mourn. If the person comes like in the States, they point Saturday, you come up next Saturday and they have to go back to work Monday. Some of these people's journeys don't end. One Pilgrim told me she went to get a letter in the post office and when she went, [she thought it was going to be] somebody she knew [and] instead of meeting this woman was a man and he told her no letter can deliver except it stamp because too much people get letter without the stamp. If you go to the end of the mourning, the full days that the Lord have for you, you suppose to get a ticket and get something to signify that your journey's ended. Some people reach to the Dragon, some reach on a hill, they stop. These are the signs that the journey end. The voice will tell you "Your journey end." I remember one time I mourn at Mother Hanoway and she had me down {i.e mourning] and [it] was not time. I saw a gentleman come in and he said, "Take up your bed and go" and the bible said, "Take up the bed and walk," but he said "take up your bed and go." The fella who was sleeping in the room with me asked why Mother don't release you. I said "I am waiting on her." He said, "if she don't take you out, you not coming back here," but *she took me out when she thought it was right*. When she come to take me out from the ground, the spirit well dismiss me already.

Q.   So you say that each person must know his/her time on the ground, not the pointer?

CP.   Not the pointer to decide, you supposed to know. I coach some people; there's a way. Some people have their plan and the devil could show some people where they are not. When the devil know what is in your heart, what is your plan, it can also bring something to you. Once I mourn a woman and it was the first time she mourning in life. An aged woman, grandmother/great-grandmother and three days I went in and she told me she travelled and she hear when she reach at Zion, "where you going?" And I know that couldn't be true. I wouldn't say she plan it but the devil try. Satan will go into the room and tell people especially in the earlier days. Most people don't get that trap now. But in the days when Converted just started they say somebody come and tell them your cattle gone, something happen to your wife, something happen to this in a malicious form as to turn their mind.

Another thing with me, when I mourn, I always train my nurses not to have any conversation with pilgrims. From my first mourning to the last time I mourn, if I discern something on my journey, something happen this side and I saw it on my mourning ground when I come back is true.

Q.   When were you consecrated Archbishop?

CP.   I was ordained a priest in 1967, 3rd November and consecrated Bishop in 1985. I was elected on the 25th January and consecrated on the 3rd March, enthroned on the 14th April as Archbishop.

Q.   How many churches do you have in your Archdiocese?

CP.   Forty churches.

Q.   How large is your Archdiocese?

CP.   It carries forty-two churches and the organisation at least thirty churches.

Q.   Which organisation?

CP.   The Spiritual Baptist Organisation of St. Vincent and the Grenadines.

Q.   Are these all the churches in St. Vincent, 72 churches?

CP.   There are some that don't belong to any organisation as yet.

Q.   I gather that you have the largest number of Spiritual Baptist churches in this island compared to the population?

CP.   Yes.

Q.   What's the reason why they have not committed themselves to the organised body?

CP.   Some are still having the old time system that they don't want to be ordained and things like that.   But it doesn't mean ordination, if you don't want to be ordained, we won't force you.   I think these are the days when everybody should be in one because Pentecostal is Pentecostal, as Apostolic is Apostolic, Anglican is Anglican.   So we Spiritual Baptists, we should be one Spiritual Baptist.

Q.   But you were telling me that this is the only island that has one Archbishop. Barbados only has one Archbishop?

CP.   Only one Archbishop here.

Q.   This other organisation, do you work hand in hand with them?

CP.   Yes, if a servant came from that side and say this person send them to me, I mourn him/her.

Q.   I gathered that you are now in the process of organising an International Spiritual Baptist Organisation, are you part of it?

CP.   Well, this started since 1993 with Archbishop Williams from Barbados as President, and I am the Vice-president.   We have others from Trinidad, Barbados, St.Vincent and so on.   But Bishop Thomas said he would take no part, he will just be an observer.

Q.   Who is he?

CP.   Bishop Thomas from America.

Q.   So are you trying to coordinate all the Spiritual Baptist churches in the region?

CP.   We have been working closely since 1991, when Archbishop Williams sent three of his members here in St. Vincent and they didn't know where they were going to, and when they reached Kingstown somebody point them onto Bishop Tree, and he point them onto Bishop John and they all came by me. Later on we took a mission-group of 38 persons to Barbados for a global revival where we spent 17 days in Service, procession, workshop, conference and so on. Well, Archbishop Williams was responsible for everything and he had people coming in from England, Canada, Trinidad and Tobago, Grenada and St. Vincent. There is where I met Bishop Noel for the first time. Archbishop Douglas, Bishop Randoo and others. So in turn we invite them to come down and any big function we have, we invite them. When we had the dedication of the Cathedral of Belmont, they were here.

Q.   This is excellent! So you are united here in the Eastern Caribbean?

CP.   Yes, and in 1994 when we had consecration of bishops they were also here and both Archbishop Williams and myself consecrate the two bishops.

Q.   I am very pleased to see how organised you all are. I was speaking with your son, Rev. Pompey, and he told me that he is involved with the younger members of the faith. Tell me more about that?

CP.   Yes, he is the Director of all the youth groups.

Q.   And I gather that you have a lot of young people in St. Vincent joining the faith?

CP.   Almost all of our churches have a tremendous amount of young people. Right here in St. Mary's, we have more young people in the church.

Q.   I observed that last right, what is the reason for this Archbishop?

CP.   We as Spiritual Baptists are trying to modernise things to encourage them [i.e. young people]. Not only just have the tie-head, but we are bringing in things to encourage them. You notice we have tambourine in the church now, but long ago they didn't have them. We don't beat drums, but most of our churches have organ and keyboard and they use them for wedding, harvest and so on. Some use them at all times.

Q. Do you hold seminars and conferences for young people?

CP. We don't miss that, from 10 years baptism age up to 30 years, they are classed as young people. The children are moving just like the adults, clapping and wanting to do everything. I even notice with the little school children, when one friend go on mercy seat to get baptise, the other friend will follow soon. They will go and ask their mother, "Mommy I want to baptise. Mary accept and I want to accept." Sometimes the mother give permission right away or sometimes wait for the next baptism.

CP. This is admirable. You mention mercy seat, can you explain?

CP. That is the front bench in the church, a special seat that only candidates for baptism or pilgrims for mourning can sit on. That seat will be there all the time and unless you have candidates nobody sits on that seat. We keep that seat and we call it the mercy seat.

Q. So each church has a mercy seat?

CP. Well yes, I suppose they do.

Q. How long do candidates sit on mercy seat?

CP. Well those of us here at St. Mary's, in fact this was my teaching from [the] early stage and *I never like to stray from anything at all, I prefer to add, rather than take away*. So at my first, my candidate will have to sit on the seat for three months. It could reduce depending on if it is school children, because they must get holidays and depending on the time they accepted, if we don't have the three months, we will get them baptised before they go back to school. Our candidates must spend nine days with their bands on their head. When you have candidates baptise Sunday, they run until the following Monday, then they come back in the morning to me and then I release them from the bands. Then they are free to go to school or to go to work or whatever.

If they baptise during the school term, I take them from school Friday, because I point them Thursday night and I have to take off the bands Monday morning for them to go to school, which is for me not really the best thing. Because when you leave off the bands you just set them free to the world, but if you allow them to settle down with the bands, after nine days you go back to school and we counsel them and caution them. And when we have candidates on the seat on Wednesday night, we choose adults to talk to the candidates. On Friday nights we choose young people from the senior section to talk to the candidates. I personally will instruct my candidates every Monday evening at 5 p.m., plus what they will get in church services. But this instruction is between me and the candidates only.

Q.   So all your churches in the Archdiocese, do they have to follow your directions?

CP.   Those who seem to show respect will stick up to anything I say to them.

Q.   Archbishop I notice that all your family are involved in the church. What is your wife's office?

CP.   A Deaconess and Pointing Mother.

Q.   You have three daughters, what are they?

CP.   Yes, they all baptise and mourn. Prudence the eldest she is a preschool teacher which is held here in the church.

Q.   Is the pre-school part of the church?

CP.   Yes, Esther is a Deaconess, she's very helpful and active. Prudence a Nurse, Melford, my eldest child, is an ordained Priest. He also has the gift of pointing, but is an Assistant Teacher. He said he's afraid of that part of work. My other son Cornelius, he also baptise and mourn; he's a Shepherd, he conducts service at times. And there's a programme in our morning service called the gospel spotlight, it's very interesting especially when Cornelius conducts it.

Chapter Six

Bishop Magna Atherly

Bishop Atherly, thank you very much for agreeing to be interviewed. I am doing this as part of my research on the Spiritual Baptist Faith, and it's very important to have the views of people like yourself who have been in the Faith for many years. How many years have you been a Spiritual Baptist?

MA. I have not been baptised in the Spiritual Baptist Faith, I was baptised in the Divine Army of the New Creation and that was in April 1949, in Point Fortin, Trinidad. I don't remember the date, but it was an Easter Sunday. I was baptised at the age of 19 years and I carried on; my elder was Elder William Duncan.

Q. You said it was the Divine Army of the New Creation. Are they Spiritual Baptists?

MA. No they are not, but it is a branch of the Spiritual Baptist, but not using certain implements which the Spiritual Baptist use.

FIGURE 18
Bishop Magna Atherly in solemn prayer after being consecrated as Bishop 1989 (Photo by the Author).

Q.   Were the services similar?

MA.   Very similar except for the ringing of the bells and the surveying of the church. They did pour water just in front of the altar, but not at the four corners. They mourn just like the Spiritual Baptists. We wore bands when we were baptised, we wore bands also when we mourn, we mourn for seven days, fourteen days accordingly and it was almost the same as the Spiritual Baptist. But just the ringing of the bell and the doption.

Q.   Are you a Spiritual Baptist now?

MA.   I became a Spiritual Baptist when I came to this country .

Q.   What year did you come to Britain?

MA.   I came to Britain on the 1st of May 1962.

Q.   How were you converted?

MA.   When I came here I tried to go to one of the churches, it was an Anglican church in Notting Hill Gate. I sent my cousin to find out the time the service would start and was told that the minister will prefer us to go to the church next door which was an *Elim* church because it would be better for us, because our people go there and that he has to consider his congregation because he didn't want to loose them. So therefore I did not bother until I came to Hammersmith and working in the Hammersmith hospital, I met a gentleman in the lift, and he said to me. "Are you a Christian?" And I said, "Why did you ask that?"

He said you look different to many people I have seen–in that calm way that you are, and it's not the first time I have seen you. I said, "Yes, I am, but I really can't find a church." Then he said to me, "There's a place in Ladbroke Grove, St. Marks Road and there's a church there where your people worship, maybe you might find that they will be suitable for you." He took me to a woman in the canteen whose name was Linda and she brought me to that church. I remained there for about two years.

Then the whole place was being demolished and in my home there was a room, and I thought if we should split up the whole church would break up, so I decided to try and get that room for the service in case we have to leave. I went to the town hall, I went to the police station and asked questions about that, if it's illegal, if it's against the law, what can I do. I was told that if we were not going beyond eleven o'clock in the night, it was okay. So we started there and we grew very strongly and many people were saved and many people were healed through the power of the Holy Spirit. And we went on for a long time until I had to do repairs.

Q.   You came here in 1962, then you spent two years at St. Marks Road. What was the name of the church?

MA.   The United Amen League of Christians.

Q.   Was it a Spiritual Baptist church?

MA.   Not fully, but there were lots of Spiritual Baptist people there, it was mixed.

Q.   When you moved the church to the room in your house, is that where you live now?

MA.   Yes, 47 Brackenbury Road, Hammersmith.

Q.   What was the church called?

MA.   The Household of Faith. That's the name that was given to the church.

Q.   How did you change to Spiritual Baptist?

MA.   Well, meeting with a Spiritual Baptist man who had no place to go. His name was Leader George and I met him and encouraged him, brought him to the church and he saw that we were having a real good time with the Lord, and he decided to join with us. He was a very strong Spiritual Baptist man, so we had another Spiritual Baptist Leader and we all joined in. I didn't have to baptise again because I was already baptised, but we continued strongly in the Spiritual Baptist Faith serving and praising God as we go along. We had about forty children and we had Sunday school .

Q.   You said to me Bishop, after meeting Leader George who was a strong Spiritual Baptist, you continued in the Spiritual Baptist way. What was your form of worship?

MA.   We worshipped like I used to in Trinidad. When the service begins we will sing three songs, then say the "I Believe." After we would survey the corners of the building, then we would, after the surveying come back and then it is time for prayers.

Q.   You said that you sang three songs when you started your service. Why three?

MA.   One hymn is not sufficient to bring that *holy* feeling within you or to give you that joy. As you sing along the Spirit of God seems to be there with you. In singing the songs it brings the Spirit deep down in you and you are lifted up.

Q.   I'm very interested in your worship. You said you sang hymns and what was next?

MA.   Then we would survey, we call it surveying of the church. It's like a garden that needs water and you go around sprinkling the water, singing the song, "When I survey the Wonderous Cross."

Q.   What was the purpose of doing this?

MA.   We water the inside [of the] church like a garden, then we go out to the door; many times people may not understand the way that we do these things, you have to explain to them. In bringing in, never mind you have Christ in you, we worship God and we have Christ in us, but there is always a stranger at the door who would like to come in and that is the reason. The Holy Spirit must come in to the church.

Q.   You said that you ring the bell when you are surveying. What is the significance?

MA   The significance of the bell is to call.

Q.   When you ring the bell at the corners?

MA.   The four corners of the earth, the angel lies in every corner, and the bells are rung in their honour.

Q.   What happens after surveying?

MA.   After surveying we go back to the altar where we started and we finish there and we start another hymn that we should kneel in prayer.

Q.   Do you have a particular hymn?

MA.   There are many hymns, but the particular ones we would sing is "Lord in this Thy mercy's day," which is 94 in the *Ancient and Modern,* or we will sing 626, "Approach my soul, the mercy-seat, Where Jesus answers prayer:" or 93, "0 Lord, turn not Thy face from me".

Q.   Would you pray as Leader of the Church? Who are the people who pray?

MA.   Sometimes according to the service we have, sometimes we have a lady's service, sometimes the men. We would have the Mother of the church to kneel and pray, then there are many Mothers, you call upon the Leader and a member of the church who are in a position to pray. They will pray aloud while the others pray silently. After prayers we rise and we greet each other in the name of the Father, Son and Holy Ghost. We will shake hands with the Leader, the Mother, the Pastor, the Deacon, but not everybody because it takes too much time.

Q.   When you say that you greet each other in the name of the Father, Son and Holy Ghost, is there a particular form of greeting?

MA.   Yes, we have a special form of greeting when we hold open hands, we kiss what we call a brotherly kiss on the right [cheek], on the left [cheek] and on the right again.

Q.   So you open both arms?

MA.   Yes, we hold right and open left so we go first right, then left then right again.

Q.   Do you say anything when you are doing this?

MA.   Father, Son and Holy Ghost.

Q.   When this is finished, what happens?

MA.   We go back to the continuation of our service which will be the reading of two psalms. After the psalms are read we will then have a foundation lesson, when the gospel will be read, or any part of the bible.

Q.   When you say foundation lesson, what do you mean?

MA.   It's like laying the *foundation for a house*, when we have that lesson, it's the lesson we have to *build upon*, to preach upon, to tell the congregations to *develop their minds*, because we are building a house, therefore we build a brick upon a brick. So in building this house we must have a foundation. So the lesson is to teach the members of the church, to exhort them, to edify them unto *good things*, and that is the way of the Lord. The things we should do, the things we should not do and so forth.

Q.   I'd like us to continue with your form of worship, what happens next?

MA.   We believe in people's participation in our church. I mean that we the leaders share the services with the congregation, but it's not practical to let everybody speak. But immediately after the foundation lesson is read, we collect the night's offering, then we ask a member of the church to conduct a testimony service of fifteen minutes to half an hour. This is a very happy time among the whole church, because we become lively, everybody sing choruses and lift their hands and praise God.

Everybody's spirit is lifted up, at times the service is so high, you speak in tongues and we dance and enjoy ourselves as the people outside. We dance as David before the Ark of the Covenant, when it was being carried along he lifted up his kingly robes and danced with joy. We feel that Christ has taken charge of us and we glorify him and sing praises to his Holy name. We have our tambourine and our shak-shak, we shake and we enjoy ourselves immensely.

Q.   You said people speak in tongues, what else happens, healing?

MA.   Oh yes, in the midst of that you may find someone with a pain or some-thing, maybe somebody will go to that person and bring them up to the altar and we will kneel there, although the joy is going on, we will pray, God hears prayer everywhere. The sick person can receive healing while we are in the testimony service.

Q.   When the testimony service is finished, what happens?

MA.   We will have another song, then we will speak on the psalms and on the foundation lesson. There are things in the psalms to encourage us. Then the foundation lesson which had great meaning to us. Sometimes the bible is read, some people don't understand, but this it the time to tell the congregation the way how to live. When we are worshipping our Lord, we need to know the things that He likes us to do and the things He doesn't like us to do, and so we have to teach the younger ones in the church about the Lord. Because remember, He had given his words to many that may pass it on.

Q.   How many preachers do you have?

MA.   We may have two people who will give their share, but a preacher is at the end, he delivers the message.

Q.   And after the message?

MA.   After the message is delivered, we may have time for two things. We may have an altar call, when we sing, clap our hands and call those outside the paling of grace, to call them in and let them know that Jesus is Lord. He is the Saviour. We call them to the altar that they too will accept Christ as the in-dwelling friend. Then again we call for whosoever needs prayer, who have pains, we call them up and pray for them. Then we bring the service to an end.

Q.   You said to me earlier that you started the church at your home as a full Spiritual Baptist church in 1964, that is almost 30 years ago? Congratulations. Tell me about the Spiritual Baptist Faith, I have heard lots of stories. Do you know where this Faith originated?

MA   I think it originated from Africa

Q.   What part of Africa? I'm interested in finding out more about the Spiritual Baptist Faith, where it originated, how it developed and spread. Could we discuss that?

MA.   The Faith came from West Africa, that is where the slaves were brought from to the West Indies. They landed some in St. Vincent, Grenada, Trinidad, these are the places where they landed. They were Christians because when they were brought there, they continued in Christianity, there fore they knew Christ and they worshipped in their own way, in their tradition; it did them no harm.

Q.   The Christian religion the slaves had, was it called Spiritual Baptist?

MA.   I don't know.

Q.   Where does the name Spiritual Baptist come from?

MA.   The reason why I said I don't know is because there were Spiritual Baptists in Trinidad, while they were called Converted in St. Vincent. They were Baptist because they baptised and Spiritual because they manifested the Holy Spirit.

Q.   Although you said that you were baptised in the Divine Army, you said they were similar to Spiritual Baptists because they wore seals for baptism and seals for mourning. What exactly do you mean when you say they wore seals?

MA.   They wore bands on their eyes and those bands had seals, and things like that. And the bands were placed on their eyes mainly to prevent them from looking here and there. Baptism is a holy thing, in those days you fast, some people are doing it, you fast three days before baptism, but in those days you will be in the church all night praying, exaltation given to you and encouraging you about baptism, the meaning, what you should do after you are baptised, giving you good teaching. About 6 a.m. you are taken down to the sea, in some places you may go to the river, but we do not baptise in ponds.

Q.   Is there any reason for so doing?

MA.   Yes, because as Christ himself was baptised by John the Baptist in the river Jordan, we ourselves are following the example. We have baptism by immersion, and we baptise them in the name of the Father, Son and Holy Ghost. The person is immersed in the water three times.

Q.   Were you aware of Spiritual Baptists before you were baptised?

MA.   Yes, in the village where I lived there were more Spiritual Baptists than Divine Army and I used to go to their services. They were always on the wayside preaching and wherever they are preaching, you stand and listen because they knew the words of God.

Q.   How did the Spiritual Baptist Faith develop in Trinidad?

MA.   Well, the Faith developed tremendously, because as time went by it grew and increased. There was a time at the early stage of the Spiritual Baptist in Trinidad, they could not have their services in the open, they had to go way out. The reason is because they would arrest them, put them in prison and charge them a lot of money which they didn't have.

The police were after them, they had a great struggle in the early days. Like Christ, even in his time on earth when he was going on with the ministry and I believe that Christ and his followers were Baptists.

Q.   I am not quite sure about what you are saying. Are you saying that Spiritual Baptists are Baptists?

MA.   Yes, when John baptised there was no Holy Ghost Spirit there. He baptised them, but not with the Holy Ghost, the Holy Spirit. Before Jesus came along, John told the people that there is one who cometh after me whose shoes I will not be able to loose and I, John, will baptise you with water, but he will baptise you with the Holy Ghost and with fire. When Peter and they baptised, they were baptised with the Spirit.

Q.   So where was the name Spiritual Baptist come from?

MA.   Now, when these folks, the slaves, came from Africa, they were filled with the Holy Ghost and the Holy Ghost is Spirit, so if you are in the Spirit, you are Spiritual. It's in the day of Pentecost when the Holy Ghost came upon them, they spoke in tongues and great things happened. Now and these people, maybe Anglican or Catholic, the churches that were [there] when the slaves came over, they were afraid of these people, because these people were healing and doing things they never saw before. They were Spiritual, they could have seen things, they had Spiritual eyes, which caused them to behold things to come. I remember reading a book about the slaves, how they worked so hard, and when they went into their little camp, you know what we will call *doption*, they were groaning in the Spirit, they became strong. When the slave master met them groaning, they would beat them with a whip, but the power of God was so strong that the whip would fall to the ground. This used to happen. That's why they used to mix up the slaves with different dialects, so that they wouldn't have the power that God give them. There was a slave master whose son was very ill and the doctors couldn't do nothing for him, and the wife of the slave master said why don't you call one of the slaves, and they did. These slaves went down in prayer and groaned and one got up and went outside and got some bush.

Q.   Any particular bush?

MA.   I don't know, but if you remember in Revelation, Jesus said the "leaves of the trees, will be the healing of the nation." So he boiled the bush, bath the child, give him to drink and he was better the next day. So these people were powerful people of God, but with society and everything they changed.

Q.   So you are saying that the name Spiritual Baptists were given to the slaves because they were Baptists and because they were Spiritual?

MA.   Because the Spirit of God was in them.

Q.   I also learnt that the Spiritual Baptists are called Shouters.

MA.   Yes, they are called Shouters. In some of these churches, they were cold in Spirit and remember Jesus said he wants us to serve him hot, not lukewarm. So these people were not like Spiritual Baptists [who] will shout in praising God, with the power of God in them, they bring up the *doption*, which is shouting.

Q.   What is the *doption* like?

MA.   The *doption* is something which they bring up from their stomach and it sound like a drum beating from in their chest. Like a trumpet coming out from their throat.

Q.   Can you still do the *doption*?

MA.   Yes, in a way. And when you bring that *doption* up, you can then through that *doption*, call on anybody and say, you have been doing an evil act yesterday, or [you] did such and such a thing the day before.

Q.   Is this prophesying?

MA.   Prophesying, yes. They will start to read you out while they puffing the *doption*, and besides that *spiritual sight* is given. They can then pick you out with their eyes closed and tell you what you did. Today society has killed such a power.

Q.   It doesn't exist any more?

MA.   It does exist in the Faith. But it is not as strong as it used to be when the people were in one accord. They supported each other, they made sure they help each other in all forms, they supported and strengthen you. It is due to supporting, when they were driven far out in the bushes and police were after them, all they were doing was preaching, they believed strongly in the Holy Ghost.

Q.   You said these people still exist in the Faith. Do you have them here in London?

MA.   Yes, here in London, not as many as they were before, but there are still.

Q.   We will continue to discuss the development of the Faith.

MA.   When slavery was abolished, under the colonial rule, they did not want them to worship. So they went in the bushes among the snakes, building their tents to serve God and none of them was bitten by the snakes. But the police kept after them and they continued worshipping in the spiritual way until the government gave them freedom. Today the churches are registered in Trinidad and they are everywhere and carry on their services like anyone else.

Q.   How did they survive?

MA.   They survived by Faith. I believe their survival came because of their Faith in God. When Paul was in trouble and he prayed to God to remove the thorn from his flesh, what did he do? He said, "My grace is sufficient to keep you from falling" and so by the grace of God they survived until now. The Faith is everywhere. In England here it is not well accepted, because they do not understand, they do not know. Spiritual Baptists are called Pocomania in Jamaica, there's a little difference between them. And the people of Jamaica who were in that Faith and come to England, they too have turned. In London you find all Spiritual Baptists tie their heads, they are called tie-head people only because they do not want to leave their heads uncovered. According to the words coming from Paul in *Corinthians*, a woman should not leave their head open and should not pray with their head uncovered. So the Baptist have that way in them, just as the Indians or Arabs.

In Jamaica, the one they call Pocomania tie their heads, but when they come in

England they criticise us. Now Spiritual Baptist people do not work for money, but those who are looking for money and things like that, leave the Faith and join up with others. They criticise the Spiritual Baptist people and call them all sorts of names.

Q.   Is your head always covered?

MA.   Always covered, even when I'm in my bed sleeping.

Q.   Tell me, you are a Teacher, a Mother, you were consecrated a Bishop. How did you get your gifts?

MA.   In the year 1966, this was my first throne of grace, this is mourning. Again you have your eye band, you go into deep fasting and praying for 7 days or 14 days and when you go down into deep fasting which is mourning, you travel out, not the same as if you have a dream. A dream is something different, with mourning it is so deep when you go down, you don't forget whatever you come in contact with. It is praying, you pray in your mind, there are others always there to pray with you and to go along with your eyes band. The first three days you will not have anything to eat nor drink. After the third day you rise.

In baptism we say you baptise in Christ, but in mourning it's like when Christ went to the wilderness and had fasted for forty days and forty nights. He had nothing to eat whatsoever, so it's like having a taste of what Christ felt when he fasted for forty days and forty nights. Although your time is shorter, it helps you to understand. It's not a bed of roses, you have pains in the ground, at times you feel hungry. When you pray your strength comes back.

I will give an account of myself. When I started to travel I found myself going through a place, according to what my Pointer told me, if I see a dog, ask the dog a question and if you see a leaf ask the leaf a question. And as I was going along to this place I saw a dog, it was a spotted black and white dog and I heard something grumble in a little distance away from the dog, it sounded like a plane, but then I still didn't bother. Then I stood there, I heard like if the plane flew away; the dog said to me, "Now you have lost your transportation."

The dog was speaking to me, "now you have lost your transportation, how are you going to get to Africa?" Now, I was lying in England in my house, and this dog was telling me how am I going to get to Africa. I said, "I don't know, but I was afraid of you." I told the dog that, he [then] said nevertheless come with me and I went with the dog and the dog took me through a little track [pathway] and out there was where the plane landed.

It was a green field of thick grass and the wind was blowing them backward and forward. And he said, "come here," and there was something lying on the grass and I did not know what it was. And he said to me, "This will have to be your transportation to Africa;" and when. I saw it, it was a white eagle lying there. And he said, "Get on the eagle's back." I said but I can't; he said "Get on the eagle's back."

And I went on the eagle's back, push my hands through the wings and sat on top. And it flew away and brought me to Africa. And when I got to Africa, there was a train station and it dropped me in the train station. Then I climbed the steps and there was a train waiting there and this big African man came to me and said, "What kept you so long?" I said I missed the plane. He said, "Get in that train." I said what is your name and he said you will find my name in the train. He said where are you going? I said I'm going to Nigeria. I had on a dress of all different colours, the head-tie was the same thing. Now I got in the train and the train pulled out. I was the only passenger, the man did not get in, when I looked out he was still standing there. When I got to the station he was there again and he took me on. So all these things remain in your head and never go away.

The first throne you wait for while and then you take your flight. Then I was taken to a school and when I got to this school, the teacher said to me "Oh! you are here now!" I said yes, I am a bit late. She said nevertheless you are here now. "Come," she said and she hand me a little pointer, she hand me a book which she said was the roll book, she hand me a kit and in that kit there were lots of little things, chalk and others. And she turned to the children and said to them, "This is your new teacher."

They did not answer. She said, "I have to go, but your new teacher has come and she will make herself known to you." When she left and I said "Good morning children," they all answered "Good morning." I said I am your new teacher, my name is Teacher Atherly. They all said good morning, Teacher Artherly. Then I said I am going to call the roll and I will know you by your names.

And I started calling the roll and they were standing and answering. After that I took them out in the yard and I've never seen children like that, when two children ring the bell it was ever so sweet. The other two [bells were] in the back. One had a bell joined in two, one head but two bells, and he was chiming that bell with the other one coming in at certain times. Then he said, "Do you know what those two first bells mean?" I said no. He said, "The first bell is to call, and this bell is to silence and that bell is to consecrate. So you heard the language of calling, silence and consecration by the bell."

Q.   What do you compare this experience with?

MA.   Astral travel.

Q.   You said to me earlier in conversation that you point souls. Where did you get this knowledge?

MA.   This again is something that you are taught. You get the gifts when you travel, when you tell the Pointer what you received, then they give you the name Teacher/Pointer.

Q.   So you received all the gifts of a Teacher/Pointer?

MA.   Yes, this was in 1966.

Q.   So your church developed. How large was your membership?

MA.   About forty-four, but now it has grown. At that time in 1966 we were in a little room, then we had to break the partition to accommodate more people. So we had a bigger place like an open lounge, because every Sunday people were all in the corridor, wonderful works went on there. The members grew to something like seventy or more, there were visitors coming.

Q.   Did you baptise people here in London?

MA.   At the first place I did not baptise until I went down for the second throne of grace. That was in Trinidad, in Barataria. That was when I went through a dessert place [during] the same mourning, where there were a lot of vines tied, it was difficult to get through and somehow a cutlass came in my hands. I don't know where it came from, but I began to cut my way through until I got to the bright light of the sun and I was out of this dessert place.

There I saw a whole line of children, they were in pairs, two by two and there was a man further on standing in a long white gown. And when I got there he said, "You are late" (I'm always late), and I said to him, "The way was so hard, there was too much vine in the way, I had to chop my way through." And he said. "Yes, you had to work your [way] to come here." When I got on the top there, he had a rod in his hand and he said to me, "This is yours," and he handed me the rod and I said, "What shall 1 do with this rod?"

Because you must ask questions when something is given. Then he said to me, "Look at the children." "They all were in long white robes with a white skullcap on their heads and they each had a lighted candle. The bigger ones, six of them, two were holding a banner in front, two holding two big bells and two with two smaller bells. They started to chime the bells and it was like music itself, and he said, "Do you know the language of the bell?" I said to him no and he said, "Well, you will have to learn the language of the bell, what the bell is telling you." I said, "What is your name, who are you?" He said, "I am the I am."

That was all he said to me. He said, "Listen to the bell" and he said, "These children you have got to take them down to the water." I said but I can't swim, then he said, "You will swim because you got to take them down to the water. But first you go down to the water with the rod, down the hill" because the sea was below; and I went into the water up to about my waist. He said "Stop and measure the water where you stop." I did. He then said, "When you take them to the water, that's your mark." I told my Pointer this, then she said to me, "You will have trouble, men don't like to hear women baptise." Men think they are the only ones to do baptism, but with Christ there is neither male nor female.

Q.   So you are a Baptiser, a Pointer/Teacher, a Mother and you were consecrated a Bishop how long ago?

MA.   About four years ago.

Q.   You said that your congregation is so large, how many hundreds?

MA.   About four hundred.

Q.   Where do you keep your services?

MA.   At the Shepherd's Bush Baptist Church.

Q.   You mentioned earlier about the Council of Spiritual Baptist churches, could you tell me more about it?

MA.   That was in 1988, we had about thirteen churches.

Q.   Were all these churches based in London?

MA.   Yes in London, but from different areas. In 1989 Archbishop Griffith and his entourage from the National Evangelical Spiritual Baptist Archdiocese came to London and ordained ministers and consecrated bishops.

Q.   Do you visit each other's churches?

MA.   Yes, we do.

Q.   Do you retain African practices in your churches?

MA.   Yes, we do.

Q.   Tell me about the African retentions?

MA.   The ringing of the bells.   In our churches, we lay a table as an altar.   We use calabashes, *lotah*, drums.   Those things that come from African origin like the tying of the heads, the pulling of the *doption*, that's when you are communicating with the Spirit itself, it's all there.

Q.   Do you have a lot of young people in your church?

MA.   Yes, and we are having some new ones coming in to the church.

Q.   Do the young people understand the African practices in the church?

MA.   Yes they do, but what they don't understand we explain to them.

Q.   So do you try to keep the traditional part of the Faith alive?

MA.   Yes, regardless about what anybody say.

Q.   Is the Faith cultural?

MA.   Yes, it has a lot of culture in it.   Now you may have something and because it is not accepted you let it go.   No, no, we are Africans and we will like to continue that way.

Q.   You talked about lighting of candles, what's the significance?

MA.   When we light candles, it doesn't mean that we have not got Christ, because Christ is the light.   But lighting the candle is a reminder of Christ Jesus and when you light a candle you see light, which is Christ.   The candle without the light is like a man without Christ and a candle with the light is like when you have Christ in you. I look at the candle, I know it's wax around here that melts away. *The wick of the candle is you, with the Spirit of God in you.*   So we are *not worshipping* the candle as if it is Christ, we are worshipping because it is the symbol of Christ which is the light.

Q.   I asked you earlier and you said the Faith is not the same. Do you think there is a need to protect these practices?

MA.   People are not giving themselves fully as those in years gone by, so that they could be filled with the power. There is a lot of negligence in the church now.

Q.   Negligence by whom, the elders? Who are you blaming for this?

MA.   I must say the elders, because they are doing things contrary, not everybody. Some are doing things not to the honour and glory of God.

Q.   How can you keep this Faith alive?

MA.   The old time Baptist people were really obligated to God. They did not mess around, they fasted, prayed and came to church with the Spirit of God in them. In that way they were able to have visions. They were charged, filled with the Spirit, so when they come to church great things happened. Today you do not have the ones who are obligated to God. They don't even have time to read the bible now. However, there are still those who have the power of God in them.

Q.   You said on your first mourning you travelled to Africa, your second mourning you were given the commission to baptise. Could you tell me more about your experiences in the spirit world?

MA.   As I travelled along in Africa, now the person who met me on the train, he disappeared, so I had to find my way for myself. And as I travelled along I started to hear the beating of a drum and the drum was beating "dudum, dudum, dudum" and I got a bit puzzled and wondered where the drum beat was coming from. And at times the beat will change. So I start following that drum and as I got closer and closer, it became clearer and clearer until I met a big yard and there was a lot of African people, and there was this young woman, she was dancing with the drums. I asked them what. tribe are you? And they told me they are Igbos. And I said the drums sound very nice and I heard it from far away. He said, "Yes, we were calling and we were wondering whether you will follow the drums, because you have to learn the language of the drums." I said to him, "The language of the drums, the drums they can't speak." He said, "Yes, they were speaking to you and they brought you right here." Anyway they changed my clothes and I had on this long full skirt, and this little top and my head was tied, it was plaited, and I started to dance as the drums beat and I danced. Then they said to me, "Well, come in now," and I had to go into the house.

When I got into the house I met this big, black, giant of a looking African man and I was scared of him because he was so serious. And he said, "Who are you and what do you want?" I said that I am a pilgrim traveller seeking wisdom, knowledge and understanding. He said, "Come in and sit down." I went in and sat down. "How did you get here?" he asked. I said that I came by the train and on my way I heard the drums and it brought me here.

He said, "Have you danced?" I said yes, then he said, "OK, you sit down." And he started to Elegbu! I looked at him. He said, *"Elego Go Wala."* I said *"Elegun, Elego Go Wala."* He said. "Did you hear that on the drum?" I say, "Do dung dung, Do dung dune." He said, you heard it. He then began to sing again in African and I said I don't understand. He said, "Come on, you heard the drums, this is the language of the drums." And I started to speak in the language. Then he said, "You have joined the African religion and you have to work for us. You have to share the bread to the people." What he merit[ed] was the words.

He gave me a whole calabash and I asked him the meaning. He said "It's the first fruit of God, you have to cut, scrape and eat." When I was leaving he gave me another calabash and in that calabash had seven candies, seven different candles with flowers all in and between. The candles were standing in the calabash and he said, "When you go home you will get the right way to use this."

Q.   Were they different colour candles?

MA.   Yes, different colours, white, blue, pink, green, yellow, and brown. They were lit and he said, "This is your lighthouse." And I found myself back home in the church at Brackenbury Road and my husband, although he was dead and gone, he was there to meet me in front of the door. And he said, "Come," and he showed me where I should place the calabash and he said to me, "This is your lighthouse and your fountain." Just as he placed it down, a white sink appeared just above the calabash and there was no tap or anything. I said, "What is the sink for?" He said, "For your water, from the spring." I said, but there is no tap, and he said, "You just have to touch it and the water would come." I took my finger and touch it and the water started flowing. Then Jones' little children came and started to interfere, and he said to me, "Don't allow anybody to interfere in the things that you have" and he put the children outside and he said, "Don't allow anybody to tell you what to do. You are told what to do, you got what you have, use it and don't let anybody interfere."

Q.   That was your African experience. You said to me earlier that in the spirit you travel east, west, north and south. Did you travel to any other country?

MA.   From Africa I went to India and how I got into India was strange. I was going up a very lonely road, and when I travelled and travelled, I saw a house, it was like a schoolhouse but it was closed. And I said to myself I wonder what kind of house that is, it look like a schoolhouse, and I'm saying if we have a building like that we can have our church in it. There was a big gate and I walked up to the gate and there was a little side entrance and I walked into it. There was a sign on top of the house and I said I wonder what kind of school this is. And a voice said to me, "Read the sign and you will know." When I got nearer to it, it was [a] Seven Days Adventist church. I said Seven-Day Adventist church? The voice said, "Yes, Seven-Day Adventist church," and I said it is closed. He said, "Yes, that was a long time ago." He said, "Don't go in, just carry on."

So I went on to the sea, and as I to down into the sea, I was barefoot and I saw a big thing coming out of the sea unto the beach and I said, Good Lord, what is that! No answer, but this big object coming up to meet me. I was so frightened and at the same time I saw a brown dog, and as the dog came the dog say, "Where is your sword?" I say my sword? He said, "Use your sword," then I remember and started to use my sword and the thing just disappeared into nothing. At the same time was a step climbing up and I climbed the steps and there I found myself into a house on a real high bank and [as] I got there, the dog said come with me.

I went through the house following the dog and the dog took me to a big place and all the people there were Indians and they were dressed in a nice blue, *aqua* blue, and they had something like a cone on their heads. This old woman came to me and she started to speak in an Indian language and I said, I don't understand what you are saying.

Now, when you are in the Spirit you *can* speak the language, you must have the Spirit of God manifest in you. At that time you are not yourself when the Spirit of God take over. She took me in, dressed me in the same clothes like they all were. Then Indian music start to play and I just went away. They took me into a temple and we prayed, but our prayer was in the language. That's where I received the *Tarya* and the *Lotah*, they were on a tray, on a silver tray. Then he said, "This is for you, when you get back to church you will know when to use it and how to use it." The *Lotah* is a vessel of the Indians. I have done many marvellous works in the church using my calabash and *lotah* in the way [it] is was given to me. The *Tarya* is a tray, it's both African and Indian.

You put grains of corn, rice, peas, flour, cloves, salt, sugar—they all represent the nations. The bell is to consecrate, the bell is for peace. I was told so. When I left there I found a very old Man who said, "Come with me." I said who are you and he said, "I am." I used my sword and he was still there. He took me up some steps, a spiral stairs, and we landed inside a house, then we passed through and went to another house. He said to me, "You have to go now, I will be with you." He was then dressed in a grey shirt with yellow flap on the shoulders and gold buttons, yellow binding round the sleeves. He said to me, "I am your General, anytime you need me ring this bell and I will come."

Q.   Was he African or Indian?

MA.   Indian.

Q   Can you summon this General at anytime during your service?

MA.   Yes.

Q.   So if you summon him and he comes, he manifests in you?

MA.   Yes, manifests. That is the time I am off in the spirit with the language, his language.

Q.   When he speaks, are there people who can interpret?

MA.   Yes, there are some people who can and do so.

Q.   So you work with different powers, African and Indian.

MA.   Yes, and I manifest Arabic too. At one time on my travels I found myself in a place. I was downstairs in a place and I was going through a little track and there I saw some Arab women, but it was like by the riverside and I went down to them and said, can I have some of your water? They looked at me and spoke in this language. I cannot bring the language right now, because I am not in the Spirit, but they spoke in their language and said to me, come. I went and they took me into the water.

They poured some water over my head, three times and when they were finished [they] brought me back outside, filled a bucket of water and gave it to me to go. They told me that I have to get four buckets, with four different types of water in it and put it at the four corners of the church. I must get rain water, tap water, river water, and water from the sea, and those four buckets must be in the four corners of the church. I left them with one bucket of water and went along. I came up to a place that looks like an abattoir, I went around the building and found a door. I entered the door and I met a man and I said to him, I'm a pilgrim traveller seeking wisdom, knowledge and understanding.

He said, "Come with me," and I went in with him and he took me through this building, I didn't see any meat or so. but in the freezer there was a lot of chicken. He said, "You see these chickens, do you know you can bring all of them alive?" I said alive? but they are dead! He said, "They are dead, but you can bring them alive." I said how? He said, "Come with me." When we got out of the door, I found myself in a cemetery and he said to me, "Take this," and he gave me a rod in my hand. I said ,what am I going to do with the rod?

He said, "You couldn't bring those chickens alive, but you will bring them alive" I said how? He gave me a word and said, "Take that stick and put it on the grave and use that word." So I took the stick, put it on the grave, used the word and the grave opened. He said, "You can bring the dead to life, use this stick and that word and you can bring the dead alive."

After that I found myself in China, busy, busy streets and plenty people. I travelled for a long way in and out, in and out, then I started to climb some steps until I got on top of a hill and when I viewed behind where I came from, it was beautiful. But I couldn't stay there, so I went further down to another part of China.

When I got there I saw a shop with neon lights flashing. As I was about to enter, a Chinese man came and said, "Don't! He spoke to me in Chinese and continued speaking in Chinese. He said to me in English, "Come with me." And we went along until we got into this strange house which looked like an umbrella. I followed him through this house and he took me to his father, a man sitting and rocking on this little chair. He had no hair, but for one little plait in the middle. When I got to him, he spoke to the Man in his language and the Man stopped rocking. When I went to the man, he didn't have eyes and I got really scared. Then I said, but he can't see and my Man said, "The reflection is only in your eyes." The old man turned to me and asked, "What do you want?" I said wisdom, knowledge and understanding.

He and the older Man talked then he took me to the house where there were a lot of teachers and nuns. Then one teacher said to me that we have a miracle to work here and you must be it. Everybody is running, they had about seven pots and you had to arrange the pots in a particular way. Everybody got about three minutes to do the pots and when they couldn't, they had to go and I went way out in the back and stand up.

The nun said to me, "You never admit you can do anything, anyway come, because you did not say you can do it, I will show you what to do." As she showed me I did it and the same Chinese man with one eye was standing there and he said, "Come and I will teach you something." There was a set of buttons and little lights, he said, "Press this button" and when I press it he said "Understanding." I press the other one it said, "Knowledge" and the third one said "Wisdom." He said, "Is that what you wanted? What are you going to do with it?" I said I have so many people in the church I need to have wisdom, knowledge and understanding in order to teach them.

"There," he said, "but they will fire after you." I said fire? He said, "Yes, but when you press this button and they fire, you are going to put them down." I said what sort of button that is? He said, "The button of wisdom, when you are in danger you press this one, and wherever your enemies are you will destroy them." He said, "When you go, you have a lot of fight to fight and you did say if fight come you will fight." I said how did you know that? He said, "You told me."

But before I went to mourn I dreamt that I went into one of these Mc Donald places, when I called for the ice cream and got it, I realised I didn't take up a little spoon, so I went back for the spoon and the ice cream disappeared. The fellow who was serving said that he saw when someone took it, but never mind he will give me some more. I sat down there and three policemen came in, the first one looked at me and I asked him why was he looking at me. He said, "I heard that you said if fight comes you will fight" and he went; the second one came to me and said, "I understand you said that if fight comes you will fight." I said yes; the third one come and asked me the same question I said what you all coming and asking me this question [for], you want to intimidate me, why are you questioning me? The third one say, "We only want to be sure, for the fight is on."

Then he handed me a whole lot of paper and when I looked at it, I saw a different name. I shouted wait, wait, these are not my papers, this is not my name. Then he said, "Your name has now been changed." I said this is the name of a queen. He said no, "Your name is changed, you are now Queen Santane."

Q.   Is this why you are called Queen Mother?

MA.   When I went down to mourn that came out. [Bishop sings in Chinese.]

Before my journey ended I was taken up on a hill and there was a little building. When I got there it was a shop but nobody was in, it was like a horseshoe. I stood there waiting on somebody to come and when the person did come, I said what sort of shop is this? And the person said, "This is Zion Doctor Shop." I say Oh and where is the person who is supposed to be here? He said, "You." I said, in Zion Doctor Shop, me? He said, "All these were given to you."

Q.   What were they?

MA.   Medicine, medicines all on the shelves. Bottles of medicines, small ones, big ones. I said, I can't take all these things with me. He said, "But it is yours, all is yours, go on now, take what you have and come back for these."

Q.   Did you go back to get them?

MA.   No.

Q.   Had you gone back, would you have been a doctor in the Spirit?

MA.   Oh yes! I have been a doctor in the Spirit. When I went to mourn at Mother Milly and I was climbing up the hill, I think I told you about that hill already, and they told me that was the hill of Mount Carmel.

Q.   Is that why you named your church Mt. Carmel?

MA.   Yes.

Q.   You didn't tell me about this experience, did you?

MA.   I found myself in a place where I was riding a bicycle and as I got on the bridge there was a truck on the bridge and I couldn't pass. Eventually, I gave the bicycle to somebody and I started to walk. When I cross the bridge there was a hill to climb, but it was not a straight hill. I was climbing, not walking. You know the six million dollar man? I was going like that.

When I reached to the first tree, it was a cashew nut tree with few fruits on the tree, but I took three and went along. Climbing up the hill again in the same position, there was a mango tree and the wind just came and blow the mangoes and three mangoes fell. One was ripe, one was green and one was half-ripe. I look up the three mangoes and continued climbing, then I came to a tree looking like a calabash tree, but the fruits on it were very small and I said to myself, I don't think I would bother with you, so I continued and went up to the top. When I got there I saw a man standing, waiting. He said, "I've been waiting here for you a long time." I said yes, but I explained that I had to give away my bicycle because the truck was on the bridge. He said, "Never mind, come," and I cross to the other side and he took me to a house that was there.

You know these houses we have back home where the door is divided into two, top half and bottom half? Well, the top part was open and the bottom part closed and there was this woman standing in front of the door. A black woman wearing a navy dress and she said, "You are late." She was wearing an indigo blue dress, long, with long sleeves and you know that Queen Victoria frill around her neck, and she had an apron on, it started on top and went right down to the end of the dress. She said to me, "Come in, they are waiting on you," and again I had to explain why I was late. She said, "Never mind, you are here now, go in." When I went inside, there was a doctor and about six nurses and he said, "You have come," and I said yes. He took off his stethoscope from his neck and placed it on my neck. He then took off his uniform and put it on me. Then the nurses said, "Look now we have been here with you and didn't give us your stethoscope or your jacket, she just came and you give them to her." He said to them, "She had worked very, very hard and this has to be given to her." He said to me, "Look outside! When I looked out he said, "Tell me, what do you see?" I said, the sun and the moon. He said, "The sun and the moon, they are in eclipse."

Q.   What did he mean by showing you this?

MA.   I don't know. But he said, "When you see the sun and the moon in eclipse, I want you to take this seal," and he placed the seal in my hand, and [he] said, "Wear this." I said, what's the meaning of this? He said, "You will find out, when you find yourself among the people that do not agree, seal yourself." He said, "There is a man right now waiting for you and you will have to take care of him." I said, what is wrong with him? He said, "He has multiple sclerosis and cannot be healed by operation, the hands of the doctors cannot heal him, therefore you will have to do the job." I said how can I do that? He said, "You will learn." He took me over to a man covered in a white sheet on the bed and he said, "This is the man, you have to heal him." I left and went around; there was this woman, again she looked like an Arab, she had this little girl who was wearing a dress of stars with all the colours in the world.

This child was sick and the mother was crying because she couldn't see the doctor. I said to her, you give me the child. Then she said, "But you are not the doctor." I said I am and I took the child, got some water and washed the face and hands of the child, then I lift[ed] her up and began to pray. When the mother came in the child was better.

Q.   So after your spiritual journeys, when you returned to your church did you begin to heal the sick, for example?

MA.   Marvellous work went on, the blind received their sight, the deaf hear, the lame walk, the dumb spoke.

Q.   All with the laying of your hands?

MA.   Praying, singing, we used just water; I was given spring water in the bottle and I had that always to give to people and [the] cancer was healed at he Royal Marsden Hospital with a bottle of water.

Q.   Are there people alive who can testify to some of your works?

MA.   Yes, there's an African man who had cancer and his wife was told about the little church down there. She came and we told her it's a faith healing school. The husband was too ill to come and we put her to sit down on a chair, give her a candle, and prayed for her husband through her. We then gave her a bottle of water and told her to give him 10 millimetres three times a day. When the doctors tested him, they said something miraculous was happening. She came back the following Sunday in tears. We prepared again the same way. She herself brought water and we blessed it. The following week she returned to say that her husband was discharged from the hospital.

Q.   Are any of you ministers who work with you then still in your church?

MA.   No, one is dead and two others opened their own church.

Q.   How long have you been baptising?

MA.   Since 1983.

Q.   How many candidates do you baptise annually?

MA.   It varies, one year I had fifteen.   We baptise in the sea, not in pools. Sometimes six, ten, eight, two, three, however they come.

Q.   Who assists you?

MA.   We have our Pastors, Deacon, Shepherd, they all go into the water.

ARCHBISHOP PHILIP LEWIS, LONDON

A rchbishop, we were talking about the Patriarchs of the Faith, those who have left us a legacy. Tell me about them?

PL   What I found astonishing about Bishop Hunte, when I mourned I didn't know what it was all about. I was sitting in the mourner room after my pointing because nothing was coming to me. Then an Indian man in a *dhoti* came and said to me, "Give me your word." I said to him, "What word are you asking for? I can't give you my word. I'm a pilgrim traveller." He said, "If you don't give me your word you will not be able to move from here." So I then gave him my password and he said, "Come with me" and he took me around to the front of St. Peter's church. He said, "You see here is where I am everyday, from six o'clock in the evening to six o'clock in the morning." That amazed me very much, it means that he being the watchman of the temple, and from that time on I travelled.

Q.   What year was this?

PL.   1974.

Figure 19
Archbishop Philip Lewis, an erudite and African-centred minister whose service, ceremonies, rituals and group meetings incorporate African traditional, Kmt (Ancient Egypt) of antiquity features. He is a practitioner of deep philosophies of ancient traditions (Photo courtesy Paul Miller)..

Q.   That was when you embraced the Spiritual Baptist Faith?

PL.   Yes, because I was conducting service from my country in a spiritual manner, but I had this vision that I must go and mourn. Because in the church, in those days we read from the Book of Nehemiah about the evening sacrifice and mourning certain days, I was always curious about mourning and I spoke to Bishop Thompson and she introduced me to her spiritual father, Bishop Hunte.

Q.   Was it after your mourning that your church was called Spiritual Baptist?

PL.   The church was always the 7th Church of Melchisidec, I only added Spiritual Baptist

Q.   You said earlier that you always conducted your services in your home, Guyana, in a spiritual manner. Did you belong to the group of people called Spiritual Baptists in Guyana?

PL.   I've never heard of Spiritual Baptists in Guyana. There was a group of people in Guyana that was known as 'Ring the Bell' because they were the only church that rang bells.

Q.   Were they the people who were called Jordanites?

PL.   No, the Jordanites are not Spiritual Baptist people, because I was baptised by the successor of the person who started the Jordanites, his immediate successor, that means that I have a fair knowledge of the organisation. That is a spiritual church that is being run more like Adventists. The only difference is that they wear robes symbolising that their white robes are symbols of the saints and they have styled themselves as the Church of the West Evangelist Millennium Pilgrims. Meaning that they were pilgrims coming from the east to the west preaching the doctrine of the millennium which is the thousand years of Jesus Christ. So their doctrine was based strictly on [being] vegetarian.

The three main tenets of their faith was Baptism, Sabbath and Sacrifice. Baptism in living waters, Sabbath because it is a creative act, a memorial, man's creation, Sacrifice meaning they were non-flesh eaters. The original man did not eat flesh. They believe that for us to enter paradise, which was lost, we must go back to the beginning of time. So my church was run in that form until I met Bishop Thompson here in London.

Q.   So you must have had the first Jordanite church here in London?

PL.   Yes I did. I came here in 1968.

Q.   What attracted you to the Spiritual Baptist Faith?
PL..   I visited a lady, Abbess Barrington, in Walthamstow with some friends one Sunday morning. I was told that they were taking me to a Spiritual Baptist church. On reaching there, the service was very impressive, but what was startling in the service was that the lady was doing the invocation and when they chanted the prayers it was heaven-like. Something outstanding took place, she was backing the entrance to get in. In the midst of the prayers she said that she will have to come down because visitors have entered the church. She got up, did what she had to do, then entertained us by greeting us.

It was the first time I had been in such a service of spiritual awakening and I was intrigued by it. The Abbess was being inspired and acted the role of that of a prophet, of which I always quoted that the Spiritual Baptist Faith is both Prophetic and Priestly in that we do carry out the traditions of our ancestors and the prophets. And that of a more modem church, which is the Priestly order which is in conformity with the government and state in which you reside. So the Spiritual Baptist Faith has come a long way.

Q.   Do we still have people like Abbess Barrington in the church?

PL.   Many people have a notion that to prophesy means to tell somebody a direct prophecy of events in their lives, but the Minister prophesies while he preaches. When you begin your preaching in the church, you then lay a foundation, but somewhere along the line, the Spirit takes over that sermon, and that preacher is then inspired by the Holy Ghost. So at that stage he begins to prophesy by preaching unknowingly. So we have the Seer, who prophesies, who they call the fortune teller. But in ancient times a Prophet with these gifts was called a Seer, which later became known as a Prophet.

Q.   Is the Prophet and the Seer the same?

PL.   Yes, they are the same now, but for distinction in modern terminology [it] is that the Minister becomes the Prophet when the Holy Spirit takes over that message. He begins to prophesy by telling the people that you must flee from the wrath to come. When Saul's daughters were lost, they lost their asses and they went in search of them and they could not find them. So they went to the man of God who was Samuel and asked, is there a man of God in the city who can tell us our way? We want to define the two.

The messenger said yes, because there is a great feast today and the people will not eat, until the prophet comes and when he comes he will bless the food, and low and behold as they went up to the high place the prophet saw them and then said unto them that the ass which thou seekest shall be found, go your way. Now, that is a direct prophesy.

Whilst the ministers do not give a direct prophesy, that sort of prophesy we still have, it still exists. Why I think it still exists [is] because the spirits of the prophets are always sub ect to the prophets irrespective of time.

They need us [so] that we can inspire them, as much as they need to inspire us. But we being the physical object, they cannot project themselves at a physical level except through human organisation, and so they are still there. What happens with the church today, whenever the Spirit is about to pass over the mantle, this is what we call the passing of the mantle, because unless the mantle is passed to someone else, the work which was done by the prophets of old could not continue.

So the passing of the mantle is the passing of that dispensation, from one age, or one era to another. Hence there is a search being made to see if there is a body which has the quality, and then that transmission takes place. It's a transmission. Therefore, if that body is up to that Spiritual standing, the bible tells us "know ye not that your body is a temple of the Holy Spirit?" So if that temple is not kept to a certain degree of holiness, then that transmission cannot take place, and so we find that that sort of purity in living is very few, hence we cannot have the amount of prophetic messages, the seer- like message that we had in the times of the early church, because people are not so dedicated to the work in this time, they are picked out, they are chosen.

Q.   Tell me Bishop, do you think this Spiritual Baptist Faith has African connections?

PL.   Yes, it has, as you know, Rev. Stephens, this faith was with the exodus of Africans from West Africa. They brought with them their traditions, and one of the outstanding traditions was that of the Yorubas and most Yorubas do practice the tradition of the *Alladura* Church. One of the things that interested me when I spoke to Father Abiola, the Moderator of the Council of African and African/Caribbean churches. He pointed out to me that this Spiritual Baptist Faith and the people of the "White Road Army" are in many parts of Africa, and it was amazing, when we invited him to the first Convention of Spiritual Baptist Churches in London he told us [this].

In reading the history of the *Alladuras*, I notice that they do a lot of fasting. We must take note that fasting is another name for mourning, and anything the *Alladuras* do, they must fast. Sometimes they fast for seven days, for fourteen, for twenty-one days and they also bless things by symbolically ringing the bell. They will go about the village and proclaim the message by ringing the bell early in the morning, and those traditions have come down to the Spiritual Baptist Faith.

Q.   What saints do you work with?

PL.   The most established saints are. those of the Blessed Mother, St. Catherine, St. Philomena who is not accepted by the Catholic Church. St. Anthony and St. Michael.

Q.   Do you have, as in the Roman Catholic church, figures of these saints in your church?

PL.   No, we do not use images, but we have pictures, symbolising their presence. It has always been said in times past that if someone has the picture of someone who's departed, it brings a sort of *presence* and blessing to a place. If you have the picture of someone who lived a blessed life, you can gather a certain amount of *vibrations* by just having the picture. Hence, it is an accepted fact that one can contact lost friends by just speaking to the picture. And so, we accept in our worship again that we are contacting lost minds in the form of the saints. So we do have the pictures in the church, they are symbols of those noble lives, who have laid the foundation for our work now.

Q.   What affinity does the Spiritual Baptist Faith have with Hinduism?

PL.   I will not say that the Spiritual Baptist Faith is directly connected to Hinduism, but with India, yes. In the Book of Esther it's recorded that in ancient times there was one king, who reigned from India onto Ethiopia, so it tells us that both India and Ethiopia were under one ruler. This has brought an affinity, and still today in India, they call them the Dravidians, a very dark race of Indians, just like some Africans. The mixture of the Indians and Africans is something of the historic past. So we always accept the two outstanding symbols of the faith, the *lotah* and the *calabash*. So the faith has preserved that tradition of both Indians and Africans.

Q.   So therefore, you have retentions from Africa in the Spiritual Baptist Faith and also retentions from Asia?

PL.   Yes, very important that you take note of that.

Q.   Is there any relationship between the Ethiopian Orthodox Church and the Spiritual Baptist Faith?

PL.   The only relationship that I have learnt from my research and connections is that which have to do with the preaching of the Eunuch. When he was converted, he went to preach the gospel in Addis Ababa. Away from that there is not much of a connection. Remember that the Ethiopian Orthodox Church is the oldest Christian church. First and foremost, Christianity was taken to the East and then to the West. The only thing I can compare is the sound of *adoption*. There is a certain group in Ethiopia that brings the sound of *adoption* and I cannot recall the particular name of the group, and some research in future date will tell us why.

Q.   What exactly do you mean by sound of *adoption*?

PL.   The sound of *adoption* is a groaning sound and typically it tells us in Roman 8:15, 22: that the whole creation groans and travails in pain, waiting for the adoption of the spirit. I can rightly say that the faith can also be called "The Faith of the Adoption Rites," due to the fact that we have this sound of adoption. As children born out of oppression, this sound of adoption is something by which we can project ourselves nearer to the heart of God. For at times we need to find solace in a changing world, and the only way we can find that is to find a place of quiet rest. By projection, we are able to find that peace with God because many great experiences have been gained in the Spiritual Baptist Faith. The adoption also brings a projection, many writers have only spoken about the adoption, but whenever there is a note of adoption, there is also a projection that must go with it.

Q.   Do all Spiritual Baptists understand the note of adoption?

PL.   It is something that is being brought about by the Spirit. It is a gift and at the same time one is able to project oneself into different realms of the Spirit. And one begins to prophesy or to speak in what Paul says, some would speak in the tongues of men and some would speak in tongues of angels, or the tongues of different nations.

So, when we refer to the old creation, your spiritual and your physical connect together, and therefore the Spirit of God then takes hold of the individual because it is an accepted fact that on the banks of Jordon we are made prophet, priest and king. So whilst we are waiting for that day of deliverance, we continue to groan and travail in pain, as Paul says, waiting for the adoption of the Spirit.

Q.   Are all members of the Spiritual Baptist Faith able to adopt the Spirit?

PL.   No, not all, because there are diversities of gifts and there are degrees of unfoldment and according to the unfoldment of the individual, s/he excel [at] their different gifts in the church.

Q.   Can we go back to your structure of service. You said after the three lessons were read, there is a supplication hymn and thereafter prayers. Who prays?

PL.   We accept in the Spiritual Baptist Movement that there are different categories of members. There are certain types which are called "praying souls" and these are the ones who will lead the church in the invocatory prayer, which we call the prayer of supplication, taking the church before the throne of God, and [in] such way we need then someone who has the gift of making such a supplication that it can be answered.

You see opening a service, or beginning a service has different keys, whether it is noticed by the worshipper, but it goes through different stages. If for instance someone of less spiritual ability starts the service, it is generally noted that the service is very flat. If another person with different spiritual abilities start that service, you find at the start of the service that you feel uplifted.

And so, what we are saying here, is that when service is taken before the throne of grace, you are then knocking at the inner court. There is an outer court and there is an inner court. This was quoted by Ezekiel m the 46th Chapter when he said the gate that looketh towards the east shall be shut the six working days, but on the day of the Sabbath it shall be opened. That's the inner court, so that inner court is opened by supplication and prayer. So you must always remember there is an outer court and an inner court. So therefore we need someone to knock as the Spiritual Baptists say, at mercy door, interceding, as the writer says, "Mercy good Lord, mercy 1 ask, this is my humble plea."

Q.   Let's go back to the order of service.

PL.   I took the order of service from the Courts of St. Peter in Gonzales, Trinidad, the Right Reverend Gabriel Hunte. They have a set order that Jesus Christ styled his church as the bride of Christ, and Solomon described the church definitely as the woman, so you have an interplay as a part of "love play." If you know Solomon, he spoke so much about love and the bride.

Q.   So are there no Spiritual Baptist Churches in Guyana.

PL.   No. I took the Spiritual Baptist Church to Guyana.

Q.   What year was this?

PL.   In 1982.

Q.   Please tell me now, how you became a Spiritual Baptist.

PL.   I became a Spiritual Baptist in this country. I was a spiritual person as Abbess would tell you. She came and met me conducting my services in a spiritual form. But I could not call myself Spiritual Baptist because certain of the practices I had not known, so I couldn't say I'm Spiritual Baptist. Now, I got this dream to mourn, this is where it started in 1971. I was then recommended to Bishop Hunte in Trinidad.

Q.   Were you baptised again?

PL.   Yes, but not on the first visit. On the first visit I mourned. On my second visit to Trinidad I was inspired to be baptised and Bishop Hunte baptised me, after which I had a throne of grace.

Q.   How did you transform the church.

PL.   We had a few Trinidadian Spiritual Baptists in the church who were very willing to carry along that line, so it was very easy. And then it was a growing church, and the Spiritual Baptist movement has so much for one to learn. So being something new to them, they willingly apply it. Those who wanted to develop spiritually found the transformation quite easy, we had no problems.

Q.   So you were consecrated a Bishop in Trinidad and Tobago in March 1974, with the National Evangelical Spiritual Baptist Faith Archdiocese?

PL.   To be their representative here.
    [Continuing where he left off on likening the church with love-making, according to the words of Solomon.]
    So here is the love-making part of the service where one is entreated to have a foretaste of that which is to come which is the Psalm of Prayers which is followed by Glory Be To The Father and to the Son and to the Holy Spirit. Then we have the second lesson which is dedicated to the blessed mother, or in other words it is called the magnificat that is followed by the I Believe in honour of The Blessed Lady.

Q.   Is the second lesson also a Psalm?

PL.   No, It can be a psalm, but in our church it is an Old Testament lesson. We recognise that there can't be a father without a mother and we pay great honour to the Blessed Virgin Mother, as that womb was appointed by God to bring forth the redeemer of the world. Then we have the foundation lesson for which the entire church stands, because it typifies that we are builders. We are workmen, such as you would find in the Masonic order, workmen for Christ. So we can't be sitting idle, so we stand and give honour to the Word of God. And since the foundation lesson is taken from the New Testament, then we are giving honour to Christ on the Chief Corner Stone.

Hence the foundation lesson is followed by *Hosanna*, which typifies that the one who has just read and is about to preach is that of the very person *incarnate* of Jesus Christ himself. And so the words say "Blessed is He that Cometh in the Name of the Lord." Hence we are about to hear the laying of the foundation lesson by that authority.

Because whoever speaks then is a symbol of the authority of Christ. So we give honour, *Hosanna, Hosanna, Hosanna,* Blessed is he who cometh in the name of the Lord. This brings us to the end of what we could describe as the ceremonial part of the service. Then we have two other speakers who have read the first and second lesson, and then exaltations. This can be followed by requests for prayers, then we close the service.

Q.   How long does your service last?

PL.   About three to four hours. We have tried to stop before the time, but something, I don't know [if] it it's by divine providence, but it never closes before four hours.

Q.   Why do you say that the Jordanites are like the Adventists. Why do you make that comparison?

PL.   Well, because they carry on their church similar to the Adventists. They would keep the Sabbath and the Laws. The only difference with them is that they wear white robes and the Adventists do not.

Q.   So are they not spiritual people?

PL.   They are spiritual in a sense, because no man can serve God without Spirit, but they would not accept the manifestation of the Spirit. You could not go into that church and have a manifestation.

Q.   No speaking in tongues?

PL.   No.

Q.   Baptism by immersion?

PL.   Yes

Q.   Healing?

PL.   No, nothing like that. Just preaching of the Word.

Q.   Did your parents belong to that church?

PL.   My parents were from The Orthodox Church, The Ethiopian Orthodox, The Coptic Church

Q.   How did you become a Spiritual Baptist?

PL.   There is a sect that came out of the West Evangelist Millennium, they call themselves Spiritual People or what you will call the Apostolic Faith. That one I would say is similar to the Spiritual Baptist, but that was born out of the Jordanites, by a man whose name was Elder Williams. He was *arrested* by the Spirit and as he began to manifest the Jordanites rejected him. He then formed his own church and they called themselves The Shakers; they were not called Spiritualists in the beginning. Now this is where the birth of Spiritualism began in Guyana, with the Shakers by Elder Williams. They later took the name Spiritual Church.

In regards to how do I see the Spiritual Baptist Faith, I see the faith as having a part to play in the healing of the nations. I firmly believe that the time will come, we are not against the medical profession, but according to the scripture, the land will need to be healed, and those healers they are speaking about are the Spiritual healers, because the conditions and time that people are living in, the great depression which is prophesied will come upon all the earth. There will be the need for spiritual healing. Such healing will not be from a physical point of view, it will be concerning the mind, our emotions. And this is what people need, we need to be *restored* in that original mind whereby we are able to make contact with that spirit of our ancestors.

Q.   How are the Spiritual Baptists going to do this?

PL.   This is being accomplished by spiritual medicine, spiritual instructions. To speak to someone from a spiritual standpoint, like the prophet, [one] must be able to have a vision of the mind of the person you are speaking to. So it's a sort of a cycle. That's where the Spiritual Baptist Faith comes in very deeply; you need a spiritual perception. The scripture tells us in Jeremiah "The earth of my daughter not being healed, are there no physicians there?" Which means that although there are physicians, they still needed that spiritual healing, the restoration of their minds so that their minds can come back in the unity of the spirit, and in the faith of Jesus Christ.

So the thing is brought about even by preaching the word. The age we are entering into is the spiritual age and so, there will be no formula that I can describe at this time that we will need, because it is the Spirit who becomes the director and influences the operation, and influences the healing. All that we will have to do is to be vessels that can be used by the spirit for the work of restoring the human race.

Q.   How soon do you foresee this change coming about?

PL.   Well, we are not far, because right now the doctors are using spiritual medicines in their work, testing and investigating cases on their files to see whether the person they are dealing with has a psychological problem or whether they are possessed by spirits from another plane. So it's not far away because this has begun. It's now taken into account by the medical profession.

Q.   Is your church, the Court of Melchisidec, moving in this direction?

PL.   It's emotional and also sad to know that the Holy Spirit has used different people at different times in the church, yet the people will not grasp the knowledge. And one of the significant things that the bible spoke about is that, he said that he will destroy this nation and at one point he also mentioned again that if they fail to praise him, he would cause the stones to rise up and give praise to him.

Thirdly, those who left Egypt never reached to the land of promise because they entered not – because of unbelief. And so the pioneering spirit of the leader is always taken for granted whilst that leader is alive. People fail to recognise that authority while it exists in their presence until it is absent from them, and this is one of the things that sadden me with the Court of Melchisidec. The people have failed to grasp the knowledge that is there for them. And because of that they failed tremendously in fulfilling that role. I personally feel that another generation will have to fulfil that role. It will be accomplished m my life time, I have decreed it, that the masters who are in charge will indeed give a lengthy life.

Q.   Archbishop Lewis, I'd be delighted if you can tell me or explain some of the symbols of the Spiritual Baptist Faith. For example, the importance and the meaning of bells, candies, etc.

PL.   It is said that John the Baptist was a voice crying in the wilderness, preparing the way for our Lord and Master Jesus Christ. The Spiritual Baptist Faith acknowledges that there is a spiritual connection and also a physical connection. The bell as a symbol denotes that it is a voice proclaiming a message of calling souls to Christ.

There is a well known chorus we often sing, "The gospel bells are ringing overland from sea to sea." If I place the bell alongside the drum, because I see them both as one aspect of the church because in the beginning man spoke just thought and so therefore it's a continuation of the energy from sound, which is, used to invite both celestial and dispel terrestrial beings. Hence, since we have no abiding city here and we look for one to come, we always survey our place of worship because it is not an abiding place, and we use the bell to invite those celestial order of spirits.

You survey the church with water and the bell?

PL.   Yes, we use them both. The bell, the calabash, the *lotah* and also a jug.   It can be different in different churches.

Q.   Do you survey the church before you begin the service?

PL.   No, we do so at the third point of the service. Now Spiritual Baptist churches carry an order. These numbers are very significant to Spiritual Baptist churches, 1, 3, 5, 7, 9. In the Spiritual Baptist order it is generally accepted that the numbers 1, 3, 5 and 7 are used most times, because we look at odd numbers as being very spiritual, hence we take our first hymn, which is the opening hymn, and the second hymn, and the third hymn becomes the surveying hymn. So it goes that way three plus three plus three brings us to the number nine. So the first three hymns are what we call invocation, at the third hymn we survey the church and at that stage we are inviting the unseen host. I think here it is good to quote John in Revelation Chapter 7 when he received the letter on the Isle of Patmos, and he was told to hurt not the earth, nor the sea, nor anything that is in the earth until they have sealed the servants of God on their forehead.

Now he was referring to the four angels, he said "I saw four angels standing on the four corners of the earth." These four angels are the four *Watchers of the Plane*. And so we accept always that there are four mighty angels who watch the earth in which we live, they are the keepers of the peace of the earth, they are actually holding the winds of strife, which is destruction. And so whenever we survey the church we also recognise the four mighty angels, who at the same time are holding the winds of strife on earth. And so we also invite them to protect the work we do throughout our service. Because those four angels are very significant in the Spiritual Baptist Faith, Raphael who rules the east, Michael rules the south, Gabriel the west and Auriel the north.

So they have a great part to play and because of that we do not work without them. After the surveying, we have the hymn of supplication, then we come to another three: the Our Father, the Hail Mary and the I Believe. Then after that we have the first lesson, the second lesson and the third lesson.

So bringing us from the start to where we get to the foundation lesson, we are at number 9. We are ascending, whenever you start a service, you are taking a step up or going up a ladder, therefore the church is being lifted at various stages of the service, whereby we can lift or take off according to Spiritual Baptists.

You must take note of this, that the Spiritual Baptist church is styled as a camp and also when it begins to sail it becomes a ship, and it is at that point that we need or should bring in the lights, which is to sail us on our journey.

Q. Do you light them now?

PL. They are lit before, but it plays its relevance very much at that particular time, because it's a ship sailing on the sea, symbolising the changing scene of life. And we do believe according to Spiritual Baptist tradition, which is what really draws me to the Faith, that *it was the only Faith that you experience a combination or unity of many faiths in one*.

Q. You said that the Spiritual Baptist Faith is a combination of many   faiths in one. Can you elaborate on that please?

PL. If you go back to the beginning when you asked why we use the bell, for instance, if you go back to ancient Tibetan rituals you will see that they use the big bell and the gong in their mystic temple to invite, or tell the initiates when it's time to come in and to meditate. It is also used as an act of invocation in which they call the great spirits. Then we come back again, you will notice the calabash, which is man's first tool that he used as a plate, to drink or to eat from. We have also the *lotah* and *tarya* which are symbols used by the Indians.

We can describe it as something most sacred by Hindus, because they use it for worship, and when milk is placed into the *lotah*, it then represents the mother giving her pure milk to the children, which is the word of God. We can add many more meanings to these aspects. Now you must take note, that the Spiritual Baptist Faith is a faith that has been born out of oppression and since it is born out of oppression it is unique in its rites. And because of this we have incorporated much of the theology of other faiths such as the Roman Catholic church and the Anglican church.

So yes, it embodies the Catholic and Anglican church. The Catholic church we

acknowledge for its Saints which we use until now and the Anglican church for the hymns of inspiration which are very reminiscent of the times when we were in oppression. For instance, we would sing "Take my life and let it be consecrated Lord to thee. Take my moments and my days, let them flow in ceaseless praise", which show that in times of oppression we will
dedicate all that we have in honour and praise of God, hoping that someday we will find deliverance.

Q.   You said the Spiritual Baptist Faith was born out of oppression, where did it evolve in Africa or the Caribbean?

PL.   According to our knowledge, it started in Africa itself, remember that the Africans at some time had their own Africans enslaved, so it was just a continuation [but a far more brutal and psychologically colonising phenomenon]. I referred to born out of oppression, in the time of the great Exodus, where Africans were transported from West Africa, Sierra Leone, [Nigeria, Senegambia, Liberia, etc.] and they were taken in batches to the Americas and the Caribbean. Because of that, the oppression brought pain and agony to them, [because of] that we can even compare the sound of a *doption*, as a symbol of our groaning, which is an experience of the torture and the pain that they bear during those times that they transported our fore-parents from West Africa to the New World.

Q.   What's the role of the Catholic Saints in your worship?

PL.   We the Spiritual Baptists firmly believe that we are the Saints' last or the Apostles' last. To note Paul's writings to the Ephesians, he said we are building on the foundation of the apostles and the prophets, Jesus Christ being the chief Corner Stone. Hence, the very works of the apostles is the work of Sainthood and we are the repairers of the breach, and as Apostles' last, we are continuing the work that was begun by those Apostles and Prophets of old. Hence, we look upon the lives of those who are born in the faith, in ages past, as *symbols* of *energy*.

They do not exist in the sense of a physical manifestation, but we do believe and it is an established fact, that the lives of good men do remind us that we can make our lives sublime. And because of that, we feel by turning in to these saints which are typified or accepted as *energies*, that we can tap their wisdom, and thus continue that work of the apostles and prophets.

Hence we use saints because there is no division between the church triumphant and the church militant. For one good writer said "heaven and earth are one, one family, we dwell in Him." One church above, beneath, though now divided by the stream, just a narrow stream of death. Hence they are always in concert with us, and so by using them we are lifted to that dimension where we can behold and feel the Spirit of God in our lives. By the very fact of their projection of their *electronic* presence.

Q.   How do you close your service?

PL.   I said in the beginning of this interview that we believe in numbers and in the commencement of our service we had three different stations that bring us to nine at the point of the foundation lesson. At that point we start to go down, so it is repeated by raps. We close our service by singing "Bless Be the Tie that Binds" and say the 121st Psalm which is a protection psalm as we are about to leave, "He shall bless your going out and your coming in from this time forth and even forever more."

Then the doxology, then three raps with the Shepherd rod, three three three. This means that we begin that way and we close that way. In numbers we dedicate nine to the Order of St. Michael. We feel that he is the protecting angel, we invited him at the start and we depend on Michael to lead those who had come and take them home. You must remember that St. Michael played a great part before Christ. We understand that St Michael was the chief ruler in heaven who fought with Lucifer, so St. Michael played a role in casting Satan down. He also played a great part in protecting God's people during the time of battle. For instance in the book of Daniel, Chapter 12:1, it is said, "And at that time" which is referring to the future, "shall Michael up, the great prince will standeth for the children of of thy people."

So it simply shows that the Archangel Michael was the protecting angel of the people of Israel, and the part that angels have to play among the human family and his work in the church has not yet [been] completed. In Revelation it is said that

Michael again will protect the women and her man-child. And so we have seen here that Michael, the chief prince, played an important role before the time of Christ and so he too was looked upon as a style of the Christ. I thank you.

CHAPTER EIGHT

ELLA ANDALL: ORISHA/SPIRITUAL BAPTIST TRINIDAD

Ella Sings:

> Mojuba Baba Orisha
> Mojuba, mojuba
> Oya Mojuba
> Shango Mojuba
> Babatana Mojuba

E lla, what were you singing?

EA. *Mojuba*, is what you answer after you say a prayer and you say *Ashe Ashe*, may it be so. So even if you are asking the *Orishas* for a favour, you say please let it be so.

Q. So are we thanking God for the prayer said in the garden.

Figure 20

Ella Andall combines both the Orisha and Spiritual Baptist as one indivorceable entity (photo courtesy Joy Oryejioko).

EA.   Yes.

Q.   Explain to me Ella, you are a Spiritual Baptist and an *Orisha*.

EA   Well, you know I have to be all of it, because *all is one of it*.

Q.   Really? What exactly do you mean by all is one of it?

EA   If you deal with the history of the *Orisha* religion as fat as I know, for it to be kept, it was kept by the Baptists. What I do know is that we have to thank the Spiritual Baptist for keeping this culture alive for us.

Q.   Is this a common belief amongst the *Orishas* in Trinidad and Tobago?

EA.   I don't know if they have gotten that far. Some of the Baptists see themselves as people apart but Spiritual Baptist is believed to be a Christian religion and in the middle of the prayers, when you kneel and you pray and talk to Jesus, or you talk to Mary, some of them have it in the Roman Catholic way and soon after that when you get down in the Spirit you begin to talk in unknown tongues, like African, so it has to be that there is some meaning and some story behind that. I am still doing research on that, but the history shows that in the days when we were not allowed to practise the religion, the ancestors, they masked [that] with Christianity, keeping the Christian Saints for when the police come, but they had their things *underground*.

Q.   What were their things?

EA.   The *Orisha* religion is not a Christian religion, you know that it was [in existence] long before Christ came.

Q.   Even though you are telling me that the *Orisha* religion is not a Christian religion, why do you say that the Spiritual Baptist, which is a Christian/African influenced religion, is the same as the *Orisha*?

EA.   Because they kept it. The Baptist base is the *Orisha*, and before any *Orisha* feast start, the Baptist prayers must go on before the feast start. And after the prayers finish, then they start to *Eshu* and then to start to beat for the saints and the *Orishas*.

Q.   If you are having the Spiritual Baptist prayers before the feast and that is Christian, so therefore it is nor really a correct statement to say that the *Orisha* is non-Christian, because you have it tied up together.

EA.   But the *Orisha* is non-Christian. If you go into the trueness and purity of the religion, when you go to Nigeria you are not going to hear the Christian prayers before. So we talking in the Diaspora now.

Q.   So the *Orisha* is tinted here?

EA.   I don't see it as a minus, I see it as a plus, because it is even shown through history that they use the Christianity to mask [their true religion], but they also found what virtue there is in the Christian religion and there are arguments that Jesus Christ himself was a man of colour. So, no matter how it might be distorted, people who study history think that we now, all of us, coming through the Diaspora, have found something else.

Q.   What?

EA.   The same Christianity.

Q.   Is this why you say that Christianity and the *Orisha* are blended together?

EA.   Its not blended because it is always separate, let me tell you why I'm saying that. You do one part, you don't mix the parts, you understand what I'm saying?

Q.   You shut off the church and open the Palais?

EA.   Yes, and sometimes you reopen again, you decide to go from the Chapel to the church.

Q.   I have seen that at Sandport and Tunapuna. What religion were you before you joined the *Orisha*?

EA.   Same *Orisha*.

Q.   Were you always an *Orisha*?

EA.   No, not always. We moved to the Roman Catholic, but I came back to *Orisha*.

Q.   So you were an *Orisha* before?

EA.   Yes, the first thing I know as a child was the drum, so this is why.

Q.   What part of Trinidad were you born?

EA.   I was born in Grenada in a little village called Du Cane and we moved from there to Trinidad.

Q.   So in Du Cane, Grenada, you knew the drums?

EA.   That's right.

Q.   Was it called *Orisha* then?

EA.   I didn't know what name it was, all I know that it was the happiest time in our yard. It was great celebration and great tying of headties, cleanliness and all of that. A lot of food, but it was a high at that time. It was something to look forward to when I was a very small child.

Q.   Why did you leave the RC church? What were the attractions?

EA.   I don't think I ever stayed in the RC church, because praying to me is joyous. So I used to go and do the Holy Communion and all that but never happy to go, so I used to run away sometimes. I was always fascinated with outdoors, I wouldn't feel lonely if I'm among the trees and all of that, so I used to run away.

So by the time Sunday school over I might get a few slaps or so, but I didn't go. And I went in to a Roman Catholic church when I was a child too, and I was put out of the seat where I was to accommodate three people. I was always a bright child and six people could have sat in that pew. But I knew that those three people, a child and two adults, and the nuns came and took me out of the seat and instructed me to go at the back and I left immediately. So after that I spent enough time on the steps because I no longer will go inside. Before that Baptist people used to come to pray, we were living at Isaac Junction.

Q.   That's where?

EA.   Couva; and Baptist people used to come to pray and they would ask from time to time for water or something. And from the time they touch me, they will start off. So my mother used to say please stay at the back, let somebody else help. So in the night I lie down and feel me body moving in a particular kind of way, and my mother say."You see you, ah hope you ain't mocking the Baptist people because it isn't a good thing to do." But this time the thing happening to me and I'm telling her how I'm feeling so sick. This here shaking like this and I don't know why, but I went to sleep. And then I went to a thanksgiving and I remember that clearly. I stood up in the thanksgiving. You know you pray, you stand up, you sit. And I stood up and I wasn't feeling that I had any legs at all, and then I went so [perhaps meaning to lose consciousness]. I was told afterwards.

Q.   You went off in the Spirit?

EA.   Yes, and that spiritual person who I still call my very first spiritual mother, she lives in New York and she talked to me afterwards and all of that. But you have to prove things to me. The drums and everything is nice, but I'm looking and saying I wonder boy. Sometimes manifestations come and you try to touch them to see if they hot or it they cold, all of that. And then it came to me in a vision from my grandmother and she showed me certain things which I wouldn't put on the tape and the *Oni of Ife* was coming to Trinidad and I was commissioned as the musical director for that occasion and I met there with my spiritual mother now and when I saw her I knew that I had seen her somewhere before, because in my visions, certain things used to manifest and I saw her church. So when she invite me a couple times, I went and I saw the whole setting. I asked for guidance because I got certain instructions from my grandmother and I knew what time to do certain things and I went and I did it, and I am very comfortable where I am today.

Q.   What happened before the *Oni of Ife* came to Trinidad?

EA.   I was going to every Baptist Church, but I'm not inside of it, I'm away from it.

Q.   So you eventually got into a Spiritual Baptist church after the *Oni's* visit.

EA.   But before that falling down and all of that happen already, you know. But

I'm deciding now whether shall I go and I was directed to where I am today.

Q.   So that's a Spiritual Baptist church?

EA.   Spiritual Baptist/Orisha, both.

Q.   When you joined that church, did you join the Spiritual Baptist. Faith? Is that so?

EA.   No, no I went because of the *Orisha*.

Q.   You went to the Spiritual Baptist. church because of the *Orisha*?

EA.   Yes, because it's happening there.

Q.   You saw that?

EA.   *I know that*.

Q.   What part of Trinidad.

EA.   St. Helena.

Q.   That's you home now?

EA.   Yes.

Q.   How did it happen?

EA.   At the same time because if we give a special feast for *Ogun*, it will happen in the Spiritual Baptist church right there. They say the Christian prayers and then you begin to sing for the *Orishas*.

Q.   So you will be giving a special prayer for *Ogun* in the Spiritual Baptist. Church?

EA.   But the Spiritual Baptist Church is also the home of the *Orisha* deity. Listen to what I'm telling you, all the emblems are there.

Q.   In the Spiritual Baptist Church?

EA.   Yes, and funny enough I don't think there's a St. Michael or a St. Philomena, all of that emblem there. I don't think it is there. I saw pictures inside the Chapel, but it's by and overflowing outside. The first thing you do when you come down my street to the Shrine, you see all the *Pierre Ogun*.

Q.   And these are Spiritual Baptist Churches?

EA.   The majority, I think maybe three or four that has now taken out the Christian part of it and going straight *Yoruba*.

Q.   So let's say now, you are having a special prayer for *Ogun* in the Spiritual Baptist church, what sort of offering, is it just prayers you have?

EA.   No, you do whatever offering you have to do.

Q.   Do you kill animals?

EA.   Yes, of course you kill.

Q.   In the Spiritual Baptist Church?

EA.   You don't ever do it inside the church, outside at the *Piere Ogun*, that's where the flag are, the congregation goes there and you sing. It is established though that this Saint is Ogun and this one is *Shokpona*, but I do not share this view. I think they are different. I think that they were used at the time of the masking, when colonialism was still in play and whenever you say OK! The police coming now, the master coming, they start to use the saints. But that is how it was done. History would show you that. I have a paper on that which was researched by Roma Spencer.

Q.   When you begin to have the prayers, let's say for *Ogun* in the church itself, it can turn to be *Orisha*?

EA.   Yes, you begin to sing and you move out and do what you have to do in the Palais. I wish you could come to experience it.

Q.   If you are giving a special prayer for *Ogun*, give me the sequence?

EA.   You do the whole Christian prayers, then you start to sing for *Ogun*, then you throw the *Obi* to see if you offering is going to be accepted by the *Orishas*.

Q.   How do you throw the *Obi*?

EA.   You prepare yourself first of all, then you prepare the *Obi*, the place is clean, and you feed the *Obi* with the honey, milk, the dried food and everything, and you ask the question. Is like that I see the Baptist use the bible too, you cut the bible for a particular reason. Well you throw the *Obi* seed and [you read it] according to what direction it fall. If it fall on both sides like this, it is said to be a NO, if it falls like this it is a YES, and if it fall like this they say it's laughing, but in Nigeria they call it a royal flush, is like real YES.

Q.   And this is done in order to know what you should do?

EA.   Yes, if the *Obi* said NO, I think you are allowed three times to ask and if the third time is NO you are not accepted, you will have to take your offering back.

Q.   What do you do now?

EA.   Some people leave the Pierre Ogun and go to the Palais, they also call the Pierre Ogun the Grotto. I don't know why, or you can go back to the church. So in Trinidad, in the Diaspora, I think the people wanted to be safe, because there is the Church, the Chapel, where all the instruments are housed, and the Palais, so its like a one, two, three.

Q.   So this happens in very many places in Trinidad.

EA.   Yes.

Q.   I'm interested to know, did your parents tell you what you were seeing as a child was exactly *Orisha* or *Shango*?

EA.   At that stage I didn't ask. The drumming was happening and I was happy. But when I get the full understanding now, when I begin to grow up.

Q.   In Trinidad?

EA.   Yes.

Q.   How many years are you an *Orisha*? Do you refer to it as a religion or a faith?

EA.   It's a way of life. It has to be about 12 or 15 years.

Q.   Would you say that the *Orisha* is developing in Trinidad and Tobago?

EA.   Most certainly.

Q.   Is there any other island in the Caribbean that's practising *Orisha* as in Trinidad?

EA.   In the Caribbean, you have it in Cuba, you have it in Brazil. A friend of mine came from Montreal and she said she found something like that in St. Lucia. But you see, it was just like in the colonial days, it's still hidden; you don't go and see an *Orisha* shrine in Port of Spain, the heart of town. It's always out on the hills, because this was how the Yoruba people believe in the outdoors, in the forces of nature. I don't think there are churches, there are places to house the instruments,. But the *Ogun* shrine as far as I know is outside, so you can be passing and you can go as an *Ogun* devotee and go to your *Orisha* and salute.

Q.   *Ogun* is what colour?

EA.   *Ogun* in Trinidad, some people offer *Ogun* red, some people offer *Ogun* red and green, but in Nigeria it is black and green. That I know of.

Q.   How do you combine your religious way of life with that of an entertainer?

EA.   My source of strength, everything that I am is from the *Orisha*, so it's not a thing apart what I choose, or what I say. The statement I want to make in music, are statements of stimulations of the mind, statements of upliftment so that the children will have something to listen to, because I have come to recognise I am like a teacher in this world thing, I have come to recognise that our African people didn't go beyond the Diaspora. They did not go to the full civilisation, they did not go to the Nile, they did not go that way because they never even were interested to know. If you grow up in a system where you were not good then nothing that relate to you will be good. So your songs, the songs of the African people, because the African people were not good people, they were only slaves, so you were told that the drums were banned, and when the need for the rhythm come, that's how we get the pan. So we beat sticks then we beat the pan.

Q.   So you brought in the sticks and the pan. What has this got to do with the Spiritual Baptist Faith?

EA.   The Spiritual Baptist Faith or the *Orisha*?

Q.   Both, because you said they are the same.

EA.   Well, I have come to understand from some elders that the first panists were *Orisha* drummers and if you listen to the chantwell...

Q.   What's the chantwell?

EA.   The chantwell is the people who sing before the calypsonians, and a chantwell singer is straight from the *Orisha* yard. The chantwell sing and if you check the long time calypsoes, you hear the E Minor, but that is the sweetest form of a chantwell singer.

Q.   How will the *chantwell* sing that?

EA.   The beat, the calypso beat is there in the *chantwell*.

Q.   If you hear the Spiritual Baptist and the *doption*, it's total, total *chantwell*.

Q.   Are you saying to me that the Spiritual Baptist Faith is directly connected to the calypso, the steelband and the *Orisha* Faith?

EA.   Of course. The Spiritual Baptist kept the *Orisha* for us.

Q.   I was told that the Spiritual Baptist Faith and the *Orisha* developed side by side.

EA.   No, I don't know about it that way, because when I check the papers, research, Christianity was used as a mask, to hide our thing. So when you say, Ay! Police! they start to sing our Father and the police gone.

Q.   So the slaves covered up their African traditional religion with Christianity?

EA.   Yes.

Q.   So they were not really Christians?

EA.   No, they were Africans carrying on their African religion. Look at the move-ment when we shout, it's all African. Look at my performance, I shouldn't say per-formance, because when I go on stage I come to give myself. I honestly come to give of my African self. If you don't like it you don't like it, if you do, you do.

Q.   Now Ella, I never met you before, I met you last evening at the 34th anniver-sary of the Independence of Trinidad and Tobago, the musical performance at the Wembley Stadium. You were the star of the show. I observed that when you came on stage you began to educate people about *Orisha*, you came on with a dynamic chant, was it Yoruba?

EA.   Yes. It was a chant for *Ogun*, my personal *Orisha*.

Q.   What were you singing? It touched me.

EA.   You see it's hard to say, this is why I say that I don't think St. Michael is *Ogun*, because one word in Yoruba mean so much, so I don't think there's a translation. The point I am making here is, what I'm saying to *Ogun* is "Ogun come clear the pathway. This is a festive time, I'm coming to deal with your people, so clear the way for your daughter to come." And I would feel the force and know that *Ogun* is there.

Q.   What was this chant? I'd like the others to hear.

EA.   *Eba Oh Eba Kumele.*

Q.   So you took your audience on a journey into Africa.

EA.   Yes. And there's no better man to take them than *Ogun*, because *Ogun* is the remover of all obstacles.

Q.   Are you a primarily a Spiritual Baptist and then an *Orisha*?

EA.   You can't put it that way, I don't see them as being separate, so I don't knock it, it's one into one. Many of the Spiritual Baptists when they mourn and they reach into Africa in the spirit, in Africa there are different tribes. It's the same Africa, the same *Orisha*. The point is the understanding. Everybody will get the call in a different way, but we calling the same person.

I saw a TV documentary about an American doctor now living in Mexico. He gave up hope on a child who was supposed to die, and the child's people took the child by the river and did something for *Oshun* and the child lived. So he is saying they have something more than his medicine. Because they took the child and carried the child to the water, I saw the whole ceremony on TV: candles on the river bank, they took the fowl and feathers, incense and all kinds of thing and the child lived.

Q.   This is interesting. Now for the record, you both have agreed that the Spiritual Baptist and the *Orisha* are the same.

EA.   Yes. [If I may add] there is a Yoruba water ritual, going to the river, or going to the sea or where both the river and the sea meet, meaning that you are dealing with *Oshun* and *Yemanja*. *Oshun* is the *Orisha* for Riches and she is the seductress, it is said and she is the owner of all sweet waters. *Yemanja* is on the second layer, I think, of the sea, because *Olukon* is at the base. It is said that *Erile* is on the top of the water, but *Erile* is on the river bank so he can walk from the river bank to the sea shore. *Joja* is the same *Erile*. *Olokun* is the owner of the water. So you can call all of them together, like how we have the carnival in Trinidad, so in Nigeria they have the feast of the *Orishas*.

Q.   So Ella you are saying that there is a direct connection to Africa?

EA.   Yes, when the *Oni of Ife* came to Trinidad in 1988 and I sang and I went to a reception where all the Nigerians greeted me in their language. They all thought I was from the continent. The *Oni* was touched by the way we have kept the *Orisha* and I was told that he even said that *some of the songs we sing are so ancient that you don't even hear them in Nigeria.*

Q.   So is the SBF handed down in the oral tradition as it is today?

EA.   Yes, definitely. And there are some people who say that when the ancestors were passing on, they gave them the other bit. So there are people in the Spiritual Baptist Faith who are doing it. Rev. Mundy, she knows the African and the *Orisha*, when *Shango* take her, you see.

I have no confusion at all you know, I am just waiting for all of Africa to come home. I want to educate all children and let them know that they must say Africa with pride. They have every reason to be [proud]. When you move away from the Diaspora, I went to a thanksgiving and they ask me to pray, now I went in *disguise*. I put on all the colours on my head and I wear a brown dress. So they put me to pray and I call of my *Orishas* before I kneel down to pray and then I begin to sing "All the way from Africa land". You should hear the church in turmoil, now they give me *tarya* and the *lotah* to pray. When *Ogun* come now, he telling the man who carrying on the service to give me a calabash, and all the Spiritual Baptist began to manifest the *Orishas*. So you follow what I mean, the church was *masked*.

All of them come and manifested. A lot of times the Baptist religion have who is this, and who is that [hierarchy]. W are all brother and sister in the Faith. I am a sister, a mother, a grandmother, a friend in real life, so we shouldn't be looking for titles. If we the African people were allowed to do our prayers, you would see. We go through the whole spectrum. We manifest in Indian, we know the whole Indian part, so we could call [on] Africa, Asia. This is a serious thing today. In the Baptist we call *Elohim* and we invoke with a chant.

CAPTAIN MILLICENT GRIFFITH, LONDON

C aptain Griffith, please tell me about yourself, where were you born, where you were brought up, how old are you?

MG. I was born in Indian Trail, Couva, Trinidad and I was registered in Tortuga. My grandfather was brought to Indian Trail, he is a African and was brought there in slavery days and [he] said to me that he didn't know his parents, that they got lost somewhere and that the person who took them both, my grandfather and grandmother, brought them up and got them married as soon as they were old enough to do so. After I was about two years old, my father and mother moved to Beche, the place is called Chirome and we have a little piece of land on the main road. To distinguish that we used to say the nineteen and half milestone. There's a church there on the land now. I am 76 years old if I live to see December I will be 77. Thanking God for keeping me up to this time. What else would you like to know?

Q. Tell me about your background in the Spiritual Baptist Faith. You said that your grandfather was a Spiritual Baptist and your mother too?

Figure 21
Eighty year old Millicent Griffith holds her calabash with pride (Photo by the Author).

MG.   Yes.

Q.   Tell me about your upbringing in a Spiritual Baptist environment in those days?

MG.   I didn't know when my grandfather was baptised, but I knew when my mother got baptised by a leader whom we used to call Pastor Mazelli Crisostum. I think this was about 1930 on Pedro Estate, Grand Couva. I knew there as a child [of] about 10 or 11 years old and used to be in the church. I went there because my mother was baptised with that leader, he had four children, one died and I used to be with these people till I left Indian Trail and went to San Fernando.

Q.   What happened in those days? What sort of churches they had, what did the buildings look like, what sort of services they had, what do you remember from your childhood about the Spiritual Baptist services?

MG.   It was exciting and nice, I used to enjoy it. When you have a service we would sing, clap, rejoice, all that sort of thing. It was different to the Spiritual Baptist today. I prefer the olden days.

Q.   What was the difference?

MG.   There is a lot of difference.   When you talk about Spiritual Baptist now I know, for example, if you go to point mourners down, we sign the bands after baptism.   But in the olden days, you sign the bands when the spirit *arrest* you during the service.   As the spirit starts moving you sign the bands and put them on the mourner, not before.

Q.   You said the signing was different, what's the difference?

MG.   They had a nice sort of chant which we don't have today.   You had nice choruses, you had solemn hymns to suit the occasion.   For instance, when you baptise you come from the river straight to church to have a service, then the leader will anoint you there and we sing the anointing hymn.   Then if you sound Gabriel, and you walk in the spirit, you would know if the person did something, you would know then.

Q.   When you say you sound Gabriel what do you mean?

MG.   You ring the bell.   In those days when you ring the bell you say you sound Gabriel.   It was the first time I had been in such a service of spiritual awakening and I was intrigued by it.

Q.   So the bell was referred to as Gabriel.   How many times did you ring the bell?

MG.   Three times.

Q.   Are certain things revealed then?

MG.   Yes.

Q.   Tell me more about your grandfather who was a Spiritual Baptist and who came from Africa.   Can you recall what happened in your district?

MG.   In those days missionaries would come, they would go around and tell everybody in this village that there is [a] meeting going on under the shop and everybody will attend. Who is Spiritual Baptist would come and sing and pray.

Q.   You said that these meeting were held under the shop, they had no church buildings?

MG.   We had our little buildings made out of mud and thatched carratt leaves, they were not in the front area, they were always at the back. Somebody would give them a little spot of land to build a church, nothing like now.

Q.   So the churches were hidden in the bushes?

MG.   In the bushes.

Q.   Why was this?

MG.   Because in those days the police used to terrorise them.

Q.   What else happened?

MG.   Where I was born in Indian Trail, the African people were there and in Kanga Woods a lot of Africans were there, because they came to an estate called Milton Estate. They worked there and bought lands as my grandfather told me, the money was small but the land was cheap and they all liked to acquire land which they cultivated. Some grew cocoa, pigeon peas, cassava and most of them grew sugar cane. Then the African had something which they kept every year. We called it *Nation Dance*. It was like a feast, where they beat drums and danced. Strangely enough the only meat provided was pork, never goat or beef or anything else. They raise the pig for that occasion, the Nation Dance. And if they have people coming from different areas, they would have a special dance and the best dancer gets the bouquet. The person who gets the bouquet has to give the next feast. As I said, drums and dancing and they danced something like [the] *pique*.

Q.   What's the *pique* dance?

MG.   It was nearly like an Indian dance.

Q.   Was the Nation Dance African? Was it religious?

MG.   Yes it was African but not religious.

Q.   The people who conducted the Nation Dance were they Spiritual Baptists?

MG.   No, not that I know of. Some of them were African, some of them were descendants of Africans, but the better part of them were born there but their parents were African and grew up in that environment.

Q.   And this was in the 1930's?

MG.   Yes, around that time.

Q.   What did your grandfather do, was he a land owner in the estates?

MG.   Yes he was, and he worked on the estates as well. Everybody had their little piece of land but still worked on the estate.

Q.   What age were you when you remembered your grandfather?

MG.   About 9 to 10 years, I remember him well. At the age of eighty he was still working and I couldn't run with him. They used to call him Zeclier which means lightening in patois or broken French.

Q.   How many children did he have?

MG.   Two, my mother and a boy who died.

Q.   Did your mother work on the estate?

MG.   Yes she did.

Q.   You told me earlier that you were baptised in the Spiritual Baptist Faith at the age of 12.

MG.   Yes, we went for baptism one day and the leader gave me "head duck." I don't know why they called it so, but you go through the normal routine of baptism; the only thing you didn't have was signed bands. But everything else was the same. And the minister took pride because he really wanted to do it, but my mother would not consent. She said I was too young at that age and I should wait till I was older.

Q.   So were you actually baptised?

MG.   Yes.

Q.   Did you keep the Faith?

MG.   Yes, I always go, wherever I am and whenever I can, I always attend and visit churches.

Q.   You said earlier that the leader who baptised your mother was a great man, tell me about him.

MG.   He was a great man, his name was Mazelli Crissostum. I understand he was a Dominican and spoke broken French, and he was a staunch catholic before he got the gift, as they call it. He was an overseer at St Pedro Estate at Grand Couva and he started [with] something like an ague fever, shivering, and he thought that something was wrong with him and he had to seek help elsewhere. Wherever he went to seek help he was told that he was better than the people and that he should do the right thing. It was never revealed to him what was the right thing until a year and a half or so later. He got baptised by a woman [in] about 1930 or so whom they called Doctor Holy Ghost. In those days women were never baptisers, but [she] had to do it. That woman had a gift as well as she was a Spiritual Baptist and the Mother of a church. But she had a big belly and they said she was going to have a son in the Spiritual Baptist way.

Q.   What do you mean by the Spiritual Baptist way? Was she too old to conceive?

MG.   I didn't think she could; she couldn't have a child, she was past the age. But after she baptised pastor Mazelli, her belly went right down, she became flat and so they gave her the name Dr Holy Ghost.

Q.   Did the Spiritual Baptist mean that she would have a spiritual son?

MG.   Yes, and she delivered the son [Pastor Mazelli].

Q.   What happened after?

MG.   At the beginning he began to do a lot of things. You know the Spiritual Baptists, after you baptise you have to mourn. But he didn't have time to go to the lower ground of sorrow. He really had the gift started right away from the river bank.

Q.   What happened immediately after he baptised?

MG.   After baptism, you have a service and that same night he brought a message telling them that somebody coming and that when the person came what they should give him. And this was really true, somebody drank something, they say someone tried to poison him and the medicine that Pastor Mazelli gave them revived the person.

Q.   Were you there?

MG.   Yes, I was there as a child and you hear what the older people talking about...
and I used to be at Pastor Mazelli's house because in my family it was just me and
my sister who lived with my aunt and I was the only one at home with my mother.
Pastor Mazelli had four children and it was nice to be there with them. I used to
know a lot about the goings on.

Q.   What sort of things were going on? What was the gift called?

MG.   They only said that he had the gift, but there were lots of people coming in
for different things. Some had evil spirits on them. I know a lady who had a sore
foot and there was a *jitney* which used to transport her from Grand Couva. And
after a while they wouldn't let her [come] in the van because they found the sore
[was] too offensive. After going to Mazelli she was healed.

   Sometime later, police raided the place and took all his things, candles, sweet oil,
everything. The case went to the high court and it was dismissed. When he went
to collect his belongings at Grand Couva police station, he threw some sweet oil in
the station and they begged him to wipe it off. Later on three policemen came and
baptise with him.

Q.   So he was able to convert the police? What year was this?

MG.   This was about 1931 to 1932.

Q.   What else happened in that era with the Spiritual Baptists? You said their
churches were made of mud and covered with carrat leaves and they were in the
bushes.

MG.   Always, yes.

Q.   Were their services very long?

MG.   Yes they were. Spiritual Baptists have no special time, it amazes me how the
Spiritual Baptists nowadays tell you they are tired, we never knew that. The night

before baptism, we would have a service and by midnight we put the candidate to rest because baptism would be early in the morning. Then we would walk from Indian Trail to Monkey Town, that's over BC across the road, to the seaside.

Q.   What is BC?

MG.   Brechin Castle.

Q.   That's another estate?

MG.   Yes, Brechin Castle is next to California.

Q.   Is it true that San Pedro estate, Milton estate and Indian Trail had a very large percentage of African slaves?

MG.   Yes.

Q.   Did they all speak English?

MG.   They spoke English but could speak their language as well.

Q.   Did you learn their language a s a child?

MG.   No, there are things I don't know. My mother knew it and she told us stories that she could have learnt more but her mother never taught her. In those days when you say you are African, they call you Congo and they didn't like that.

Q.   Was it derogatory to use the word Congo?

MG.   Yes.

Q.   What did it mean when you are called Congo?

MG.   It meant you come from Africa.

Q.   How were the Spiritual Baptist services conducted? Describe the inside of the church?

MG.   You will have candles, an altar, not an elaborate one as we have now. You put a cloth and a bible and a bell there, flowers and accordingly if you are a *Shango* Baptist you must have a calabash and a centre pole.

Q.   Is that how you differentiate a *Shango* Baptist from a Spiritual Baptist?

MG.   Yes.

Q.   So all the Baptist were not called *Shango* Baptist?

MG.   No.

Q.   All were not called Baptists?

MG.   No, we have what you called London Baptist, they used to get some sort of power like Spiritual Baptist, they don't shout, but they jump 1,2,3 then they cry out. The *Shango* Baptist beat drums, then you have the Spiritual Baptist.

Q.   So in your days there were three types of Baptist. Who conducted the London Baptist services, white or black people?

MG.   Black people. You get the London Baptist in Princess Town.

Q.   So all the London Baptists were based in the companies?

MG.   Yes, as you say Company, they were in a place called 5th Company.

Q.   Please tell me exactly what do you mean when you say *Shango* Baptist?

MG.   *Shango* Baptists are the ones who beat the drums and they have feasts. There is a certain time of the year when they give a feast and if you are a real *Shango* Baptist, a highly spiritual one, they don't have to tell you when they start to feast. They usually start on a Monday night, with the beating of drums and if you are a true *Shango* Baptist you will find that place and go there.

Q.   Where did they keep their services?

MG.   They build a tent when they are going to have a feast.

Q.   Before the feast, did they keep their services in the same Spiritual Baptist church?

MG.   Yes in the same church.

Q.   Can you describe how the *Shango* Baptist conducted their services?

MG.   The same way, they cut the bible, have the bell, but then they like a lot of red. They would have the calabash and what they call a chapel. Something like a tree planted in the yard with calabash candle *poi*, you know what they call *poi*? A cutlass. Then they would have a sword and flags. The *Shango* Baptists always have flags, not one, different colours. They plant flags.

Q.   What were the Spiritual Baptists like?

MG.   They would have an altar with a cloth, always a white cloth, a bell, the bible, lotah and calabash.

Q.   You also had calabash with the Spiritual Baptists?

MG.   Yes.

Q.   So they both have calabash?

MG.　Yes, but you have more in the *Shango* Baptists. And again some Spiritual Baptists, Pastor Steven, he never wanted that in his church.

Q.　Never wanted what?

MG.　No calabash. Just a bell, *lotah* and candles, nothing else. And that church is on my land, I have to go home and do something because the previous pastor has passed on.

Q.　So he didn't want any of those African retentions?

MG.　No, he didn't use those instruments.

Q.　Did you see any difference between the Spiritual Baptists and the *Shango* Baptists? Were they the same?

MG.　There was a difference in the way the service was carried on and the way how the implements were used.

Q.　Did you have pictures of Saints in your church?

MG.　No. The old time Baptists never had that sort of thing. The modern Baptists have the beaded chaplet from the Catholic church, the crucifix and all those sort of things. In those days, no. The bible, the bell, the *lotah*. And they did not believe in all the robes you have now.

Q.　What did they wear?

MG.　They wore ordinary clothes. The Ministers wore sandals, no shoes and socks. Pastor Mazelli only wore sandals. I never saw him in a robe.

Q.　Did the Spiritual Baptists, London Baptists and *Shango* Baptists all believe in mourning?

MG. I cannot tell you about the London Baptists, but the *Shango* Baptists and Spiritual Baptists believed in mourning.

Q. They both baptise in running water?

MG. Yes.

Q. Did they use seals?

MG, Yes.

Q. Tell me about the rituals and celebrations.

MG. We didn't have all these big thanksgiving as today. But when we put down mourners, it was like a celebration. We didn't have to invite anybody. Once you hear that mourners going down, they will come to labour with you.

Q. So everything was by talking, you sent messages orally, nothing was written, did you have leaflets?

MG. No.

Q. Did you have hymn books?

MG. Yes, we had the Sankey, I always try to get one. There was a place in Canapo, Sangre Grande, and I hope to go back and get there because it has all those choruses.

Q. Was there a special format for the service?

MG. Yes, you must tie your head. Women don't go into the church with their heads uncovered.

Q.   Did they wear shoes in the church?

MG.   Some of them, some churches you have to leave your shoes by the door. But if you are going on Holy Ground like the altar or centre pole, you must take off your shoes.

Q.   Did you have candle light services?

MG.   No, in those days we didn't know anything like that.

Q.   Did you have ordination?

MG.   No. We never had Archdeacon and Bishop and all of that. When you go down to the lower ground of sorrow and you come up, according to your track of vision you get your office, a leader, a prover, a pastor, a warrior. Not any ordination as we have now, whatever you get it was given in the spirit while mourning.

Q.   Did you wear colours?

MG.   Yes, we could wear coloured band, headtie, or sash, but no coloured dress.

Q.   Did you have cords?

MG.   I can't remember cords in those days. Pastor Mazelli used to wear a red and blue sash around his waist.

Q.   How was the church run, did you have a Mother and a Father?

MG.   As I remember Pastor Mazelli and Pastor Jummette run the church. The money from collection was used to buy candles. Somebody wanted to baptise, you didn't have to bring your [own] clothes. Most times the Pastor and the Leader would give you your clothes. When you go to mourn nobody paid for anything in those days. Everybody would bring things, candles and food would be supplied for the labourers because the mourners ate no food. There was no money passing in those days, that's why when I asked about mourning in Moruga and Mother Hockey told me that "salvation is free" and there was no charge, I felt happy and went to them. When you finished mourning and want to give anything you can do so.

But now if you go to the country parts of Trinidad you feel the real Baptists. You can still find out something going on as what I used to know. But in the town, the Spiritual Baptist Faith is commercialised. When you go to a Spiritual Baptist church in the town now is like going to a Catholic church. I don't know if the Baptists in olden days was wrong or right but they never had all this praying to saints. All they said was pray to God. You call no man father, you have your carnal father and the Father in Heaven. We never called any Spiritual Baptist leader Father in those days. We had Pastor Mazelli, Leader John, Pastor Steven.

Q.   You keep referring to men, what was the role of women?

MG.   They were Mothers in the church or Pointers.

Q.   What was the role of the Mothers and Pointers?

MG.   If you have any problem you can talk to them and they would try to help you. If somebody want to mourn or baptise the mothers will get financial help for the candidates. But we are in a modern world now and you have to pay for everything in the church. The things I am seeing in the church now we didn't have in those days.

Q.   Compared with today, what's the difference, was the old Spiritual Baptist faith better?

MG.   I think the people were more faithful, more truthful and most honest.

Q.   When you say truthful, what are you referring to?

MG.   In the old days if somebody told you something in the spirit you better believe it was true. They were truthful and honest. It was so different from now, if you find somebody in the faith to help they try to rob you instead. In the old days when you got help it was left to you to give a present or so, but you were never charged a fee. People would go to Pastor Mazelli for help and if you are a smoker he would send you to the shop and buy you cigarettes, he would feed the people who came to see him. There were some days when people seeking help had to stay over a day or two until the spirit worked and he would look after them.

Q.   So is there a vast difference between the Spiritual Baptists of 1930's and the Spiritual Baptists of today?

MG.   Yes, a vast difference, they worked with the Spirit.

Q.   So whatever they did then was under the guidance of the spirit? How were you sure then that they were working under the direction of the Holy Spirit?

MG.   The things the did, the way they did it, you must know there is a difference. Nobody didn't jump up as they do now, when somebody moved you know they move in the spirit.

Q.   What happens now?

MG.   Everybody jumping and everybody have spirit all throughout the service. Some people now as soon as you sing a hymn they have Spirit. If you go to a Spiritual Baptist service, we have a lot of chorus singing and we feel nice in the Spirit. It's all right to dance, we dance, but that doesn't mean to say you have Spirit. When Spiritual Baptists sing an inviting hymn, you feel something move, you enjoy yourself. I am talking about *rejoicing*, when you feel the presence of the Spirit, everybody feel lively as though you went to a party. Christianity that going on now, I don't know what it is.

CHAPTER TEN

ARCHBISHOP JOHN NOEL
CHILDREN OF THE LIGHT SPIRITUAL BAPTIST SHRINE, GRENADA

You spoke about the period of sanctification for the people who were baptised yesterday. What exactly is your sanctification?

JN.   We learn that when David was in Babylon mourning, he sanctified for twenty-one days. During this time certain practices he did not do. We want to prepare the candidates for Baptism with seven days prior to Baptism which is called Repentance. In that seven days we are instructing them and letting them realise the importance of what they are about to do. Some people get the notion that when they baptise, they have accomplished their goal. We are teaching them that when they baptise they begin the process of trying to accomplish the goal and not that they have accomplished anything.

They have now begun the process. They are now born again and begin to grow in the spirit. So we have them to sanctify themselves – that means they partake of nothing worldly for seven days prior to their baptism and seven days after.

When we go to the inner chambers, [for a purpose] like mourning, then we do it for twenty-one days. This is seven days before they go to mourn, seven days while they are mourning and seven days after they mourn. So that is what constitutes the period of sanctification.

Q. I thoroughly enjoyed the baptism yesterday. Can you tell me something about the other rituals? Any special Thanksgiving or candlelight service?

JN. Yes, we have candlelight and Thanksgiving services. We believe in giving thanks in the traditional and cultural way. That is, the fruits of the land are placed on a table, all the little gifts that God make us privileged to acquire, and we are aware of the fact that we cannot give these things to God. For the Earth is the Lord's and the fullness thereof, the world and they that dwell in it. But we feel we can put it on a table and give thanks. Say Lord we thank you for all these things and we pray that you will bless it and multiply it for us. So we do these things in that sense.

We must remember anything you do, you must bear in mind your faith makes you whole. He say you must do and believe. If you believe placing all these dainties – we put peanuts, bread, honey, apples, whatever we put on the table, based on how God bless you, it can be reflected on the table.

The candlelight service we also do. This reminds us, yet again, that Jesus was the light of the world. Symbolically, we use the candles to remind us of the situation.

Q. How do you place the candles? Lit, on the table or on the floor?

JN. We put candles on the table, on the altar, on the centre pole. We put candlelight everywhere to show the illuminating power of God. He say when you light a candle, don't put it under a bushel but you must put it up where people can see it. The Bible justified the lighting of candles so we do light candles.

Q. You talked about the inner chamber to do with mourning. How important is mourning in the Spiritual Baptist Faith?

JN. Very important. If we go back to what Jesus said to Nicodemus. He said:You must be born of the water of the Holy Spirit?. If we go back to Moses, every time he wanted to communicate with God, we learn he used to go down in sackcloth and ashes. We learn that Jesus went into fasting for forty days. We learn Daniel mourned for twenty-one days.

So we practice this as a means of giving ourself some time to search ourselves and reflect on our personal relationship with God, to speak to him personally to have a closer communication with him spiritually. In so doing he instructs us through visions, dreams and revelations. This is why when people go to mourn, we place bands on their eyes so they would not be able to be looking around and taking pictures.

As you know, your eyes snap pictures as the movements go by. In order for you to remember what they were doing here in ten years from now, you will have to go to the shelf of the brain and pull out this picture that will tell you that you were speaking to me, he was dressed in a black pants and white shirt. [That is] because you went back now to take out this picture.

Now if we cover your eyes you won't be taking these pictures. So therefore you will be looking within. So the picture you will be putting on the shelf will be that one you took within because you cannot look out.

If we look at the third chapter of *Ezekiel*, [we can see] he was given a commandment to go and close himself within a room and there the Lord will speak with him and will even tell him what to say.

During this time he should not be communicating with anyone, his tongue will cling to the roof of his mouth and he will be like if he is dumb. So this is the same practice that we go through in building ourselves spiritually. So when anyone comes from in there they have a more committed spiritual life and better understanding. During this period, we spend a lot of time instructing them on the life of a spiritualist. What is required of a spiritualist, the charity and everything that is necessary to make you walk in the footstep of Jesus Christ.

Q. How long does a member stay in that inner chamber?

JN. For seven days. As I said, they sanctify for seven days seven days in the inner temple and when they come out they sanctify for another seven days. This brings us to twenty-one days.

Q.   So everyone who is baptised goes to the mourning room at some stage?

JN.   Well not necessarily everyone. One must have the calling. As the scripture again declare: those who I fore-know?. This means that I know in advance I am called. Those who I call, I justify. Those who I justify, I glorify. People get their calling in different ways. You could get it through dreams. Someone might come here with a dream to me based on the dream, I would say to you it appears that you should go into mourning.

Another person might have a disturbed mind, confused with what is going on in the world. You know some people take on the problem of the people in the world and think they can solve it and throw their mind off track. When we take them into the inner chamber, we put them on track. When they come back out, they are a bit more confident. They have a little more faith in God. Anytime you can take somebody who is confused and transform their gaze from this carnal world unto the heavenly kingdom, then you have cast out the devil.

Q.   So to you mourning is very important?

JN.   It is vital to some people.

Q.   Is there a procedure for baptism? You went there first without the person you are going to baptise, what did you and your assistant go in the sea to do?

JN.   To symbolically sanctify the spot that we are going to be using. As you see, a lot of people are in the water bathing. So we go to sanctify a spot, to bless it and seal it in Jesus name. So it will be used for the baptism.

Q.   Then you had two sticks?

JN.   We had a cross and the shepherd rod which we used to measure the area from the cross we going to be sanctifying to use for the baptism.

Q.   I should have asked you this earlier. You said you sealed your candidates before you took them to the sea, you use white handkerchiefs. What is the purpose of those sealed handkerchiefs?

J.N   Well according to the seventh chapter of Revelations, when God had sent out the destroying angels, he gave them a specific order. He said the destroying angel must not touch the earth, nor the sea, nor the trees until we have sealed the servants of God.

Everyone who receive Jesus Christ as their personal saviour, receive a seal. We give them a symbolic seal. We can't seal them really but we can give them a symbolic seal. Everything we do in Jesus name, including the laying of bands is only symbolic because He will do it through the Holy Spirit.

When Jesus was baptised, for example, he was sealed in a different sense. He was sealed by the spirit coming down like a dove and remaining upon him.

So we go through the same sealing and at the same time we take bands, sanctified pieces of cloth that was blessed and sealed to cover the eyes. Again to give them an opportunity to put themselves and their minds on Jesus and reflect on their own relationship.

We do the same thing because it was done to Paul. When Paul was on his way to Damascus, the bright light blinded him. He couldn't see anymore so he was unable to look within and to listen to the instruction of God. God instructed him to look for a man to teach him all the things God wanted him to do.

Q.   You seal the bands with pencil or chalk writing?

JN.   We use chalk.

Q.   These are writings as ....?

JN.   Revealed to me.

Q.   Is it in English?

JN.   No, it's not in English and to be honest it is not in a language I can identify. Although sometimes when we seal bands there are people who are able to translate it in Greek and in Arabic and can read it and say that it is what you write there. This is not intentionally, these things are by the Spirit and are written without our knowledge.

Q.   So when you seal these bands, you seal them as the Spirit leads you?

JN.   Personally, if I have to seal bands I get the bands, bless them, cut them and I leave them there. While praying, the Spirit will show me something to put on No.1 band and so I go and put it. It may not necessarily be the same for No.2 band.

This is where the sanctification comes in. During the time this member is sanctified for the first seven days, I too as the person doing the pointing or baptism, have to be sanctified as well. So we will all be praying. Because of this utterances will come and I will do as it is revealed to me.

Q.   We have agreed that the style of the worship has changed. Is this copied from the Roman Catholic or Anglican Church? I mean your format of worship.

JN.   You mean the changes?
Q.   Earlier you said they went away when they were free and they said their prayers. Now there is a structure for doing things, isn't there?

JN.   During the time they went away and said the prayers they had a structure. They used to have a spiritual way of doing things but it was not similar to the Roman Catholic operations as now. In fact, now one of the reasons most people are not in the Spiritual Baptist Faith, is because they [would] rather be in a faith that has a little more European flavour. So they could go to church and show off their pretty skirts and their nice shoes, their stockings and their hair-do and so on, where in the Spiritual Baptist Faith you have to be more humble, your head covered, a long skirt. In some circumstances you come bare feet. So you find modern girls especially don't want to do that. So they look for a church with a little more European flavour where they can do these things and think they are happy.

Q.   How do you as a Spiritual Baptist person see yourself?

JN.   We see ourselves as humble, meek people. The scriptures says the meek shall inherit the earth. We don't go out there and put our priorities on the material things in the world or live according to emotion and ego. But in attempting to be in total submission to the will of God through the direction of the Holy Spirit.

Q.   You said the Spiritual Baptist Faith is not Europeanised, would you say that you are more Africanised?

JN.   Yes, the Spiritual Baptist Faith has always been more Africanised and therefore more down to earth, more humble than in the European churches where you have to put on your suit and tie.

If you don't have the proper tie in some of these churches, you have to go in a back pew. When you have the proper tie, you can walk right up to the front of the pew. That is because you are well dressed.

In the Spiritual Baptist Faith people come right up to the altar and shake the hands of the leaders. It doesn't matter the humble manner in which they are dressed.

Q.   Can you describe the Spiritual Baptist Faith in your own words? What sort of religion is it?

JN.   The Spiritual Baptist is not a religion. It is a faith – that is by calling. A fella could call himself a Roman Catholic and yet he can be called into the Spiritual Baptist Faith because he calls them from everywhere to be in this Faith. But he doesn't call them from this Faith to be everywhere.

Q.   I have been told that the Faith is not developing in the Caribbean. Yet it is developing abroad. You mentioned Panama. When did the church reach Panama, for example.

JN.   All the churches big in Panama. The Universal Spiritual Baptist Archdiocese has its headquarters in Panama.

Q.   What Spiritual Baptist?

JN.   The Universal.

Q.   So they are the same Spiritual Baptist as you are?

JN.   The same Spiritual Baptist. As the bible will tell you there are diversities of gifts and different methods of operations but it is the same spirit. This is what you will find. This is one of the reasons that some of the Spiritual Baptists, even here, try to condemn one another. This is a lack of understanding. This is one reason for different units of churches.

They do not understand that the directive given you as a leader in the church will not necessarily be the direction given to me. The way I carry on service would not be the way Archbishop Pompey will carry on service. This does not make us different because we are going by the spirit. The Bible tells us that obedience to the Holy Spirit is heaven's first law.

For example, suppose I'm supposed to sing a few hymns before I come into church. That is my normal setting. One morning the Spirit says go straight into prayer and we come in there and is praying time, obedience to the Spirit. We are not here to be conformed to a situation but you find people will say, My leader doesn't do it like that or leader so and so doesn't do it like that, so he is wrong, he is not doing it right. And that's where people make the mistake.

Q.   Therefore you are telling me there is no set pattern of worship?

JN.   For the Spiritual Baptist? No.

Q.   So these manuals that are coming into being are not absolutely necessary.

JN.   I won't say not necessary. It might give one the basic method of operating *in the absence of the directive of the Spirit*.

Q.   How big is the Spiritual Baptist Faith here in Grenada?

JN.   The Spiritual Baptist Faith here is very big. If you are talking about actual participation, here in Grenada they still at the stage where they are sceptical to identify because people still label the faith with names like "obeah," "voodoo." Because of this, people baptise but don't want to openly come to church because the neighbour will say they working obeah and so on.

Not until some of them travel and come back and they see how professional people participating in the Faith, they become more serious. Even people like myself. So I think this is the only church you find people like the Commissioner of Police, the Prime Minister and other ministers come to openly. They participate in a lot of our activities. This is why we try to teach and set a standard because the bible say we are the light of the world.

When you meet a spiritual brother or sister in church they look like a saint and then people want to be part of them so they look at them. Then they go to town in the market and they hear this same brother and sister using some heavy dirty language, dressing in a compromising situation and they withdraw. I don't want to be part of that. If you want to shine a light for God, people must look at you and admire you and say I would like to be like that Reverend.

For example, you come down here and somebody says that's the Reverend that was in church yesterday talking proper. So they will be talking about your head is uncovered today and Captain always say when you come around the church your head must be covered. I told them don't cross it with pants or untie head.

Q.   Had I known your Rules. I must apologise.

JN.   It's not a problem.

Q   Now the covering of the head is this African?

JN.   Not necessarily.

Q.   I apologise for coming with my head uncovered and wearing a trouser suit, because my mobility is impaired it is more comfortable to wear trousers. Usually I have someone assisting me, so I would have had my head tied.

It means in spite of all the transformations, there are still leaders who are sticking to the hard and fast old time rules?

JN.   Yes, I consider myself young but I stick to it. The Bible justifies that a woman's head must be covered. Growing up, I remember all my grandparents, my great-grandmother who could have traced her relationship right back to Africa, we used to call her Ya-Ya. She was 106 when she died.

Q.   Was she a Spiritual Baptist?

JN.   I can't remember if she was a Spiritual Baptist. Let me put it this way, I remember her never having her hair untied. Even when she was dying, I remember as a little child she had all of us lined up the night and she wanted to speak to us one by one.

She was very big and she had a big bed made of mahogany with a big canopy over it and she was lying there and she ask which one I am. I told her and she said right. Ya-Ya is going to a place called heaven and you will meet Ya-Ya again only if you give your life to God. If you don't give your life to God, you are not going to be in the same place as Ya-Ya. So if you want to see Ya-Ya again make sure you give your life to God.

I can remember coming out crying and my grandmother was saying to me don't worry with her, her head not good, she just saying those things. They were only trying to calm us. All of us were sleeping in this house. About two nights later she called out and.....

There was another old woman in the village called Tayfam who walked with a stick and didn't go out. But they had an agreement that which one die first will dress the other one. *In those days when you die, they didn't keep you for more than a day. They bury them the same evening.* So she said to them, go and get Tayfam and tell her to come, I'm going. Her voice was very strong and my grandmother say "Ya-Ya what you worrying...?...She said go and get Tayfam. So she went. Tayfam took a while to get there but she came. From the time she reach up the hill Tayfam will call out, "Lillie, I am coming girl, I am coming. I hear you are going home?" She said who calling? Tayfam. Tell her come quick. And you know is not like people who was sick. So I now was convinced that she head is not good. So Tayfam come and went inside. She prayed and then they both prayed. When they finished she say to Tayfam, "Dress me, girl.".

So Tayfam call my grandmother and say, "All you open the drawer? she dress down there." And [it was] something she used to call a chemise which is a slip made out of cotton with frills on it.

She say get the chemise, the apron. In this sense I think she is a Baptist because I didn't know what I just saying.

They were dressing her. The room door was slightly open. Being nosy I will go to the crease to see what they doing to Ya-Ya. They were tying the head and she was saying, "Is not so I tell you to tie my head, don't tie my head like that. Is how ah doing, I want you to tie my head this way." Tayfam say, "Is me that tying the head. You going home and you making all this fuss!" She say, "Is not so I tell you to tie my head. Tie it how I tell you." When she tie the head and everything she say, "How I look?" So Tayfam say, "If I look like that you mean you going before me. I say you woulda dress me let me look like that. Well I have to look for somebody to dress me now because you well dressed." So my great-grandmother said, "Band my jaw. I want yuh to band meh jaw now." So Tayfam take the cloth, looking like what we does use for the bands and she put it under the jaw and she tie it to the headtie.

I fell asleep but about 4 o'clock in the morning I head them start to bawl. When I wake up they said Ya-Ya dead. So I went in the room, this is the first dead I have ever seen and I look, to me I see her moving as usual. So I say "She eh dead, she moving." So my grandmother say "Shut your mouth!"

That was the first funeral I went to. I never advise people to take little children to funeral. Some people does think because there are evil spirits. My experience was when they cover the coffin with the dirt. When I went home, my mind was locked on one thing: how they could cover her down there. How is she going to breathe? Then imagining that I am down there and I started to scream. After that happened people were saying they have to bathe me and as different things with me because [they thought] maybe some spirit is around. I know what I was going through. I would go into a deep meditation and imagine is me they put down there and they cover me and when I get the realisation of it I would scream out. It's like I'm losing my breath. I would get over it for a few days and even a few days later I go back into it and I remember her.

Q.   So you said your great-grandmother never ever uncovered her head?

JN.   Always covered. They had something they used to call calico cloth. Some nice flowers. I don't see that these days. You could see them for miles.

Q.   Would you link this to African tradition?

JN.   Yes, I would and I do and also it is reflecting the Spiritual Baptist Faith.

Q.   You said people are in the Faith here but are not coming out. What percentage of the population is Spiritual Baptist, approximately?

JN.   I would say a good 60% of these people are Spiritual Baptist, baptised. Some of them for the sake of relatives, friends and neighbours are going back into the Roman Catholic and Anglican churches. They are at some time in their life baptised in the Spiritual Baptist Faith.

Q.   Would you still say it's not developing?

JN.   Oh yes. I wish I could have said there's a little more unity in the Faith. The lack of unity is because of the lack of understanding of the different methods of the operation within. The Spiritual Baptist Faith is the most divided faith you could find, all this is because of the obedience of the Holy Spirit. Now the Roman Catholic church is uniformed. Whether you go to a Roman Catholic church in St. George or Port of Spain, you would expect the same procedure to take place because it is written down.

In the Spiritual Baptist Faith it is not really written down. Although it is good to be guided by a manual, the Spiritual Baptist Faith is divided. We are a peculiar people in other words. It's not a situation where you can have a set [procedure].

Q.   Is this the reason for not having a unified church here?

JN.   To some extent people seem not to understand. The other one has always been wrong and seen as wrong. Rather than admit that it is diversity of the Spirit and different methods of operation and then work from there. We are working towards unity. For example, in America we have the United Spiritual Baptist

Ministers Council. They are functioning at a level where they are not interfering with the actual function of the unit church but they come as an umbrella for these churches. Here in Grenada, in our next celebration, I will have a Council of ministers with a view of having a Council of Elders which will encompass all the unit churches and still not interfere in their method of operation.

I came here and single-handedly erected this shrine. I have a weekly radio programme. We visit the prison on a regular basis, every fourth Sunday of the month. We visit and feed the old people on a quarterly basis. We do a yearly pilgrimage up the Grenadines to Cairacou and Union, St Vincent, Barbados and Trinidad. This is without the operation of an Archdiocese. I do not see the Archdiocese functioning in a manner in which I can associate myself.

Q.   How do you foresee this unity then since you are in different operations?

JN.   As I say we are going to have a conference and to form a Council of Elders. We would not interfere with the operations of any church. The function of the Council will be basically to solve problems with the churches instead of going to court.   Being splintered and not having an umbrella group does not make us exempt for tax purposes. If we can come under an organised group we can then be eligible for tax exemption status. There is some real benefits to derive from being a member of the Council when it is formed.

Q.   Do you have many Spiritual Baptist members who are marriage officers?

JN.   Yes, I am a marriage officer. I do weddings. There are other ministers in the Spiritual Baptists who do.

Q.   Can your ministers sign birth certificates saying Spiritual Baptist?

JN.   Yes.

Q.   You never had the problem that St Vincent and Trinidad had with the suppressing of the Faith by law?

JN.   No not really. We suffered in the sense of the degrading of the name but not with police arresting you and so on. That never took place here.

Q.   It's been very interesting talking to you. I look forward to being in Grenada again. You said you were having some big event soon here?

JN.   Our celebration is normally every June around the 15th.

Q.   You have it here?

JN.   Yes.

CHAPTER ELEVEN

MRS MABEL SALAZAAR,
85 YEAR OLD CULTURE CARRIER,
HER SISTER MRS MARY MUNROE AND
MRS SALAZAAR'S DAUGHTER, MAJORIE CREIGHTON

You said to me earlier that your mother was a Spiritual Baptist.

MS.   Yes.

Q.   What was here name?

MS.   Eliza Salazaar.

Q.   When did she die and how old was she when she died?

MS.   She died 15 years ago at the age of 110 years.

Figure 22
Majorie Creighton, eldest
daughter of Mabel Salazaar
(Photo by the Author)..

Q.   What do you recall of your mother? You said that she was a Spiritual Baptist,
if she died 15 years age she would have been 125 years old now. Was she always a
Spiritual Baptist?

MS.   Always a Spiritual Baptist.

Q.   So this goes back to around the 1870's, that the latter part of the 19th
century. So you mean that the Spiritual Baptist Faith was around all this time?

MS.   All this time.

Q.   What do you remember of your mother and the Spiritual Baptist Faith?

MS.   My mother had something like a tent and there we used to keep the church
and sometimes we keep it inside the house. When we had to feed people we used
to keep it inside the house.

Q.   Who had the church? Your mother had the church?

MS.   Yes, my mother. She and Arthur, they had the church, that was her son-in-
law.

Q.   What sort of building did you have?

MS.   They make it with carratt.

Q.   Carratt leaves?

MS.   Yes, and then they used to bar it around with coconut leaves, they used to put around the tent. When they used to keep the feast, they used to keep the church in it.

Q.   Now I am getting a bit confused. The Spiritual Baptist church in these days, did you hold feasts in it? Prayers and feasts?

MS.   Yes. They used to keep the prayers first. Oh, I see. We used to keep the prayers first and after the prayers, the whole night, you see like Monday night, Tuesday night, prayers; and after the prayers we start on Wednesday morning. Wednesday, Thursday and Friday is the African feasts.

Q.   Did you remember this as a child, how old were you?

MM.   About 16 or 17 years.

Q.   You are Mabel Salaazar's Sister Mary?

MM.   Yes

Q.   How old are you?

MM.   Can't remember.

Q.   How much younger are you than your sister?

MM.   I'm quite lower.

Q.   Are you a Spiritual Baptist?

MM.   Yes.

Q.   Were you always a Spiritual Baptist?

MM.   Always, my mother had us baptise.

Q.   What age were you when your mother had the church? How old were you then?

MM.   Maybe about 9 or 10. I was very small.

Q.   And you remember your mother having the church?

MM.   Yes. It wasn't directly a church. It was a tent in the yard. It's only when she invite people she will put a table, and the leaders will sit there and there and they would say prayers. So it wasn't a church.

Q.   What did you call it, a prayer house?

MM.   No it was just a tent in the yard. It's only when she go to keep African feasts the people will come and have prayers.

Q.   How often did your mother kept this feast?

MM.   Every year, August month.

Q.   And what was this feast for?

MM.   African feast.

Q.   And what did this have to do with the Spiritual Baptist Faith?

MM.   We were Spiritual Baptists and we used to keep feasts otherwise.

Q.   Do you mean the Spiritual Baptist Faith and the feasts were all the same thing?

MM.   You keep the Spiritual Baptist prayer first, you had to call on God first. You keep the prayers and in the morning five o' clock, you get your goat, your fowl, your animals them, we get them ready. Wash their feet and wash the beak and so on. You sing the African and then you start to kill.

Q.   What African did you sing?

MS.   First we start to sing when you go round.

> Eshe parakbo ye
> Mojouba
> Aye Aye mo de
> Eshe parakbo ye
> Lo lo ye
> Ya manda kori
> Eshe parakbo ye
> Mojouba
> Ba ba la goluna

[They demonstrated by singing Yoruba choruses which were sung at the African feast.]

Q.   What was the meaning of this song?

MS.   The meaning is that we are going to keep a sacrifice. We have fowl, we have goat, we have sheep, anything you want to kill we go right away round with the animals.

Q.   You walk with the animal when you are singing?

MS.   Yes, right around, all the people that come will join in and sing and the drums will beat.

Q.   So you are calling the names of all the deities as you sing?

MS.   Yes. You give offering [of] a goat. You give [to] *Erile*.

Q.   So this was not part of the Spiritual Baptist Faith, was it?

MS.   No, this was African.

Q.   So the Africans were Spiritual Baptist and they practised the traditional religion?

MS.   Yes, from Africa. You keep your prayers in the night, you sing your hymns, and when it is 4.30 to 5.30 [in the morning] you start the *Eshe parakbo ye, mo jouba*.

Q.   So this went on once a year. Where did you go to church on a Sunday?

MS.   Anglican church. My mother was Anglican and my father was Roman Catholic, so we went to the Catholic [church] first and when it was over we went to the Anglican Church and meet all the other family.

Q.   When did you go to the Spiritual Baptist church?

MS.   Anytime the Spiritual Baptists have prayers we go, but we have it in our feast. But we used to go to church in Diamond.

Q.   Where were you baptised?

MS.   In Diamond, in Sum Sum Hill. They had churches. Pastor Crisostum, he has a big church, up to now they have that big church there.

Q.   So you were baptised with Pastor Crisostum?

MS.   No, I was baptised with Leader Chase and Juba.

Q.   I have heard of Juba – where was he from?

MS.   Juba belongs to Chase village – wherever he get people to baptise he went.

Q.   How old were you when you were baptised?

MM.   I was seven or eight years.

MS.   I baptised at about twenty. I made my first child very young and I baptise after that. I used to go to church all about. I used to dance. Then after that I follow the African dance so I couldn't dance again. Sometimes, I had to go to Moruga, sometimes quite Mamoral.

Q.   Where were you born?

MS.   I was born at Kanga Woods.

Q.   The whole family was born there?

MS.   Yes, the whole family.

Q.   Were there only Africans in *Kanga* Woods or was it a mixed community?

MS.   No, you had Indians. The whole place was one family. Mother, sister, aunty, everybody had their own land but lived together.

Q.   Why do they call the place *Kanga* Woods?

MS.   *Kanga* is an African name and they now call it Kanga Woods, but it used to be called Kanga settlement.

Q.   Was it because the freed slaves settled there?

MS.   My great-grandparents, the Coles, didn't come here as slaves. He told us that he came to show the people how to make roads. Because right now I could carry you to Kanga Woods and show you a place called Makadam. They used to take the soft stone from the river to make the road, throw the dirt on both sides and get gravel from the river. They didn't come here as slaves. My great-grandfather was a man who showed me lots of things through visions and I had to explain to my mother and them. He show me plenty things. Makadam red, I could show you.

Q.   Why did they call them Yarrabas?

MS.   They were called Yorubas. Anybody could dance Yoruba. You could go to a dance and get up and dance. They throw hat on your head, towel round your neck; when you dance they spin you. Sometimes you dance and come out queen of the Yoruba dance. My mother was a queen in it. When you see my mother throw her hands and feet and hold her dress...!

Q.   What sort of dress would she wear?

MS.   Duet. You have to make a dress for that purpose and get nice flat shoes – no high heels, soft shoes because you dance until 4 o'clock. When my mother go to that Yoruba dance...when she is finished...Madam! handkerchiefs, hats, towels, all kind of things on her head. They make things for the people who dance good.

Q.   What sort of songs did they sing when dancing? Do you remember the songs?

MS.   No. The African dance is different from the Yoruba dance. When you dance the African dance, you are in spirit, a good spirit. I could pick up a man who is sick and dance with him on my back, When you see I put a man on my back and dance and when I put him down I take sweet oil and fix him up, when he is ready to go home, he is better.

Q.   Is this what you call *Shango*?

MS.   Yes, this is *Shango*. And when you see they dance up this *Shango* they get a big blaze of fire and dance in it. When you see they go to start it, they clap.

Q.   So tell me something now. Is the *Shango* and the Spiritual Baptist the same thing?

MS.   No.

Q.   What is the difference?

MS.   Plenty difference. In the Spiritual Baptist you drum with your hands, you sing and clap. The Spiritual African is drum and the ceremony. African is Yoruba. When you have your African business you sing your hymns first, then you get outside with a calabash of water, you get some ashes and you put it down on the ground and you walk your drummers. You sit there and when you and your singers start to sing, now who fall down they will pick them up and everybody begin to *Ehsu* right around. When we get the signal me and my sister would throw the calabash and no evil can enter here.

Q.   What were you throwing?

MS.   While they singing and everybody group around, just at the entrance of the tent, where they have to pass, I have the calabash with the ashes from the coal and the water. When they are ready to change the song, I and my sister throw what we have to throw and light a candle right there.

Q.   What are you throwing?

MS.   We have two calabashes, one has ashes properly formed, no coal dust in it, clear salt and sweet oil and rum in the water and we are group with that. When we put it down at the side of the road, we light the candle and nobody interfere with that. Because if they interfere and something take them, well!... So nobody interferes with that. You have to get rum, puncheon rum to throw in the calabash too.

Q.   What was the reason for the rum?

MS.   For the spirit. You have to call them with the rum and you have to give them the rum.

Q.   Are they Ancestral Spirits?

MS.   They come and they can tell you anything. If you going to die tomorrow they will tell you. Anything they tell you look out for it. When you catch this spirit, you don't know anybody, you are not here. The spirit can tell you from the day your mother made you. If trouble will take you, they will tell you, and you have to ask what you must do and what you shouldn't do. If you didn't ask questions and you ignore the spirit when trouble take you then your friends will remind you of what you were told. Then you will be advised to go back to the place where the spirit spoke to you. Well, my mother, she would just go outside and throw sweet oil, she would throw her water and light her candle and she sees everything and say what happened. The African Spirit take you, then he or she will start to tell that person what happened again and he will ask for help. You just tell him what to get. No goat or sheep, just candles, rum, sweet oil and every six 'o' clock they will offer prayers. If you have a bad case in court, then the case is dismissed.

Q.   So this is what you call the *Shango* or *Orisha*?

MS.   Yes. They harm nobody, they just help people.

Q.   Does this mean now that the Spiritual Baptist and *Orisha* are the same?

MS.   They all work together. But you see some people are Spiritual Baptist and they don't have to have African dance. Well if you want to let it go, let it go [i.e., relinquish your connections to the African dance/religion].

Q.   Some Baptist people just have prayers alone?

MS.   Some, [it's] just [that] they have to give it up. They don't understand it, they let it go, everybody don't carry it on. If your parents show you what to do and how to do it, when they die you could carry on.

Q.   Do you know how to carry on these prayers?

MM.   No. Only one sister could carry it on, Martha, she was after Mabel. When my father died my mother used to keep it and when she couldn't manage that sister took over. We carry on a portion, but that sister died.

Q.   So some Spiritual Baptists gave it up and some carry it on?

MM.   Yes, as long as they are alive. I never kept any, my parents kept it. When time came my husband prepared what he have to give and took it to my mother. My cousins, the Coles, used to give prayers and we would go to them and they would come to us.

Q.   I have been talking to both your aunts about the Spiritual Baptist and the Yoruba dance and African feasts. You are a Spiritual Baptist. Now tell me what is the relationship between Spiritual Baptists and the others?

MC.   Well, I would say that the *Shango* is worshipping God in the African way, the way they know but to me the Spiritual Baptist is a more modern something. The *Shango* feed, beat drums and kill animals. But in the Spiritual Baptist when you go to feast they give you the drum, but we don't kill animals and do this outside business. The *Orishas* have their altars outside but the Spiritual Baptist, if the Holy Spirit gave you an altar, [it] has to be inside the house. We use a glass of water and so on, we just don't use the things that they use. But there are those Spiritual Baptists who use the rum and the things that the *Shango* use. I use olive oil, clean water and *Kanaga* water, we use calabash too. They work a lot of miracles, you know, the *Shango* people.

Q.   Do you remember your grandmother and the Yoruba dance?

MC.   Not so much, I more remember the African yearly feast. When I first baptise I danced. I remember I was looking up one morning when they were preparing the animals and so on, eventually I just swayed from side to side and I wasn't there. I was completely out of myself.

Q.   Was this on the day of your baptism?

MC.   No, the day of my baptism it was different. I am talking of the first day that I danced *Shango*, I was in a feast and I stood there while they were dancing in the morning. I was a praying soul then, I was already baptised; that morning they were passing around something with olive oil, *obi* seed chopped and guinea pepper. Everybody will take a little, put it to your mouth and chew it. I remember when they reached me they put some olive oil on my head, they rubbed my face and my hands and throw some on my feet. And the next thing when I came to myself I was really out [there] dancing.

Q.   You were out of self for a while?

MC.   But to say I knew what was going on at the time I did not. I was completely out in the spirit.

Q.   Does this happen to you since your baptism?

MC.   Since I baptise I don't beat drums, I go to church. But my baptism was very nice. I baptised with Teacher Warren. My old spiritual leader was Cyril John from Gasparillo. My baptism took place right down here on the seaside. I was in Caracas when I got my call for baptism. I saw this woman in this blue dress, she said I come for you and all your children, but I didn't understand it. I saw the clouds cover up the earth and this woman walking from east to west, I asked her if she was not afraid because the clouds were covering the earth. I was so afraid I thought I was going to die. I called out to the woman again and asked her if she was not afraid and she said no, because I'm baptised. I held on to my head and began to scream and was awaken by the screams in my dream. I couldn't catch myself until daybreak. There and then I was in the spirit in Venezuela, people speaking Spanish and I speaking English, nobody can't help me except for one Trinidadian girl who was there named Jean. She was a Baptist and had the eyes to know that I was walking on that road. I didn't know, but I was a praying soul in a country all by myself, no mother, no father, no husband, no brother and sister. So I got *convicted* in Caracas and came home.

Q.   Were there any other Spiritual Baptists in Caracas at that time?

MC.   Yes, this was about 1967. It was there I began to communicate with one Mother Rita; she have a church in St Croix. They were in a place called San Augustine and I would attend her prayers. I had to leave everything in Caracas and come home. I was ill and thought I was going to die. But it was when I reached home here the spirit gave me the date in a vision one night and the woman came in a pink dress and showed me three letters. I went straight to my spiritual mother and asked her for a private baptism; it will be a private baptism in a public place. My spiritual mother broke her leg for breaking the first date of my baptism. So I got up early to bath and she put me on the sheet. So when the leader reached, he brought another pilgrim just as the mother said, that it would be two of us. When they placed the bands on my head, I started to travel instantly. The next day they told me all that I did. But I knew that they had showed me the time for baptism. I was running in a road and I saw the time was 4 p.m. The leader said to teacher Warren, this pilgrim has to be in the water at four, so we are leaving here at two because of the distance we had to walk. My spiritual mother said she cannot go because of her foot. When she said that I turned around and told her that she will have to go even if it meant going on my back. She said 'what'?

Q.   Did you take her on your back?

MC.   No, she went very well walking. It was the spirit talking, not me. When I reached in the sea I never felt my feet touch ground and I came out shouting. After I was anointed in the church, I had on a white lace dress, I felt so clean, so new, so nice that people said that I looked like a 16 year old. This time I was a married woman, 30 years old, with five children. Mother Marie was there, I meant to call her so that she could tell you what went on. I could give you the very proof I took. "Thou art a priest forever after the order of Melchisidec." I still have that very bible. I went down to mourning one year after I baptised, it was good. From then to now, I keep walking forward. And mourning is a serious thing.

Q.   Is it?

MC. Yes, people take it for a joke. Now, anybody can baptise but everybody cannot mourn. The pointer will point you, but if your heart is troubled you cannot mourn. I do not eat when I am mourning. Just a little bush tea. I mourn about eight times.

Q. What's your office now?

MC. I'm Mother Marjorie.

Q. So the whole family is Spiritual Baptist?

MC. All my children are Spiritual Baptists, not my husband, but he's a good supporter. He's spiritual, whenever I go to mourn he stays at home here and track me.

Q. What's the name of your church?

MC. St Francis Mt. Zion. We have baptism at 4a.m. on Sunday.

Q. Do you still baptise at that early hour?

MC. No, she requested it. Normally, we start our baptism service early on Saturday evening and according to how the spirit moves, we put down the candidates to rest about 10 p.m. because we avoid late services. About 5 a.m. we wake up the candidates, because they are young, very young people joining the faith.

Q. So you have many young people joining the Spiritual Baptist Faith?

MC. I find that lots of 12 –15 year olds joining up.

Q. What's the attraction?

MC. I don't know, because our church have a lot of rules. You cannot live as you like, do as you like, then come to church. You have to live as a Christian and some people reject the rules, even some of the members fell away because of this. You can't go down carnival with a beer in you hand and in your short pants wining, then you come in a brown dress and a broad belt around your waist and say you are a mother? We cannot tolerate that. So if we have to have a member they must be Christians. It's no point having a full church with people who do not have respect or try to lift up the faith.

Spiritual mothers and elders today must look up. I remember God wanted to call David, he didn't just say 'David I need you,' he didn't even speak to David at all. He spoke to Samuel and told Samuel to fill his horn with oil and to go down to the house of Jesse. Samuel being a man of God got his vision and I believe, the bible didn't say this, but being a man of God he went down in prayer and waited on the Lord. In our churches we have too much favouritism and too much, 'I get this and I get that.' When the Lord speaks to you alone, he also speaks to someone else. And he said he choose the foolish things to confound the wise.

A certain man had to go to battle, I can't remember the name, but as he went down in prayer, the message came to a little boy, the battle is the Lord's. God choose whom he wants and God chose David to do his bidding. People are just straying from the bible, but the bible tells us how to live. So many people cannot control their own homes, cannot control their own lives and they want to hold office in church. If you were living a wretched life and you baptise, you must keep your light shining on a candle stick.

Q.   What is your membership like?

MC.   About 25 attending service. We have plenty members but they fell away. My life is dedicated to God, we have to live for God.

Q.   Do you belong to any organisation?

MC.   No. We have had support from the West Indian United Spiritual Baptist Sacred Order Archdiocese, but their services are different from us. We clap and build up our preachers, ring bells, raise hymns spontaneously. But they don't do that. We cannot shout and sing and dance as we want at their church. But with the Archdiocese we have to hand over our money. But if we have a marriage or dedication we have to contact them for a minister in order to get the certificate under their name. So Pastor Mc Millan comes to our church from Pond St, Mt. Paran Church, La Romain.

Q.   What do you think of women Bishops. and Archbishops?

MC.   I think we have a guideline but a woman can never override a man in God's work. You see as Christ is the head of the church so the men should be the head of the church. I don't mind women being robed as mothers, but I feel a bishop is a man's job. You can have a woman working side by side with a leader, but the head must be a man. Now if Christ likened the church into a body, there must be one head and two arm bearers, who would be equal and they can deputise for the head. A lady buried yesterday, she was Archbishop, Spiritual Baptist just doing what they want. There is family lineage not spiritual lineage. I remember a certain mother was given a command by God to hand over certain things and she said *not even to my children*, because she felt her daughter should get it. She refused; she didn't crown that person, but we must remember only God chooses. We Spiritual Baptist people who can be here and pick you up [i.e., spiritually] in Port of Spain. I am asking God for that kind of communication.

Q.   Do you have these gifted people in the church?

MC.   No. Long ago we had provers, divers, pointers, hunters.

Q.   What's a hunter?

MC.   A person who goes out and meet people and talk to them, then according to their conversion these people get eager to come to God.

Q.   Do you have hunters?

MC.   Yes, there are still people who God call to bring people in but when you bring people in they want them for themselves. They get big, they want to be Ministers. There are mothers who are classified [i.e., directed] to the mourner's house and can stay here and pick up what's happening to the mourner, then there are mothers who are called to evangelise. I had a taste of this as a young person in the faith. I will go to church and during prayers I will pick up the pilgrim and converse with the pilgrim in tongues. Then I would go to No. 2 and start to shout.

Q.   What is the meaning or significance of shouting then picking up?

MC.   My shouting comes to me in a language. There are people who don't talk in tongues, but will shout.

Q.   Is shouting a gift of the spirit?

MC.   Listen to me. When you shout something comes from inside, deep within. It comes in a alphabetical order. I was taught to shout on the mourning ground. The lady came to me and screamed. I stayed on that beat all day, then the following day I changed to first note and started to walk on a road until I reached a junction. As you grow in the Spirit you bring different notes and it changed again the following morning. The last note I was taught was much faster.

Q.   Is this part of the Aficanisms in the Faith?

MC.   They teach you to change your notes on an instrument at times.

Q.   How do you see yourself?

MC.   I'm on a Holy Ghost track. I feel alienated in some of the churches here, they are too commercialised. We have to look to God and live, I made a promise to God, so I have stopped doing a lot of things.

REFERENCES

CHAPTER ONE

1. *Trinidad Guardian*, 21 January, 1980.

2. Mother Virginia Sandy (1996), Interview by the author, Georgetown, St. Vincent.

3. Simpson, G. E. (1980). *Religious Cults of the Caribbean: Trinidad, Jamaica and Haiti*. Institute of Caribbean Studies, University of Puerto Rico. p. 141.

4. Elder; J.D. (1988). *African Survivals in Trinidad and Tobago*. Karia Press, London, p. 16.

5. Pearse, Andrew (1958), "Afro-New World Cult Dances , unpublished paper, p.4.

6. Elder; J.D., op. cit., p. 37.

7. Connor; Edric (1943). "Folk Music of Trinidad and Tobago," a lecture given at the Bishop Anstey High School, Port-of-Spain, Trinidad (unpublished), p. 2.

8. Warner-Lewis; Maureen (1991). *Guinea's Other Suns: The African Dynamic in Trinidad Culture*. The Majority Press, Dover, Massachusetts, p. 10.

9. Mbiti; John (1975). *An introduction to African Religion*, Heinemann, London, p. 13.

10. Brereton, Bridget (1979). *Race Relations in Colonial Trinidad 1870-1900*, Cambridge University Press, p. 159.

11. Pearse; Andrew op. cit.

CHAPTER TWO

1. Williams, Eric,(1962), *History of the People of Trinidad and Tobago*, Trinidad

p. 41.

2.   Ibid.

3.   Carrington, Selwyn, *Econocide, Myth or Reality*.

4.   Stewart; John (1976), "Mission and Leadership among the 'Meriken' Baptists of Trinidad," Contributions of the Latin American Anthropology Group, 1976, p. 17.

5.   Douglas; Raymond Oba, "The Bible and the Spiritual Baptist Church," Mt. Pisgah Spiritual Baptist Archdiocese International Ltd. (undated), p. 2. See also Huggins A,B., "Saga of the Companies."

6.   De Verteuil, A, *Sir Louis de Verteuil, His Life and Times, Trinidad 1800–1900*, p. 145.

7.   Brereton, B., op.cit., pp. 9–10.

8.   De Verteuil, A., op.cit., see chapter, "Champion of the Catholics."

9.   Warner-Lewis, M. (1991), *Guinea's Other Suns*. The Majority Press, Dover, Massachusetts, 1991, p. 51.

10.   Brereton, B., op.cit., p. 10.

11.   De Verteuil, L. A., *Trinidad*, Ward & Lock, London, p. 173.

12.   Ibid.

13.   Ibid., p. 191.

14.   Underhill, Edward B. (1862), *The West Indies, their social and religious conditions, 1862*. Jackson, Walford and Hodder, London, p. 16.

15.   East, D J. (1892), *Baptist Missionary Society the Centenary Volume*, etc, London, p. 212.

16.   Wood, Donald (1986), *Trinidad in Transition - The Years After Slavery*, The Institute of Race Relations/Oxford University Press, London, p. 239.

17.   *Port of Spain Gazette*, 1st November 1844.

18.   Clarke, *Sierra Leone*, quoted in Donald Wood, *Trinidad in Transition*, p. 239.

19.   Thomas, J.J. (1969), *Froudacity*, London, New Beacon Books, (new edition, first published 1882) p. 142.

20.   Trotman, David, "The Yoruba and Orisha worship in Trinidad and Tobago and British Eugane - 1838-1870." African Studies Review, Volume I2, No.2, September 1976, p. 6.

CHAPTER FOUR

1.   Herskovits, M.J. (1941), *The Myth of the Negro Past*, Harper and Bros., New York/London.

2.   Herskovits, M.J. (1947), *Trinidad Village*, Knopf, New York.

3.   *Legislative Council Debates*, Trinidad and Tobago, 28 October 1949; Thomas, E. (1987), *A History of the Shouter Baptist in Trinidad and Tobago*.

4.   Brereton, Bridget (1981), *A History of Modern Trinidad 1783–1962*, Heinemann, Jamaica/London, pp. 138–9.

5.   Ibid., p 139. See also: James, C.L.R., "The Case for West Indian Self-Government," (first pub. 1932), in Grimshaw, A., ed., 1992, *C L R. James Reader*, Blackwell, Oxford.

6.   See: Dr. C. Joseph, "An Address on the Opening of the Spiritual Baptist Cathedral," Port of Spain, Trinidad, 29th September, 1974; Archbishop Raymond Oba Douglas (1991), *The Spiritual Baptist Handbook*.

7.   *The Trinidad Guardian*, 9 January 1918.

8.   *Legislative Council Debates*, Trinidad and Tobago, 16 November 1917.

9.   *The Trinidad Guardian*, Friday 30 March 1951, p. 6. Editorial observed that "The Ordinance for some reason avoided calling them [the Shouters] a religious group, but includes references to the initiation ceremonies and other things."

10.   "Shouters Prohibition Ordinance," enacted 28 November 1917, Chapter 4, No. 19, *Laws of Trinidad and Tobago*, 1940 edition, pp. 558–560.

11.   *The Beacon*, August 1931 edition, reproduced in Gomes, A. (1974), *Through a Maze of Colour*, Key Caribbean Publications, Trinidad, pp. 74–80.

12.   Ibid., pp 74-80. Incidentally, 1931 was the year of the passage of the Statute of Westminster, which repealed the 1865 Colonial Laws Validity Act, but only as far as the Dominion Legislatures – Canada, South Africa, New Zealand, Australia, Ireland, were concerned, not the Crown Colonies.

13.   *Legislative Council Debates*, Trinidad and Tobago, 16 November 1917.

14.   *The Holy Bible*, The Open Bible Edition, Thomas Nelson Publishers, Nashville, Camden, New York, 1975, p. 1110.

15.   Ibid.

16.   Thomas, E. (1987), *A History of the Shouter Baptists in Trinidad & Tobago*, Calaloux, p. 24.

17.   Rohlehr, G. (1990), *Calypso and Society in Pre-Independence Trinidad*, UWI, Trinidad.

18.   Ibid.

19.   Ibid.

20.   Herskovits, M. (1941), op. cit., p. 222.

21.   Herskovits, M.J. and F.S. (1947), *Trinidad Village*, Knopf, New York, pp. 184–5.

22.   Reddock, R. (1988), *Elma Francois: The NWCSA and the Workers' Struggle in the Caribbean in the 1930's*, New Beacon Books., London, p. 24.

23.   Joseph, Cuthbert, op. cit.

24.   Gomes, A. (1974), op. cit., p 164–71.

25.   Lovelace, E. (1983), *The Wine of Astonishment*, Heinemann, London, p. 35.

26.   Herskovits, M.J., and F.S. (19470), op-cit., pp. 187–8.

27.   Archbishop Clarence Baisden, unpublished paper.

28.   Ibid.

29.   Thomas, E., op. cit., p 40.

30.   Ibid., p. 25–6.

31.   Herskovits, M.J. and Herskovits, F.S., op-cit., p 172.

32.   Thomas, E., op. cit., pp. 25–6.

33.   Ibid., p. 26.

34.   *Legislative Council Debates,* Trinidad and Tobago, 30 March 1951, Morning Session.

35.   Ibid.

36.   Henney, J.H., "A Spiritual Possession and Trance in St. Vincent," in Bouguinon, Erika (1973), *Religion, Altered States of Consciousness and Social Change*, Columbus, Ohio State University Press.

37.   *Minutes of the Legislative Council*, St. Vincent, 13 April 1939.

38.   Reddock, op. cit., p. 9.

39.   Ibid.

40.   Thomas E, op. cit., p. 20.

41.   *Minutes of the Legislative Council*, St. Vincent, 13 April 1939, p. 23.

42.   Henney, J.H. (1973), *The Shakers of St. Vincent: A Stable Religion*, Ohio State University Press, p. 225.

43. Ibid., p. 222 (Henney quoted the *Caribbean Monthly Bulletin*, February 1967).

Chapter Five

1. Makandal Daaga was centrally involved in the 1970 popular uprising and army revolt in Trinidad. A national political figure, he is currently leader of the National Joint Action Committee (NJAC).

2. Williams, Eric (1964), *Capitalism & Slavery*, Andre Deutsch, London.

3. John, Gus (1996), "Thy Kingdom Come, Thy Will Be Done," Address to the Annual District Convention of the Church of God of Prophecy, Moss Side, Manchester (unpublished).

Conclusion

1. Lanternari, Vittorio (1965), *Religions of the Oppressed: A study of Messianic Cults*. New American Library/Mentor Books, N.Y. p. 254.

BIBLIOGRAPHY

Anderson, Allan (1993). *Tumelo: The Faith of African Pentecostals in South Africa*, The University of South Africa.

— (1992), *Bazalwane: African Pentecostals in South Africa*, The University of South Africa.

BBC TV-Time Life Books (1972), *The British Empire*, Time Life International (Netherland) NV.

Bonnett, Aubrey W and Watson, G Llewellyn. *Emerging Perspectives on the Black Diaspora*, University Press of America.

Bourguignon, Erick (1967), *Ritual Dissociation and Possession Belief in Caribbean Negro Religion*, New York, Free Press.

Brereton, Bridget (1981), *History of Modern Trinidad 1783-1896*, Heinemann, Kingston/London.

— (1979). *Race Relations in Colonial Trinidad 1870-1900*, Cambridge University Press.

Carr, Andrew (1989). *A Rada community in Trinidad*, Parie Publishing Company, Trinidad.

Connor, Edric (1943), "Folk Music of Trinidad & Tobago," Lecture given at Bishop Anstey High School, Port-of-Spain, Trinidad.

Cox, Edward (1996), *Rekindling the Ancestral Memory: King Ja Ja of Opobo's exile in Barbados and St Vincent (1888-1891)*, Department of History, Rice University, U.S.A.

Curtain, Philip (1968), "Field Techniques for Collecting & Processing Oral Data," *Journal of African History*, 9 (3).

— (1969), *The Atlantic Slave Trade: A Consensus*. Mekison, Milwaukee, The University of Wisconsin.

(1978), *African History*, London, Longmans.

De Verteuil, Louis A. (1858), *Trinidad*. London, Ward and Lock.

–   (1888). *Trinidad: Its Geography, Natural resources, Administration, Present condition and Prospects*. London, Ward and Lock.

–   (1973), *Sir Louis De Verteuil: His Life and Times 1800-1900*, Columbus Publishers, Port-of-Spain, Trinidad.

Douglas, Raymond Oba (1990), *The Bible and the Spiritual Baptist Church*; known as *A Spiritual Baptist Handbook*, Mt Pisgah Spiritual Baptist Archdiocese International, Port-of-Spain, Trinidad.

Elder, J D. (1988), *African Survivals in Trinidad and Tobago*. Karia Press, London.

East, David Johnathan (1982), *The Baptist Missionary Society. The Centenary Volume*, London.

Finnegan, Ruth (1970), *Oral Literature in Africa*, Oxford University Press.

Furley, Oliver (1965), "Protestant Missionaries in the West Indies: Pioneers of a non-racial society," *Race*, Volume 1, No.3.

–   (1965), "Moravian Missionaries and Slaves in the West Indies," *Caribbean Studies*, 5, 2.

Gibbs-De Peza; Hazel Ann (1996), *Call Him by His Name Jesus. Spiritual Baptist Christians moving into the 21st Century*. Fishnet Publications, Trinidad.

–   (1966), "Affirmation of the Spiritual Baptist Faith as part of the Christian Fraternity."

Glazier, Stephen (1982), "African Cults & Christian Churches in Trinidad: The Spiritual Baptist Case," *Journal of Religious Thought*.

–   (1983). *Marching the Pilgrims Home*, Greenwood Press, West Port, Connecticut, U.S.A.

Gomes, Albert (1974), *Through a Maze of Colour*, Key Caribbean Publications.

Gopaul-Whittington, Viola (1984), *History and Writings of the Spiritual Baptists*, Ministry of Community Development, Trinidad.

Grimshaw, Anna, ed., (1992), *The C L R James Reader.*, Blackwells, Oxford.

Hackshaw, John Milton (1993), *The Baptist Denomination. A Concise History 1816–1991*, Amphy and Bashana Jackson Memorial Society.

Handler, Jerome (1992), *Slave Medicine and Obeah in Barbados*, Department of Anthropology, Southern Illinois University, U.S.A.

Hastings, Adrian (1976), *African Christianity*.

Henige, David (1982), *Oral Historiography*, Longman Books, London.

Henney, Jeanette (1973), *The Shakers of St Vincent: A Stable Religion. Altered States of Consciousness and Social Change*. Ohio State University Press.

—   (974), *Spirit Possession: Belief and Trance Behaviours in Two Fundamental Groups in St Vincent*. Goodman, Henny and Pressel, New York.

Herskovits, Melville J (1944), *The Myth of the Negro Past*, Harper and Bros., N.Y./London.

Herskovits, Melville and Frances (1947), *Trinidad Village*, Alfred A. Knopf, New York.

Idowu, E. Bolaji (1962), *Olodumare: God in Yoruba Belief*, Longman, Green & Co.

Jacobs, C M (1996), *Joy Comes in the Morning*. Elton George Griffith and The Shouter Baptists Caribbean Historical Society.

Jakobsson, Stiv (1992), *Am I not a Man and Brother?*, Almquist and Wiksells, Germany.

James, C. L. R. (1980), *The Black Jacobins, Toussaint L'Ouverture and the San Domingo Revolution*, Allison & Busby, London.

John, Gus (1996), "Thy Kingdom Come.......They Will be Done." Address to the Annual District Convention of the Church of God of Prophecy, Moss Side, Manchester. (Unpublished.)

Joseph, Cuthbert (1974), Address Delivered at Ceremony to Lay Foundation Stone and Blessing of St Peter's Spiritual Baptist Cathedral, Port-of-Spain. (Unpublished.)

Lanternari, Vittorio (1963), *Religions of the Oppressed: A study of Messianic cults*, trans. from the Italian by Lisa Sergio. New American Library/Mentor Books, N.Y..

Lovelace, Earl (1983), *The Wine of Astonishment*, Heinemann, London,

Lummis, Trevour (1987), *Listening to History: The authenticity of Oral Evidence*, Hutchinson, London.

Mbiti, John (1975), *An introduction to African Religions*, Heinemann, London.

Millette, James (1985), *The Genesis of Crown Colony Government. Society and Politics in Colonial Trinidad*. Third World Books, London.

Mintz, Sidney W. and Price, Richard (1976), *The Birth of African-American Culture. An anthropological Perspective*. Beacon Press, Boston.

Moore, Zelbert (1989), "Out of the Shadows: Black and Brown Struggles for Recognition and Dignity in Brazil 1964-1985," Journal of Black Studies.

Oosthinzen, G. C. (1979), *Afro-Christian Religions*, E.J.Brill, Leiden. Institute of Religious Iconography, State University Groningen.

Parris, Ralph (1996), *Religious Tolerance: A case study of The Spiritual Shouter Baptist in the Rupublic of Trinidad & Tobago*, Bowie State University, U.S.A.

Pearse, Andrew (1958), "Afro New World Cult Dances," University of Warwick, (unpublished papers).

Pretorius, H. L. (1995), *Historiography and Historical Sources regarding African Indigenous Churches in Southern Africa*, The Edwin Mellen Press, N.Y.

Raboteau, Albert (1978), *Slave Religion*, Oxford University Press.

Ranger, T. D. (1973), "Recent Developments in the Study of African Religions: and Cultural History and their Relevance for the Historiography of the Diaspora," *Ufahamu*.

Reddock, Rhoda (1988), *Elma Francois: the NWCSA and the Workers Struggle in the Caribbean in the 1930s*, New Beacon Books, London.

Robinson, A. N. R. (1989), Address by the Prime Minister at the 38th Anniversary of the Liberation of Spiritual Baptists, Trinidad. (Unpublished.)

Simpson; George E. (1980), *Religious cults of the Caribbean: Trinidad, Jamaica and Haiti*, Institute of Caribbean Studies.

—   (1978), *Black Religions in the New World*, Columbia University Press, New York.

Spear, Thomas (1981), "Oral Traditions: Whose History?" *History in Africa 8.*

Stanley; Brian (1992), *The History of the Baptist Missionary Society 1792-1992*, T & T Clark, Edinburgh.

Stapleton, Ashram (1983), *The Birth and Growth of the Baptist Church in Trinidad & Tobago and the Caribbean*, Stapleton, Trinidad & Tobago.

Stewart, John (1976), "Mission and Leadership among the 'Merikin' Baptists of Trinidad," Latin American Anthropology Group.

Thomas, Eudora (1987), *A History of the Shouter Baptists in Trinidad & Tobago*, Callaloux Publications.

Thornton, John K. (1983), *The Kingdom of the Kongo – Civil War and Transition*, University of Wisconsin Press, USA.

Trotman, David (1976), "The Yoruba and Orisha Worship in Trinidad & British Guiana 1838-1870," *African Studies Review*, Vol. IX, No.2.

Underhill, Edward (1861), *Emancipation in the West Indies*, Two addresses by Underhill and J.T.Brown, John Thurland Brown, London.

—   (1862), *The West Indies: Their Economic and Religious Condition*, London, Jackson Walford & Hodder.

Vansina, Jan (1985), *Oral Tradition as History*, University of Wisconsin Press, USA.

Warner-Lewis, Maureen (1991), *Guinea's Other Suns: The African Dynamic in Trinidad Culture*, The Majority Press, Dover, Mass.

—   (1972), "Yoruba Religion in Trinidad: Transfer and Reinterpretation," *Caribbean Quarterly*, Vol. 24.

Williams, Eric (1942), History of the People of Trinidad and Tobago. A & A Books.

—   (1964), *Capitalism and Slavery*, Andre Deutsch, London.

—   (1971), *The Negro in the Caribbean*, Haskell House, N.Y.

Wood, Donald (1968), *Trinidad in Transition*, Oxford University Press.

Worsley, Peter (1957), *The Trumpet Shall Sound*, Mac Gibbon & Kee, London.

Yow, Valerie R. (1994), *Recording Oral History: A Practical Guide for Social Scientists*, London, Sage Publications. London.